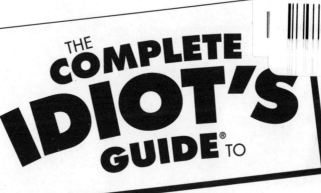

THE
COMPLETE
IDIOT'S
GUIDE® TO

Cheeses of the World

D1033796

This book is dedicated to my husband, Kyle, and my parents, Tom and Mary Hurt, who have supported my cheese habit.
—Jeanette
Dedicated to my father Lawrence Ehlers—the ultimate salesman!
—Steve

ALPHA BOOKS

Published by the Penguin Group

Penguin Group (USA) Inc., 375 Hudson Street, New York, New York 10014, USA

Penguin Group (Canada), 90 Eglinton Avenue East, Suite 700, Toronto, Ontario M4P 2Y3, Canada (a division of Pearson Penguin Canada Inc.)

Penguin Books Ltd., 80 Strand, London WC2R 0RL, England

Penguin Ireland, 25 St. Stephen's Green, Dublin 2, Ireland (a division of Penguin Books Ltd.)

Penguin Group (Australia), 250 Camberwell Road, Camberwell, Victoria 3124, Australia (a division of Pearson Australia Group Pty. Ltd.)

Penguin Books India Pvt. Ltd., 11 Community Centre, Panchsheel Park, New Delhi—110 017, India

Penguin Group (NZ), 67 Apollo Drive, Rosedale, North Shore, Auckland 1311, New Zealand (a division of Pearson New Zealand Ltd.)

Penguin Books (South Africa) (Pty.) Ltd., 24 Sturdee Avenue, Rosebank, Johannesburg 2196, South Africa

Penguin Books Ltd., Registered Offices: 80 Strand, London WC2R 0RL, England

Publisher: *Marie Butler-Knight*
Editorial Director: *Mike Sanders*
Senior Managing Editor: *Billy Fields*
Acquisitions Editor: *Tom Stevens*
Senior Development Editor: *Phil Kitchel*
Production Editor: *Megan Douglass*
Copy Editor: *Cate Schwenk*

Cartoonist: *Steve Barr*
Cover Designer: *Bill Thomas*
Book Designer: *Trina Wurst*
Indexer: *Johnna Vanhoose Dinse*
Layout: *Ayanna Lacey*
Proofreader: *John Etchison*

Contents at a Glance

Contents

Introduction

Let me start by saying one thing: you're not an idiot. When it comes to cheese, the only idiots are those who think they know everything. Although most everyone has experienced and eaten cheese, once you learn more about cheese, you'll better savor and enjoy it.

And there's a lot of cheese out there to enjoy. In fact there are hundreds, if not more than a thousand, different types of cheese in the world. France alone boasts approximately 750 different cheeses. That means you could spend your whole life eating cheese and never taste every single variety. Add to this the fact that dozens of new American cheesemakers are creating new cheeses, and the diversity becomes almost dizzying.

But don't let the exciting variations of cheese wind you up into a tizzy. Learning about cheese isn't that hard, and it's actually a lot of fun. Open your mind—and your mouth—to the possibilities and dig in. A little desire to learn will take you a long way. Ten years ago, I started out just where you are. A freelance writing job at a gourmet food store introduced me to the wide world of cheese. Little did I know that it would become a new passion—I was hooked as soon as I began. Some women might buy shoes. I bought—and still buy—a lot of cheese.

I hope that you'll discover that same enthusiasm in *The Complete Idiot's Guide to Cheeses of the World* and uncover your own passion along the way. If you haven't spent much time exploring different cheeses, you may be a little perplexed. But stick with it, and taste by taste, your palate for cheese will expand. Learning about cheese is all about paying attention to what you try and what you like. Use your own sense of taste—and smell—as a guide. This book is meant to help you along in your own quest for cheese, and I hope that you do taste the cheeses that you read about. By the time you finish this book you should have degusted a lot of wonderful cheese.

How to Use This Book

Part 1, "It's Easy to Be Cheesy," covers just that—what cheese is, how it's made, and what the differences are among cow's milk, goat's milk and sheep's milk cheeses. It also details the rich history of cheese and explores the different types of cheese.

Part 2, "Old World Favorites," explores the best and most famous cheeses of Europe, from the big cheese regions of France and Italy to the lesser-known varieties of Sweden and Finland. It covers cheese on the continent, from top to bottom.

Part 3, "American Artisans and Other New World Delights," tackles the history and delicious variety of American cheeses. This part also delves into the interesting world of artisan cheesemaking and the new and old American "originals." It also covers Canadian, Mexican, and Latin American cheeses.

Part 4, "Shopping and Enjoying Cheese," gets to the best part—shopping, storing, and cooking with cheese. Here's where you'll learn how to navigate the cheese aisle, but you'll also learn how to pair and taste cheese. You'll even learn the "whey"—as in curds and whey—to make cheese in your own kitchen.

Extras

I have to admit—I'm a super cheese geek, and I dearly love to share my knowledge and spread my enthusiasm to anyone who cares to listen. For your special benefit, I've added some interesting tidbits and facts in each chapter, which you'll find under these headings:

A Cut Above

This is a space for little bits of interesting extra information that might help you better understand the information in a chapter; I also include some funny stories I thought you might enjoy.

Stinky Cheese

These are warnings about challenging or confusing details in the cheese world, with tips on how to identify the issues and avoid or understand them.

Say Cheese

Words that might be unfamiliar to you but are frequently used in the cheese world are defined here.

Acknowledgments

This book could not have been written without the loving support of my husband, Kyle Edwards. He never realized that his first job, working at Highlands Cheese Basket in Racine, Wisconsin, would come in handy. I also owe a huge debt of gratitude and a big wheel of cheddar to my parents, Tom and Mary Hurt, and my sisters, Julie and Karen Hurt, all of whom sent any cheese-related information my way. My in-laws also are owed a debt of gratitude: Jeanne and Ed Potter and Craig and Sally (Dowhower) Edwards, along with Marcie Hutton and her two boys, Eric and Ryan. And I have to add a special thanks to my "adopted" grandparents, Ellen and Dick Haynes, whose love, support, and wisdom have been invaluable.

Monica Gotomo, food scientist and writer, not only helped me understand the finer technical points of cheesemaking, but her research was invaluable—I owe her some Brie. Jill Prescott, chef extraordinaire and dear friend, offered not only inspiration but practical wisdom in the kitchen. I owe some wine and cheese to my writing-goal buddy, Damon Brown, whose encouragement kept me going when the writing was not flowing. Damon also introduced me to my wonderful agent, the lovely Marilyn Allen, who made this possible. I also owe some fine Stilton to Tom Stevens, who is as excellent an editor as I could have hoped for. Extra thanks also goes out to editors Phil Kitchel, Megan Douglass, Cate Schwenk, and Christy Wagner, whose eagle-eyed edits were much appreciated.

My dear friend and colleague, N. Marie Dries, is also owed some sweet chevre for her eagle-eyed research and thoughtful suggestions. Shannon Luckey, another writing friend, also needs to be singled out for her support. I also owe special thanks to the Bay View Writers Group: Lisa, Kristine, Ricardo, Carrie, Elke, Ginny, Harold, and the rest of the bunch. Other cheesy kudos go out to my cousins Barb and Julie and friends Bec, Jen, Jennie, Krissie, Paula, Suzie, Susan, and Sue.

This book also would not have been as up to date or as informative without the support of Heather Porter Engwall, Marilyn Wilkinson, Patrick Geoghan, and everyone else at the Wisconsin Milk Marketing Board; Jeanne Carpenter and Norm Munson at the Dairy Business Innovation Center; Korinne Munson, Kiaran Frietag, and Lynne Devereaux at the California Milk Marketing Board; Gregg Marston, Paolo, and Sylvie at VBT for helping me with my Italian research.

Lastly, I would like to thank all of the wonderful cheesemakers who welcomed me into their creameries—you do such a wonderful, wonderful job! Thank you for sharing your wisdom (and great cheese) with me.

Special Thanks to Co-Author

The Complete Idiot's Guide to the Cheeses of the World was reviewed by Steve Ehlers, who double-checked the accuracy of what you'll learn here, to help us ensure that this book gives you everything you need to know about cheese.

Trademarks

All terms mentioned in this book that are known to be or are suspected of being trademarks or service marks have been appropriately capitalized. Alpha Books and Penguin Group (USA) Inc. cannot attest to the accuracy of this information. Use of a term in this book should not be regarded as affecting the validity of any trademark or service mark.

It's Easy to Be Cheesy

Most of us eat cheese, and we probably eat a lot of it. But eating cheese and knowing about cheese are two different things. Otherwise, we'd already have eaten our way into knowledge.

Eating cheese is part of learning about cheese, and if you just read about cheese without ever tasting it, it's sort of like learning French without ever traveling to a French-speaking country. But without a little background about cheese, you really won't know what you're eating, nor truly appreciate it in all of its glory. It's sort of like going to France without ever listening to a French language tape. You might get by, but you'll never fully experience its delights.

In this part, you'll get a solid foundation in the fundamentals of cheese: what it is; where it came from; and how to really define the basic cheese types and milks that go into cheese. Armed with this knowledge, you'll be ready to get the most out of the rest of the book—and every bite of cheese thereafter.

1

What Is Cheese, Anyway?

In This Chapter

- ◆ Defining cheese
- ◆ Explaining how cheese is made
- ◆ Exploring the art of aging cheese
- ◆ Discovering the different tastes of cheese

Cheese. It's not milk gone bad. Cheese is milk taken to another level. Although cheese is at once familiar, it can also be surprising or even mysterious. Indeed, Clifton Fadiman once described cheese as "milk's leap to immortality."

Cheese is, in fact, a living organism. It shares this characteristic with wine, and it is perhaps the food that most closely mirrors wine. Like wine, there are endless varieties of cheese, and as with wine, geography, or terroir, also plays an integral role in the final product. No two cheeses are exactly identical. A master cheesemaker cannot make the same cheese in different locales around the globe even if he or she uses the same recipe and milk from the same breed of animal.

Indeed, people have had a love affair with cheese since the earliest civilizations. That romance not only continues today, but it grows increasingly passionate as new artisan cheesemakers from Hawaii to Poland continue to push the boundaries of cheesemaking.

The Cheese Stands Alone

Ask a simple question—what is *cheese?*—and several images might immediately come to mind. A bright orange wedge of cheddar, crumbling slightly on a plate. Bloomy wheels of brie, oozing creamy goodness. Gooey strands of mozzarella being pulled from a slice of pizza. Single slices melted over burgers. Or even a sea of cheering Green Bay Packers fans.

Say Cheese

The word **cheese** comes from the Latin word *caseus*, probably derived from the word *kwat* of the Proto-Indo-European language, a language linguists believe could be the common ancestor tongue of today's Indo-European languages. Kwat means to ferment or become sour.

We all know what cheese is, what it tastes like, and we all have several sensory images of this dairy delicacy stored in our brains. But of course there's more to it than that. Real cheese is actually a living organism because it contains microorganisms, and it changes over time. It's a high-energy food that starts out as milk and, in a sense, it's a solid form of milk. But even though milk is the basic ingredient and the foundation for cheese, leaving plain milk to sour will not necessarily make cheese!

How Cheese Is Made

All cheeses start with the same basic process, but cheesemaking is a very complex endeavor involving both chemistry and art. The cheesemaking processes all start with the milk, usually from cows, goats, or sheep. To make good cheese, it's imperative to start out with very good milk. With good milk, you can still make a bad cheese; but with bad milk, you cannot possibly make a good cheese.

Cheesemaking is basically the separation of milk into solids (curds) and liquid (whey), with the final cheese being a product developed from the curds. Milk left to spoil will separate on its own, but that process is unpredictable at best and unsanitary at worst. Still, cheesemaking is the controlled spoilage of milk.

It All Starts with the Milk

Milk is either first pasteurized or used unpasteurized as *raw milk*. After the milk is pasteurized, or just after it arrives at the cheese factory if it is to be used raw, the cheesemaking process starts. There are three main parts of cheesemaking: transforming the milk proteins into curds or solids, concentrating or intensifying those curds, and then aging or ripening the resulting cheese.

The first step—the making of the curds—is often called *acidification,* or the controlled souring of the milk. Bacterial cultures, often lactobacilli or streptococci, are added. Different cultures, or starters, as they are also known, are used to create different cheeses. *Artisan* or specialty cheesemakers often experiment with new or different cultures to create new or different cheeses or improve upon a basic cheese's flavor profile. Food chemists also develop new cultures for cheesemakers to try.

Say Cheese

Cheese made from unpasteurized milk is called **raw milk cheese.** In the United States, all raw milk cheese must be aged for at least 60 days. No unpasteurized Brie for you (unless you happen to know the rare cheesemonger who skirts the law).

Master Cheesemaker Bruce Workman tests the readiness of the curd.

After about 45 minutes of letting the cultures work their magic, rennet or another coagulant is added. Rennet is an enzyme that comes from a calf's stomach, but most rennet used today comes from microbial rennet or rennet produced by yeast or microbes. Sometimes, cardoon thistle or artichoke is also used as a coagulant, especially for cheeses made in southern Spain and Portugal. A coloring agent, usually the vegetable-derived annatto, is also added at this point in the cheesemaking process. After a period of 30 minutes to two hours, the milk begins to coagulate. Its texture becomes similar to that of custard or gelatin and wobbles if you touch it.

Say Cheese

Acidification is the process in which bacterial cultures change the milk sugar or lactose into lactic acid. The lactic acid causes the milk protein or casein to coagulate when a coagulating agent is added.

Artisan is a term that gets tossed about in gourmet conversations, describing everything from cheese to olive oil. Artisan cheese, in the strictest sense, is specialty cheese crafted in small batches, but not all specialty or high-quality cheeses are artisan-made. Indeed, most European imports are made in large factories, and some of the best American cheeses also come from medium to large factories. Artisan, in this case, describes the care that goes into making the cheese. Artisan also indicates that the cheeses are made using traditional, by-hand methods rather than automation.

The next step begins with the cutting and stirring of the curds, using a *cheese harp*. Depending on the type of cheese, the curds will be handled or cut a bit differently. For some cheeses, another mold or bacteria can be introduced at this point. Curds are cut so that the whey will begin to separate—this is likely the stuff Miss Muffet was snacking on. A little cream is also separated at this time, and some cheesemakers will sell that to butter makers. Whey, a by-product of cheesemaking, can be used to make cheeses like ricotta, which actually means "re-cooked." In years past, most cheesemakers considered it a waste, but today whey is a hot commodity, and manufacturers of this concentrated protein add it to everything from snack bars to animal feed.

Say Cheese

A **cheese harp** is a metal, harp-shaped paddle, strung with linear blades.

Cheddaring, Salting, Molding

After the whey is drained off, some cheeses go through a process of cheddaring. The curds are piled up and cut into pillow-shaped slabs. Then these slabs are piled on top of each other and turned every 15 minutes or so to expel more whey. After the pillow-piling turns the cheese into thin, thin slabs, the slabs are then fed into a mill. That process of pillow-piling and milling is called cheddaring.

Master Cheesemaker Bruce Workman and his assistant use cheese harps to cut the curd.

Cheesemakers at Fiscalini Cheese Company mill and salt curds of fresh cheddar.

(Jeanette Hurt)

For other cheese, the curds are reheated or cooked while being stirred. After cooking, the curds begin to develop a tender, stringlike consistency. At this point, the cheese-making process ends for spun or stretched curd cheese (pasta filata) like mozzarella and string cheese. Not every cheese has reheated curds; as you'll discover, different cheeses go through slightly different processes.

Whether cooked or cheddared, at this point the cheeses are ready to be salted and put into molds. Cheeses that are dry rubbed or brined are molded, then salted. Cheddars are salted, then molded.

A Cut Above

Fresh cheese curds are a popular snack food in Wisconsin that have begun to spread to other parts of the country.

Cheeses are salted in three different ways. In cheddar, the pillows are cut or milled and then sprinkled with salt—a process called dry salting. For cheeses like Emmentaler or Gruyère, the cheese curds are pressed into molds and then the molds are brined in a bath of salt water. Other cheeses such as Roquefort and Parmigiano-Reggiano, once they are molded, are rubbed with salt in a method call dry rubbing.

Cheesemaker Marisa Simoes hand-packs fresh curd into molds at the Three Sisters Farmstead Cheese Company.

(Three Sisters Farmstead Cheese Company)

When cheeses are pressed into molds, they begin to take on the shape of the molds. Most molds are made of stainless steel. Sometimes cheesecloths are laid into the molds first, sometimes not. For some cheeses such as brick cheese, actual bricks were traditionally used to press down the molds and drain additional whey out of the cheese.

Aging

Lastly, cheeses undergo the ripening or aging process. Traditionally, many cheeses were aged in caves, and some still are, but natural caves aren't always geographically convenient, and man-made caves aren't always feasible. Many cheeses are instead aged in custom-built, special temperature- and humidity-controlled storage rooms.

Fresh cheeses at this point are simply packaged and sent off to stores or sold directly to consumers. But others continue their "treatments": some are rubbed or washed with olive oil, wine, or herbs; some are aged in cloth bandages or sealed in wax; and still others sit on shelves bare, just aging. Many blue cheeses have holes poked in them at this point to allow air to circulate more freely so their molds can develop more evenly. Soft-ripened cheeses like Brie are washed with bacteria to create their traditionally bloomy crusts and gooey, soft interiors.

During the aging process, many cheeses are turned periodically so that they age evenly. In the first few days and weeks, they need to be turned more frequently, as the turning also presses out remnants of whey. The frequency of turning decreases over time as the cheeses age.

In France, the art of aging cheese is called *affinage*, and the person who ages the cheese is the affineur or affineuse. Aging not only helps the flavors of the cheese develop, but also allows the rinds or the rusts of the cheeses to develop. Commodity cheeses—block cheddars, mozzarellas, and the like—can be ready in as little as two weeks of aging. Other cheeses must be aged for several months or even several years.

Many cheesemakers produce cheeses of varying ages; for example, some cheddar producers make a year-old cheddar, a 4-year-old cheddar, an 8-year-old cheddar, and a 10-year-old cheddar. A good cheesemaker knows which cheeses will age out over time; like an expert vintner, a cheesemaker needs to know which batches will age gracefully and which ones should be served fresher. Different cheeses have optimal ages at which they should be served.

Processed cheese is another food entirely, and it doesn't require any aging at all. Processed cheese starts out as regular cheese, and then different ingredients and chemicals are added. According to governmental standards, at least 51 percent of products labeled "cheese foods" must be real cheese. So-called "American cheese" is a processed cheese product that must contain 90 percent cheese, often cheddar.

Say Cheese

Affinage is the art of aging cheese, and affineurs or affineuses are the artists who perfect the cheeses until they are ready for consumption. An affineur not only ages the cheese, but also corrects any potential defects in the cheese before it develops.

Processed cheese typically melts more smoothly, and processed cheese products such as cheese spreads obviously spread more smoothly, too. Unlike processed cheese, which has real cheese in it, imitation cheese does not.

Stinky Cheese _____

Imitation cheese is not real cheese. It's a nondairy product that is supposed to taste like cheese, but is a concoction that usually contains soy, often tofu, as well as a calcium caseinate (a milk protein), starch, and other additives.

The Gouda and the Bad, or How to Taste Cheese

Most cheese connoisseurs remember tasting that very first cheese that made them fall in love with cheese. For some, it might have been a sharp cheddar, for others a silky Camembert, and still others might have enjoyed a tangy chevre. Cheeses that make grown men swoon all have one characteristic in common—they have a depth of flavor to them.

To truly get the most out of your cheese, you must learn to taste cheese properly. When we taste food, we are actually absorbing its flavor, and flavor not only involves the sensations that the taste buds on our tongues tell us, but it also involves the smell, texture, and appearance of the foods we eat.

A Cut Above _____

Cheese is one of the most chemically complex and flavorful foods on the planet, just behind wine. More than 700 different chemical components create the flavors in wine; cheese has more than 200 different chemical components that create its flavors.

Flavors traditionally have been divided into the categories of sweet, sour, salty, and bitter, but a fifth taste or sense called *umami* has recently been added. Umami, a Japanese word, basically means "savory," and it refers to the taste that naturally occurring monosodium glutamate (MSG) brings out in foods. Umami often refers to foods that cannot completely be described by the other flavor categories.

The Nose Knows

You might think taste begins with taste buds, but your olfactory sense is also integral to the process. Our sense of smell directly relates to how we taste things. For example, if you have a cold, foods taste blander to you, but it's not because your taste buds aren't reacting; it's because your sense of smell is impaired.

We smell our foods both before we put them in our mouths and after we begin chewing them. Before a piece of cheese even reaches our tongue, we have a sense of what it might taste like. That sense might change after we place it in our mouth because the aroma of the cheese that first traveled into our nose is now going from the mouth to the back of the throat and up to the receptors in our nose.

Some cheeses have very strong aromas, but once we place them in our mouths, the aromas change. A good example of this is American Limburger. Limburger is a semi-soft cheese that many describe as having an earthy pungency. It smells really strong, but once you place it in your mouth, it has more of a mild flavor.

A Cut Above

In Monroe, Wisconsin, near where Limburger is made today, it used to be said that the smell of Limburger was the smell of money because so many cheesemakers in the area made their livelihood from limburger.

Sometimes a cheese might smell "bad" or unpleasant to you. If a cheese truly has gone bad, it will smell more and more like ammonia, and that means the cheese isn't good to eat. If a cheese smells too strong to you, check out its appearance and texture. If it doesn't look good to you, then you probably shouldn't eat it.

Other times, cheese might just smell too pungent for your liking. If you are unsure, ask your cheese seller (good cheesemongers will even take phone calls) if your cheese is okay to eat. The more you try different cheeses, the more your tastes will grow, and the more pungent cheeses you might enjoy.

Taste Is Everything

After smelling a cheese, the next step is to consider both its visual and textural appeal. Visually, consider the rind of the cheese—is it uniform or cracked? Texturally, what does it feel like in your hand? What does it feel like in your mouth? Is it smooth or crunchy? Professional cheese judges often first inspect the exterior of a cheese and its packaging. Next, they poke a hole in the middle of a large round of cheese with a tool called a *trier*, then they touch it, smell it, and finally taste it.

Say Cheese

Professional cheese judges use a tool called a **trier** to "plug" a cheese. That means they plunge a skinny, hollow tool with a T-shaped handle—think apple corer—into the middle of a cheese, rotate for one complete turn, and pull out a plug or a sample of the cheese. This tool is also used by cheesemakers as they check their cheese as it ages.

To truly taste cheese, you use all your senses—your sight, your taste, your smell, your touch, and perhaps even your hearing (the sound cheese makes in your mouth). The more you taste cheese, the more you will notice different flavors and aromas that good cheese has. Fresh chevres tend to have a tangy flavor, as they have more acid in them. Some cheddars develop a crystalline sort of bite to them because as they age, calcium deposits form in the cheese.

You will begin to see different patterns in cheeses, and you discover what you particularly are fond of. At cheese stores or knowledgeable delis and grocers, ask to sample the different cheeses. Start with what you know you like, and then ask for recommendations. Begin to branch out and try different kinds and makers of cheese.

The Language of Love

Like wine lovers or *oenophiles*, *caseophiles* or cheese connoisseurs spout a bodacious vocabulary to describe how they experience a cheese. They can wax poetic about the ochre shade or the rusty rind; or talk about the bleaching—shiny, pale, or otherwise—how white a cheese is. They will tell you a cheese is runny, compact, tight, or elastic. A cheese might also be gummy, greasy, gooey, or rough. The flavor might be nutty, earthy, buttery, spicy, woodsy, or acidic. It could also be strong or weak, biting or timid, unctuous or zesty.

Say Cheese

Cheese connoisseurs or cheese lovers can be called both **caseophiles** or turophiles, while wine lovers are called **oenophiles**. The French love their cheese so much that they have a special vocabulary to describe cheese. Sometimes they call a cheese *nerveux* or nervous to explain a cheese's tartness. They also call some cheeses *noisete* or nutty.

But don't let a cheese snob's verbosity keep you from describing a cheese the way you experience it. Although cheese has begun to rise to a level of gourmet tasting like wine, it should never be intimidating. The whole point to tasting cheese is to enjoy it.

The Least You Need to Know

- Cheese is a living organism, and like wine, where it is made and how it is handled affects its taste.
- The process of cheesemaking combines both chemistry and art.

◆ Cheesemaking is basically a three-step process: transforming the milk into curds, concentrating the curds, and then ripening the cheese.

◆ All cheese is made in a similar fashion, but different variables within each stage of the process determine the kinds and variations of cheese.

◆ Tasting cheese involves all the senses, and to truly enjoy cheese, you should take your time.

A History of Cheese

In This Chapter

◆ The accepted legend of cheese

◆ Legend versus historical evidence of cheese

◆ Tracing back 12,000 years of cheese in history

◆ Historical highlights of cheese

Cheese has been around almost as long as we've inhabited Planet Earth, or at least since we domesticated and began milking animals. It is a food that predates recorded history. Ancient Egyptians ate cheese, the Romans spread the art of cheesemaking throughout their empire, and monks preserved and honed cheesemaking techniques throughout the Dark Ages. Cheesemaking references have popped up in Homer, in the Bible, and even Shakespeare waxed poetic about its protein prowess. This ancient food boasts a tasty history!

A Delicious Accident: The Mythic Origin of Cheese

Legend has it that cheese was discovered by a nomad, perhaps of Arabian descent. This nomad packed some milk to quench his thirst during his journey, storing it in a saddlebag made from the stomach of a young animal, perhaps a lamb or a kid goat. The bumpy ride, combined with the day's hot sun, jostled the milk, and the enzymes in the saddlebag separated the milk into curds and whey. When he stopped for a drink, the milk was no longer milk. Though puzzled, this nomad tentatively sipped the liquid and tasted the curds, finding them to be very good indeed.

There's no concrete, historical evidence to back up this myth as fact, but it could very well have happened that cheese was discovered by accident—an accident with a very practical outcome. While milk spoils quickly, cheese does not, and in the many centuries before refrigeration, this was one method of preserving food for leaner times. It also provided a use for excess milk, as good milkers produced more milk than a baby animal and the human owners could consume.

The Real Roots of Cheesemaking

Whether or not cheese was the result of a delicious accident or deliberate experimentation after dairy animals were domesticated, what is known for sure is many ancient peoples have left behind evidence of cheesemaking. Dairy animal domestication occurred around 10,000 years before Christ, and cheesemaking is believed to have evolved sometime between 10000 B.C.E. and 8000 B.C.E.

The ancient Sumerians of Mesopotamia left behind bas-reliefs showing cows being milked and cheese being made, dating back to around 3500 B.C.E. The ancient Egyptians were also into cheese art, and they painted murals in tombs around 2000 B.C.E. depicting cheesemaking. And archaeologists have discovered milk-curdling artifacts dating back to around 5000 B.C.E. near the shores of Lake Neuchâtel in Switzerland.

A Cut Above

Forget spinach. For strength and endurance, nothing beats cheese. In the Bible, when David escaped across the River Jordan, he ate cow's milk cheese. Historical records also show that at one time, a place outside Jerusalem was dubbed "The Valley of the Cheesemakers." That valley is not to be confused with Egypt's "Valley of the Kings."

Historical writings on cheese also abound. Homer, around 18 B.C.E., referred to goat's milk and sheep's milk cheese being crafted in the mountain areas of Greece. Aristotle (384–322 B.C.E.), talked about mare's milk cheese. And the ancient Greeks held the belief that Aristaeus, son of Apollo and Cyrene, invented cheese.

It isn't conclusively known, however, which ancient civilization first developed cheese. Many historians credit the fertile valleys in the Middle East as the birthplace of cheese. Others believe that cheesemaking was first developed in central Asia, and that traveling tribes brought it to the Middle East and Europe.

The ancient tribal communities in Europe knew how to make cheese before the Romans conquered them. But the great armies of Rome not only refined cheesemaking as a skill, they also spread it to every land they stomped on.

Cheesemaking Conquerors

The ancient Romans knew how to get things done, and their legendary efficiency not only extended to chariot making and army building, but also moved into the agricultural arenas—into the fields for raising dairy flocks and into the kitchens where cheese was made.

The Romans, in fact, turned cheesemaking into a highly skilled craft. By this time in history, ripening cheeses had become more refined, and people understood that different methods in the making and aging of cheese resulted in different flavors and textures. Large Roman households had separate cheese kitchens called *caseales*, and they also had special cheese storage rooms. They often smoked cheeses in town centers, too.

By this time, rennet had become commonly used, and cheesemakers now had more control over their curds. This allowed cheese to be better transported, and the trade of cheese grew along the Mediterranean Sea. Rennet was not the only curdling agent that the Romans used. In fact, the Romans experimented with various other curdling agents, including thistle flower, safflower seed, and fig bark.

A Cut Above

Marcus Terentius Varro, a Roman scholar considered "the most learned of all the Romans," described different cheeses in his writing. He particularly noted the way that different geographical locations had an effect on the tastes and kinds of cheese.

The Roman Empire Falls, but Cheesemaking Still Spreads

The Romans couldn't hold their empire together, but its collapse did not mean the end of cheesemaking. Regional cheeses and cheesemaking techniques really began to take root from the Mediterranean through the Adriatic Sea and various river valleys across the continent.

Different dairy animals began to flourish in various geographic areas. In the more remote mountains, goats and sheep were easier to raise, while the fertile lowlands provided the perfect environment for breeding cattle.

Different tribes across what is now Europe began specializing in different cheeses. The caseus Helvetica, a dry, hard cheese of Roman times made by the Helvetii tribe in the Swiss Alps, evolved into sbrinz and spalen cheeses, for example. Gallic tribes in what is now France began developing soft-ripened cheeses like the predecessors of Brie, while the tribes in what is now the Netherlands began developing hard, wax-coated cheeses—the forerunners of Edam and Gouda.

A Cut Above

The enterprising Dutch dairy farmers also began cultivating a certain black-and-white breed of cattle known to be high producers of milk. Today, the biggest dairy breed in the world, which began showing up 2,000 years ago, is known in the United States as Holstein, and in Europe as Friesian.

Wars and other such occurrences slowed the progress of cheese development. Just as they preserved books, enterprising monks in monasteries preserved and continued to innovate the production of cheese during the Middle Ages. In fact, monks in the Po Valley of Italy created Gorgonzola in 879 C.E. while monks in Conques, France, made Roquefort in 1070. Here are the earliest recorded dates of some commonly known cheeses:

Cheese Variety	Year
Gorgonzola	879
Roquefort	1070
Gruyère	1115
Emmentaler	1200
Grana	1200
Cheddar	1500
Parmesan	1579
Gouda	1697
Gloucester	1697
Stilton	1785
Camembert	1791

During the Middle Ages, the Italians became the most well-known and specialized cheesemakers. In 1579, they even branded a cheese called *La Luna* (the moon), which today is known as Parmigiano-Reggiano.

Outside of monasteries, cheese was mostly made by farm women, and during the thirteenth century, the earliest farm cooperatives were formed, as people realized that combining milk and then sharing the cheeses resulted in greater efficiency. The first recorded cooperative was listed in 1267 in Deservilliers, France.

The development of harder, aged cheeses occurred in the British Isles. While King Arthur was busy uniting England, the process of making cheddar was developed. Stilton and Gloucester were also developed. The English word *cheese* comes from the Middle English word *chese*, which evolved from the word *cese*.

Cheese also began showing up in litera-ture. In John Heywood's *Proverbes* (1541) he wrote, "The moon is made of greene cheese," with greene meaning new or unaged, not verdant in color. This line of poetry was probably not meant to be inter-preted as scientific fact, but rather poetic license.

Shakespeare also used cheese as a poetic metaphor. In *All's Well That Ends Well* (1623), Shakespeare wrote, "Much like a cheese consumed itself to the very pairing." In *Troilus and Cressida* (1609), Theresites refers to Nestor as a "mouse-eaten dry cheese," and Achilles also exclaims, "Why, my cheese, my digestion, why hast thou not served thyself into my table so many means?" But perhaps the biggest cheese insult Shakespeare penned was in *Henry IV* (1598): "His breath stinks with eating toasted cheese."

> **Say Cheese** _____
>
> The Romans not only spread cheesemaking, they also left behind a linguistic mark. The Latin words for cheese, **caseus,** developed into the Spanish **queso,** the Italian **cacio** and the Portuguese **queijo.** The term the Romans used for hard cheese, **formaticum,** became the French **fromage.**

On the various trips of exploration and settlement of the New World, cheeses and cheesemaking went along for the ride. Columbus might have munched on Manchego during his long voyages, but we do not know for sure. We do know, however, that the Pilgrims packed some wheels of cheese onto the *Mayflower*. They also tucked some beer into the ship. Cheese is also believed to have been served at the very first Thanksgiving.

Big Cheesemaking Develops

For many years, cheesemaking remained a family, farmhouse tradition in the United States, and New York State became dairy central. As the industrial age began to dawn, the very first cheese factory was built in 1815 in Switzerland. But factory cheesemaking didn't get going until Jesse Williams, a dairyman in Rome, New York, decided to set up shop. Williams built the first assembly-line cheese factory in 1851, using his neighbors' milk.

Feeding these small factories were the first batches of mass-produced rennet, which began being produced in the 1860s. Scientists refined this process so that by the twentieth century, microbial rennet had been developed. A purer coagulant meant that cheeses and cheesemaking could become more standardized.

From Pasteurization to Processed

Around the same time, the French scientist Louis Pasteur began studying diseases and the transmission of diseases. His studies of fermentation led him to believe that microorganisms carried out the fermentation process, and that led him to believe that these "germs" might also be responsible for contagious diseases. His hypothesis, called the germ theory, led to the development of pasteurization for wine and beer making. Pasteurization of milk did not become widespread or mandatory until 1908, when the first compulsory pasteurization law was enacted in Chicago.

As pasteurization of milk was beginning to spread, a certain James L. Kraft began a wholesale cheese business in Chicago in 1903. In 1915, he developed what he called "process" cheese. To make his cheese product, he ground up an assortment of cheddar cheeses, pasteurized them, and then added emulsifying salt to the mixture. The mixture was heated and then poured into foil-lined containers, which were sealed. The resulting cheese sliced easily, and it could also be kept without fear of spoilage in a time before refrigerators.

Kraft's company continued to research cheese and its related products, including whey, which led to the development of Velveeta in 1928; just three years later, Velveeta received the seal of approval from the American Medical Association. In 1937, Kraft released Kraft Macaroni & Cheese dinner, which, during a time of rationing during World War II, was a welcome product. Kraft Macaroni & Cheese has since influenced the palettes of generations of children.

The twentieth century not only saw a huge growth in processed cheese products but in factory-made cheeses in general, as they became the norm in both Europe and North America. In fact, many of the great handcrafted cheeses in Europe were first affinaged and then both affinaged and made in factories. From the 1920s through the 1980s, factories grew in size, as many smaller factories consolidated. The invention of refrigeration and tanker trucks affected cheese production, as milk could now be transported longer distances.

In the 1970s and 1980s, great European cheeses also became more regularly imported to the United States. Specialty cheese production and artisan cheese production in the United States also started up in the 1980s.

Today, worldwide consumption of cheese continues to grow. The Greeks eat the most cheese, with about 56 pounds per capita; and the French come in second, consuming about 54 pounds per capita, followed by the Germans who eat 46 pounds; the Italians who eat 44 pounds; and the Swedish who eat 38 pounds. Americans only eat about 31 pounds a year.

Today there is a movement to return to the cheesemaking methods of the past, with many cheesemakers here and abroad making cheese in smaller batches using a more hands-on process. This artisan cheese movement has led many people to rediscover the ancient art of cheesemaking.

The Least You Need to Know

- Cheesemaking predates recorded history. Historical records show that many ancient peoples, including the Sumerians and Egyptians, made and ate cheese.

- The Romans perfected and then spread more modern methods of cheesemaking.

- Monasteries preserved cheesemaking during the Middle Ages, and different geographical regions began developing distinctive cheeses and cheesemaking methods.

- Factory cheesemaking became widespread after a New York dairy farmer set up an assembly-line production in 1851. Factory cheesemaking grew, pasteurization became an established practice for cheesemaking, and processed cheese also was created in the twentieth century.

The Big Three Milks of Cheesemaking

In This Chapter

- ◆ How milk serves as a building block for cheese
- ◆ Exploring the three main milks for cheese
- ◆ Reindeer milk, buffalo milk, and other exotics
- ◆ What happens to the milk happens to the cheese
- ◆ Fast health facts

Milk might do a body good, but it also does a cheese good. Although it might be obvious to say so, milk is the main ingredient of cheese, and as such, quality milk begets quality cheese.

But there's a little more to it than that. What animals are milked, what time of year they're milked, what the animals ate … these are all factors that not only affect the milk, but will affect the cheese, too. How the animals are cared for and whether they are allowed to exercise can also affect the quality of the milk.

Most people are familiar with cow's milk cheese, but goat's and sheep's milks create some of the world's most famous cheeses. The fat and protein contents vary from milk to milk and create very different conditions for making cheese. Experienced cheesemakers know the nuances of the milks they use and how to work with them to achieve the perfect balance.

The Milk Is Where It's At

This white, viscous liquid has sustained humankind for generations. In fact, devout Hindus have even offered milk to their gods. And who can blame them—especially when it's been transformed into the even more ambrosial form of cheese.

All milk, however, is not created equal, and different milks need to be handled in distinct manners in order to create cheese. Milk is mostly water—about 80 percent—and the rest is made up of protein, fat, lactose or milk sugar, vitamins, and minerals. All milk contains these components, but in different amounts.

Here's a nutritional breakdown for the main milks, minus some trace elements (plus a couple more):

Mammal	Water %	Fat %	Protein %	Lactose %
Cow	87.3	3.7	3.4	4.7
Goat	88.7	3.5	3.5	4.5
Sheep	80.7	7.4	5.5	4.8
Buffalo	82.5	7.6	4.2	4.8
Reindeer	66.9	16.9	11.5	2.8
Camel	86.2	4.5	3.6	5.0

Milk production varies from animal to animal. Cows are the most prolific milkers, whereas ewes or female sheep are the least; but sheep's milk is the most rich and concentrated of the big three milks. That means while cows produce more milk than sheep, less sheep's milk is needed to make cheese. As a general rule, one pound of cheese requires about 10 pounds of cow's milk or goat's milk, while only 6 pounds of sheep's milk is needed.

The variations in fat, protein, and lactose among the different milks means cheesemakers must handle the milks differently. For example, goat's milk and sheep's milk can be frozen and then used in cheesemaking, whereas cow's milk cannot be frozen because the cream separates from the milk.

To understand milk production and how it translates to cheese production, consider these famous cheeses: it takes about 12 pounds of milk to make a 2-pound round of Roquefort, and it takes about 3,000 pounds of milk to make a 220-pound wheel of Emmentaler (a Swiss cheese). Doing the math, it takes six pounds of sheep's milk to yield just one pound of Roquefort cheese, while it takes almost 14 pounds of cow's milk to yield just one pound of Emmentaler.

A Cut Above

Though we consumers measure milk in terms of cups or gallons, in the dairy world, milk is measured in pounds, with one pint of milk being almost the equivalent of a pound.

Mooving Milk

Worldwide, cow's milk makes more cheese than the other milks combined. Gallon per gallon, beautiful bovines out-milk other farm animals. Cows also naturally lactate almost year-round, or an average of 300 days. That means if you selectively breed portions of a herd you can easily have fresh milk year-round. (You'll have plenty of baby calves, too.) If you inject cows with hormones, it's even easier to drive up milk production. (More on that in a bit.) Certain types of feed also may increase production.

Cows greet visitors at the Three Sisters Farmstead Cheese Company.

(Jeanette Hurt)

Breeds

All cows are not created equal. Different breeds produce differing amounts of milk. Worldwide, Holsteins are the breed of choice for both milk and cheese because they are the biggest milkers. Jersey cows come in second, but other breeds such as Guernsey, Brown Swiss, and Ayrshire are also valued. All told, there are about 50 different bovine breeds whose milk is used in cheese production. In some countries, only certain breeds can be milked to produce certain types of cheese. For example, Reblochon is only made by the milk of the very French Montbéliard cows. Among the different breeds, milk fat content can also vary, but it doesn't vary as much as it does between the different species of milking animals.

A Cut Above

Milk production is not just affected by breeding. According to a scientific study of dairy cows subjected to music, softer music increases milk production by as much as 3 percent.

The University of Leicester determined that cows who listened to slower-paced music, including R.E.M.'s "Everybody Hurts" and Beethoven's *Pastoral Symphony,* produced more milk than those who listened to Wonderstuff's "Size of a Cow" or the Beatles' "Back in the USSR."

Breed to breed, the milks are more similar to each other than, say, camels or sheep, but the variations can be enough to make cheesemakers take notice. Raw, unprocessed, and unpasteurized cow's milk tends to be off-white or ivory in color, darkening in the summer season when bovines browse on more beta-carotene enriched pastures than winter silage. Ayrshire cows, however, are the exception, as this particular bovine produces a pure-white milk.

Hormones

Cows naturally produce a hormone called bovine growth hormone or bovine somatotropin, but in 1993, the FDA approved the use of synthetic bovine growth hormone or recombinant bovine growth hormone (rBGH), to increase a cow's milk production by at least 10 percent. Although the American Medical Association, the World Health Organization, and the FDA all agree that milk from cows receiving injections of this hormone is safe for human consumption, many advocacy groups disagree, saying not enough research has been done.

Canada and many European countries forbid the use of rBGH in their countries' cows, but they do allow imported milk and cheese from hormonally enhanced American cattle. Health Canada banned the hormone because of its adverse affects on cows, while hormone proponents point out there is no chemical or nutritional difference between milk produced from treated and untreated cows. Anecdotally, though, many artisan cheesemakers say milk from bulked up cows just doesn't taste as good, and a growing number of American cheesemakers are choosing to use rBGH-free milk.

Homogenization

In cheesemaking, cow's milk can be used raw or pasteurized; it may also be whole, skimmed of cream, or with added cream. Milk can be *homogenized* or *unhomogenized*, although most cheeses are made with unhomogenized milk. These various treatments of the milk add or remove characteristics that cheesemakers use to their advantage in cheesemaking. For example, raw cow's milk is used to create the famed Swiss Gruyère, while pasteurized milk is used to create the bright orange French cheese Mimolette. Italy's Asiago is made with partially skimmed milk.

Say Cheese _____

Homogenized means that milk fats have been broken down until they are evenly distributed throughout the milk. With **unhomogenized** milk, the cream separates and rises to the top, and the milk must be shaken to recombine the cream or fat with the rest of the milk. That's where the saying "The cream rises to the top" comes from.

Pasteurization

Two main pasteurization processes are used in cheesemaking. The first is gentle pasteurization, in which milk is heated up to 145°F for 30 minutes then rapidly cooled. The second, high temperature, short pasteurization or HTST, requires milk to be heated to 161°F for 15 seconds, then rapidly cooled.

A third type of pasteurization, ultra high temperature pasteurization or UHT, is not often used; in UHT, the milk is heated to 200°F, then cooled and packed into containers that don't require refrigeration. In the United States, all cheese that is aged less than 60 days must be pasteurized, and as such, pasteurization is used not just in cow's milk cheeses, but also in goat's and sheep's milk cheeses.

A Cut Above _____

In the United States, the majority of raw milk or unpasteurized cheese is made from cow's milk. Not only because quantitatively more cheese is made from cow's milk, but also because there are proportionally fewer aged goat's milk and sheep's milk cheeses produced.

Goat's Milk

Goats are curious creatures, and unlike both sheep and cows, goats are willing to be *browsers* and try anything at least once. Tin-can consumption jokes aside, goats prefer to forage or search out their nutritional intake rather than idly be *grazers* in pastures like their bovine and sheep counterparts in the barnyard.

Say Cheese _____

Browsers eat leaves, bark, twigs, shrubs, and vines.
Grazers primarily eat grass and clover.

More acrobatic than sheep and cows, goats will stand on their hind legs to reach tasty treats. If you ever happen to visit a goat farm, the goats will climb up their pens to sniff you and invite you to pet them. They also will pickpocket anything within their reach, and they might even taste your clothes, especially if there are any hanging straps, strings, or buckles.

Goats browse on fresh California pasture.

(Marin French Cheese Company)

There are dozens of different dairy breeds of goats, but in the United States, primarily six breeds are used for milk: Nubian, French Alpine, La Mancha, Saanen, Toggenberg, and Oberhasli. All but the Nubian and the La Mancha are considered "Swiss" goat breeds, or breeds developed in Switzerland and the Alps. The Nubian was developed in Great Britain and the La Mancha was developed in California from Spanish ancestry. The Nubian is the most popular breed in North America, as they are more heat tolerant and tend to be more out-of-season breeders, allowing for greater winter milk production.

Goats can not only survive but thrive in areas that are completely inhospitable to cows. Therefore, traditionally, they've been the cheesemaking milkers of choice in sparse, rocky regions of the world. An anomaly to this rule are the well-fed goats of the pastoral Loire Valley of France, where some of the most decadent goat cheeses on the planet have been perfected.

Though the fat content of goat's milk is similar to that of cow's milk, the fatty acid composition is quite different. Goat's milk has a higher proportion of caproic, caprylic, and capric acids, which create the characteristically tart flavors in goat cheese. With no carotene, goat milk always boasts a pure, chalky white color.

Goats produce milk for an average of 240 days or about eight months, but the first milk, called colostrom, isn't suitable for cheesemaking, as its purpose is to support the newborn kids' immune systems. Goats breed in fall, giving birth in late winter or early spring. The best milk for cheesemaking tends to be in the spring and summer months. Traditionally, goats are milked twice a day, with the evening milking offering a richer liquid with a higher fat content. But unlike cow's milk, goat's milk can be frozen to be used at a later date for cheesemaking. Of course, frozen milk is never quite as good as fresh.

Sheep's Milk

Like their billy counterparts, sheep can survive in more adverse terrain than cows. But unlike goats, sheep are pasture grazers, so sheep are traditionally grazed in rocky pastures in areas such as Spain, southern France, and Italy. Like cows, sheep are grazers; but sheep can graze in pastures that cows would find inhospitable. Think rugged, windswept, rocky pastures in Spain, Portugal, Italy, and Greece.

Sheep are, in fact, believed to be among the first animals to be milked in history. There are about two dozen breeds of sheep used in dairy production, and unlike cow's and goat's milks, which are often used to drink or make butter, yogurt, and ice cream, just about all of the sheep milk produced in the world is used for cheesemaking.

Worldwide, the East Friesian breed is the most common dairy sheep. Other popular breeds include the Awassi and Assaf from Israel and the French Lacaune.

A Cut Above

Because female sheep are called ewes, sometimes sheep's milk cheese is labeled as ewe's milk cheese.

A Cut Above

Unlike goat's milk cheeses, many sheep's milk cheeses are more well known by their names, than by the milk making them. Think of Italy's Pecorino Romano, Greece's Feta, Spain's Manchego, and the king of all cheeses, France's Roquefort.

Sheep tend to produce less milk than either goats or cows, but sheep's milk is richer than either cow's or goat's milk. Because part of the cheesemaking process is separating the water from the good stuff in the milk, ewe's (female sheep) milk is one step closer to becoming cheese, in a sense, than either goat's or cow's milk. For this reason, some people say sheep's milk is the best milk for cheesemaking. It's also nutritionally denser, and it's pure white in color. Sheep's milk is richer in vitamins A, B, and E, as well as calcium, than cow's milk, and it has a different proportion of fatty acids than cow's and goat's milks. The milk also has more linoleic acid, a member of the omega-6 fatty acids, which are believed to help prevent cancer.

Like goat's milk, sheep's milk can be frozen and then used in cheesemaking. Because sheep lactate, on average, about 150 to 240 days a year, that prolongs the cheesemaking season and allows cheesemakers to stock up on milk until they have enough to make cheese.

Cheeses Made with Exotic Milks

Some cheesemaking milkers do not cut a common figure in farms across the globe. In fact, although all mammals produce milk, not all mammals' milks are used for human consumption. Still, we need to discuss a few other animals when it comes to cheesemaking. Water buffalo, reindeer, yaks, camels, and even horses and donkeys can be and are milked for cheese production.

Perhaps the most well-known and most common "exotic" in cheesemaking is the water buffalo. Mozzarella might be synonymous with Italy, but the mozzarella they eat in Italy isn't the stuff that comes shredded in bags. In fact, it's not even the fresh mozzarella common in upscale Italian groceries and delis in the United States. The fact is, Italian mozzarella is really *Mozzarella di bufala*, or buffalo milk mozzarella, made in the central-south region of Italy—in Caserta and Salerno, as well as parts of Benevento, Naples, Frosinone, Latina, and Rome.

Because it's so rich, buffalo milk is not used for drinking and is reserved exclusively for making fresh cheese. Fresh Mozzarella di bufala offers a richer-tasting cheese with more depth than the fresh mozzarella made from cow's milk. Some farmers in the United States are beginning to raise water buffalo, including Woodstock Water Buffalo Co. Cheese in Vermont.

A Cut Above

Though Mozzarella di bufala is a bit harder to come by in North America, one place you can experience it is at a small bed and breakfast in British Columbia, Fairburn Farm, which makes it fresh. But unless you stay at this B and B or attend the farm's cooking classes, you won't get to taste this wonderful mozzarella.

Reindeer milk could be considered the next most prevalent exotic milk for cheesemaking. In Finland, reindeer milk is used to make Juustoleipa, which can be translated to mean "cheese bread." Pronounced *HOO-stah-lee-pah*, this is made by draining and pressing the curds into a flat dish that is then toasted on an open fire, giving the cheese a brown, breadlike crust that looks more like toast than cheese.

Apparently, though, Rudolph's female counterparts aren't that easy to milk. The yields of milk are low, compared to other milking mammals, and it takes two people to milk a reindeer—one to do the work, the other to hold the horns. Traditionally, Finnish mothers have served the cheese to their daughters' suitors, and if their suitors approve of the cheese, then they are deemed suitable.

A Cut Above

Though we haven't come across any Juustoleipa made from reindeer's milk imported here, several Wisconsin creameries, including Brunkow, Bass Lake, Carr Valley, and Pasture's Pride, make a version from cow's milk. Pasture's Pride also produces a version with added jalapeño peppers, which probably is not a Finnish tradition.

Mélange of Milks

Mixed-milk cheeses are aptly named because they're made from at least two, sometimes three, types of milk. Traditionally, most European cheeses are made from a single milk. As with most areas of cuisine, the locals made do with the ingredients on hand, and most regions had either cows, goats, or sheep.

The exception to this rule is Spain. Though most of the Iberian cheeses come from single milk sources, there is a tradition of mixing milks, especially in the Castilla-Leon and Castilla-La Mancha regions.

Perhaps the most well-known mixed-milk Spanish cheese is the blue cheese Cabrales, which is made of cow's, goat's, and sheep's milks and aged in caves in northern Spain. Other Spanish milk medleys include Picón and Valdeon. Some fetas in Greece are a blend of cow's and sheep's milk. The Italians make a blend of sheep's milk and cow's milk, sprinkled with truffles called Caciotta al Tartufo, and the Portuguese make a three-milk blend called Toledo.

But much of the mixing is going on in the United States, where artisan cheesemakers such as Sid Cook of Carr Valley Cheese in Wisconsin, Soyoung Scanlan of Andante Dairy in California, and Eran Wojswol of Valley Shepherd Creamery in Vermont all make cheeses that involve the mixing of milks. These and other American artisans are combining sheep with goat, cow with goat, sheep with cow, and sometimes sheep, goat, and cow.

> **A Cut Above**
>
> The first mixed-milk cheese to achieve prominence in American cheese circles is Sid Cook's Gran Canaria, a blend of sheep's, goat's, and cow's milks that's cured in olive oil and then aged. This nutty, deeply flavored cheese was the first mixed-milk cheese to win the Best of Show honors from the American Cheese Society in 2004.

Mixed-milk cheeses can be created by directly blending the milks together or by creating separate layers of milks within the cheeses. Although there is a trend of more American artisans trying out mixed-milk cheeses, there will probably not be huge numbers of them creating these cheeses simply because it's a challenge to obtain milks from all three types of animals.

The Geography of Cheese

Talk to any winemaker, and they'll wax poetic about the minerals in the soil the grapes are grown in, the sun and wind conditions of the vineyard, the seasonal anomalies that affected this year's vintage, and so on. Cheesemakers can be equally verbose.

But unlike wine, which has a direct relationship to the soil and the weather conditions, cheese has more of an indirect relationship to the geographical and environmental conditions in which it is produced. Cheese is, of course, related to the milk, and the milk is directly affected by anything that affects the animal being milked.

What the animal ate, where it fed, what part of the lactation cycle it was being milked in—these are all factors that can come into play in cheese. Cheese produced from the milk of cows that are fed formulated silage tastes different from cheese from the milk of cows that nibbled on grass in the pasture. And if those cows in the pasture ate clover, too, well, that can also come out in the cheese. We don't necessarily taste clover in our cheese (unless it's added to the cheese afterward the way peppercorns and jalapeños are mixed in some cheeses), but the quality of milk is affected.

Some cheesemakers, especially farmstead producers who milk their own animals, can be quite fussy about what their animals snack on. Mike Gingrich, of Uplands Cheese Company in Wisconsin, went so far as to specify the grass seeds used to feed his cows so that his Pleasant Ridge Reserve, an American artisan cheese, would have the taste profile he was looking for. Simply put, what happens to the cow or the goat or the sheep, happens to the cheese.

The *terroir* of the milk is affected not only by what the animals consume, but also by the natural bacteria and molds in the area that might come into contact with the cheese as it's being made. This is not always as true today as it was in the past, as modern technology makes it easy for cheesemakers around the globe to use the same mold used in Roquefort to make different blue cheeses. But some cheesemakers, both in Europe and North America, encourage natural flora and fauna to affect their cheeses.

Say Cheese

Terroir is a French term that denotes the effects that geography and distinct environments have on food products, particularly wine and coffee. It also can be used to describe the way a region imparts flavors to cheese.

A Bit About Cheese Nutrition and Reading Cheese Labels

Okay, it's kind of obvious to say so, but cheese is typically a more calorie-dense food than, say, broccoli. But eating cheese—especially good cheese—is not necessarily the precursor to gaining weight that some people think it might be.

Good cheese—cheese that's not processed—does contain fat, but because it usually tastes richer, it fills you up faster than slices of fat-free processed cheese. Some recent studies show that the fats that make you fat are trans fats—the kind of fats that are in processed and highly preservative-laden foods—not the kind of natural fats found in dairy or meat products.

Milk, and thus cheese, does contain quantities of vitamins such as A, D, E, and K, as well as B vitamins, a small amount of vitamin C, as well as calcium, phosphorus, and magnesium—all things that do a body good, especially when it comes to bone health.

Not only is cheese good for bones, but it is especially good for your teeth. Recent studies by the British Nutrition Foundation have discovered that eating cheese after a meal can help prevent tooth decay. Apparently, eating cheese increases the amount of saliva in your mouth, which helps wash away the food particles that get stuck to teeth and cause decay. The phosphorus and calcium in cheese are also thought to replace the minerals in tooth enamel, which further strengthens teeth. Cheese is one of the few foods that's been proven to be good for your teeth.

A Cut Above

One especially confusing point is that some cheeses are considered double or triple creams, which does mean that there is more butterfat in those cheeses. But those cheeses are soft cheeses, and soft cheeses actually have less fat than hard cheeses. A dense hard cheese like Parmigiano-Reggiano actually has more calories than a creamy Brie.

Reading cheese labels can be a bit confusing because some labels indicate a cheese is "50 percent" butterfat. But that doesn't mean that half of every slice is fat. Fat content on cheeses is calculated on the percentage of solids in the cheese, with the liquids excluded, and most cheeses are between 50 and 70 percent water.

Lastly, good cheese can be seen as a fine indulgence, and as with any indulgence, it is best consumed in moderation. Most dieticians and doctors endorse moderation.

The Least You Need to Know

- Cows, goats, and sheep are the most common animals to be milked for cheese production.

- Other exotic animals such as water buffalo and reindeer can also be milked for cheese.

- Cheese tastes and characteristics not only vary from milk to milk, but they also are dependent on the geography and environments in which the animals are raised.

- Cheese contains many important nutrients.

Chapter 4

The Main Cheeses

In This Chapter

- ◆ Different classification methods for cheese
- ◆ Texture versus milk versus rind classifications
- ◆ Fresh cheeses
- ◆ Bloomy and washed rind cheeses
- ◆ Semi-soft, firm, hard, and blue cheeses
- ◆ Processed cheese products

How do you classify cheese? … let us count the ways. There are plenty of hard-and-fast rules for making cheese, but there isn't one be-all, end-all system for classifying the different types of cheese.

Sometimes cheese is classified by its milk; even the name chevre, which refers to fresh French goat's milk cheese, means goat in French. Other times, cheese is classified by its color—blue cheeses, are, in fact, blue. Then, raw milk versus pasteurized milk sometimes comes into play. Most cheeses, however, are classified by texture and rind.

The Basic Types of Cheese

The rind is where it's at. Just as the art of affinage develops the various types of rinds and textures of cheese, how a cheese is aged largely determines its classification.

The main types of cheeses are fresh or rindless, bloomy and soft-rinded, semi-soft, firm or semi-hard, hard, washed rind, and blue. Cheeses in each category can be made using different milks and methods, but within each classification there are similarities in tastes and textures.

> **A Cut Above**
>
> Some of the earliest classi-fiers of cheese were those enterprising Romans. Regular or softer cheeses were called caseus, but when they began aging cheese so that it could be more easily transported by their armies, they named that formagium.

Some cheeses—often cheeses made from goat's milk or sheep's milk—can be classified not only by their rind but also by their milks, whether the milk is raw milk or pasteurized. For example, Mt. Sterling Cheese Company in Wisconsin makes a raw goat's milk cheddar. But many famous cheeses—such as Manchego and Roquefort—are classified by their texture or their color, rather than their milks.

Fresh Cheeses

Fresh cheeses were probably the first kinds of cheeses ever developed. Made fresh and sent off to be consumed within days of making, these cheeses generally are creamy, young, and almost juicy, as they contain much more whey than other cheeses. Fresh cheeses have no rind, and they can be so soft that they can be scooped and packed into containers. They can also be gently molded. These cheeses have a fresh flavor, and they taste distinctly of the milk from which they are made. Extremely soft, these are the mildest cheeses.

Think of the fresh chevres of the Loire Valley in France; these cheeses are poured into containers or gently formed into logs, which are sometimes rolled in cracked pepper-corns or herbs. Herbs and spices can also be mixed into fresh cheeses as well.

Another famous fresh cheese is mozzarella. Mozzarella is a cheese that is spun into balls and then preserved in whey. The Italians call this pasta filata. Feta is another fresh cheese, and its creamy crumbles are preserved in a salty brine. Simple cottage cheese, which showed up on diet plates in restaurants everywhere in the 1970s, is also a fresh cheese, just cow's milk curds dressed in cream. When cottage cheese is pressed, it becomes farmer's cheese.

Bloomy Rind Cheeses and Triple Crèmes

Luxury knows no bounds when it comes to the creamy beauties of bloomy rind and triple crème cheeses. Brie, Camembert, and other famed cheeses belong to this class. These cheeses are created by a mold and soft-ripening process that typically goes from the outside of the cheese and moves inward to the cheese's interior. During the cheesemaking process, many times, bacterial cultures are sprayed on the outside of the pressed rounds of cheese to create the rinds. Some cheesemakers, like Marin French Cheese Company in Petaluma, California, mix the bacterial cultures right into the milk instead of spraying them onto the cheese rounds.

Besides the well-known Brie and Camembert cheeses, double and triple crèmes also belong to this class. Double and triple crème cheeses are cheeses that are enriched with cream. Double crème cheeses have a minimum fat content of 60 percent while triple crèmes have a minimum fat content of 75 percent.

Brillat-Savarin and Cremeaux de Bourgogne are two famed triple crème cheeses. Buttery rich, the cheeses in this class have edible rinds, and they are soft to the touch. They often also have a silky mouth feel and a buttery taste. Don't let the double or triple fat content trip you up. These luscious cheeses actually have less calories per ounce than hard cheeses like Gruyère or Parmigiano-Reggiano. Hard cheeses have more calories because they have less moisture and are denser.

A Cut Above

Brillat-Savarin, one of my favorite triple crème cheeses, is named for the famous French gastronome, Jean Anthelme Brillat-Savarin, and it was first created in the 1930s by cheesemaker Henry Androuet.

Washed Rind Cheeses

Washed rind cheeses are the original stinky cheeses. These pungent cheeses are so named for the process of washing them during their affinage period. If you ever get the chance to walk into a cellar filled with these aromatic rounds, you'll get more than a whiff of ammonia.

They can be washed in brine, beer, wine, spirits, or even olive oil. Often, their cheesemakers have their own special recipe for a wash. Early on in their process, these cheeses are washed every day, and less frequently as they age. Cheeses in this aromatic category include: Taleggio, Livaro, Limburger, and Maroilles, which is a washed rind cheese made near the border of Belgium. One version, Gris de Lille, boasts the nickname of *Ouant de Lille*, which translates to "stinker from Lille."

A cheesemaker at Roth Kase washes the rind of Gruyere.

(Roth Kase)

A Cut Above

Limburger, an oft-maligned cheese, was described in 1880 by John Luchsinger as "a premeditated outrage on the organs of smell." Its smell so upset a mail carrier in Iowa in 1935, who claimed its aroma made him sick, that the postmaster of Independence, Iowa, barred Limburger cheese from being mailed. This upset the postmaster in Monroe, Wisconsin, where the cheese was made. The ensuing brouhaha resulted in a "Limburger trial" in which judges deferred to the cheese.

What's interesting to note, however, is that these smelly cheeses are not usually the strongest tasting. When you place those cheeses in your mouth, their aromas are toned down, and they often taste much milder than their smell would indicate.

Semi-Soft Cheeses

Semi-soft cheeses are easily recognized by their texture. Not quite hard but not really that soft, they are aptly classified as semi-soft. Semi-soft cheeses often have earthy undertones, and gentle yellow or soft-white colorings. Sometimes these cheeses have a gentle mold on the rind, and they also might be coated in wax. Think Edam, Young Gouda, and fontina.

A Cut Above

Though most fontinas you'll taste in the United States could be considered semi-soft, the name-controlled Fontina d'Aosta is a washed rind cheese made in the Piedmont region of Italy. The version more commonly found in the United States is a semi-soft, Danish style of the cheese.

Firm (Not Too Hard) Cheeses

Cheese classification by texture sometimes gets a little complicated. Under some systems of classification, hard and firm cheeses are combined under hard cheeses. But there are distinctions, so how can one tell the difference?

Firm cheese, just by touch, has a little more give to it if you press your finger into it. Hard cheese is, well harder, and it crumbles more easily. Many great Swiss cheeses fall into the firm realm, including Emmentaler and Gruyère, as well as the French Alpine cheese, Beaufort. The Swiss cheeses are also more commonly referred to as Swiss cheese or Swiss styles of cheese: pointing not only to their place of origin but to their characteristic holes. The holes or *eyes* are caused by carbon dioxide pockets emitted when certain bacteria eat the lactose in the cheese. This secondary fermentation is called *propionic acid fermentation.*

Say Cheese

Propionic acid fermentation is named after the propionic bacteria that grows two weeks after the cheeses are first made. At this stage, the cheeses are moved to a warmer room, and propionic acid bacteria (*propionibacterium shermanii*) grow and emit carbon dioxide. This develops the **eyes** or holes in the cheese after three to six weeks. After the eyes develop, the cheeses are aged at a cooler temperature.

Other firm cheeses include the cheddars of both England and the United States, as well as Spain's most famous cheese, Manchego. Firm cheeses often have a nutty flavor. They can also have sharp or tangy flavors, as aged cheddars do. Their rinds should be cut away and not eaten.

Hard Cheeses

Hard cheeses are the big boys in the world of cheese. Dry, hard, grainy, crunchy, and crumbly, these cheeses are typically aged longer, and they boast intense and complex flavors.

Stinky Cheese

Forget those little green shakers of cheese in the pasta aisles of grocery stores. If you read the label on these canisters, you will see that although real cheese might be an ingredient, this is a processed cheese product; one that does not taste at all like real Parmigiano-Reggiano.

Think Parmigiano-Reggiano, dry Monterey Jack, and aged Goudas. These are not cheeses for the faint of heart. Milk itself is made up of 80 to 88 percent water. As a cheese ages, its water percent declines. Hard cheeses typically have a 30 to 35 percent water content, and fresh cheeses can be 70 to 80 percent water.

A little of these cheeses goes a long way. They are great to grate (pun intended). What spaghetti with marinara sauce could not be improved with some Parmigiano-Reggiano? Purists, however, will stress that these cheeses should not be tainted by other flavors but instead savored alone or perhaps just on a slice of bread.

Blue Cheeses

Blue cheeses range from delicate blues to distinctive blue greens in color, but it's easy to see how they get their name. The color of blue cheeses puts them in a category all their own. Famous blues include Roquefort, Gorgonzola, and Stilton.

A Cut Above

The penicillium molds used to ripen cheese are slightly different species than those used in antibiotics. For the production of penicillin, the species *penicillium notatum* and *penicillium chrysogenum* are used.

What they have in common, besides color, is that they all boast a mold that gives them their characteristic coloring. Perhaps the most famous mold used in their making is *penicillium roquefortii*, first found in the caves of Combalou, outside the village of Roquefort, France.

Though some blue cheeses get their molds from their aging environments, many of them are "inoculated" during the cheesemaking process; that is to say, the molds are mixed directly into the milk. To make the molds grow, the cheeses need to be exposed to air. Many blue cheese rounds have holes punched in them to allow the blue veins to develop more evenly throughout the cheese as the air better circulates around the cheese.

Blue cheeses typically are strong and full of flavor. They offer a complex array of tastes, both piquant and pungent notes. Because they are often brined, they also have a distinct saltiness.

Some cheeses aren't naturally blue during the affinage process, but they develop a bluing that can begin even after they are delivered to stores. That can be good or bad depending on the cheese connoisseur. Some English cheddars, for example, are prized even more highly when they attract a little of the blue mold because only the richest cheeses ever turn blue.

Processed Cheese

Processed cheese isn't exactly cheese, but it is closer to cheese than, say, a granola bar. Processed cheese or "cheese food products" all start out as cheese or have cheese as the primary ingredient. But a lot of other ingredients, some of which gourmets disdain as junk, are also added.

Cheese is shredded and melted down, and then various fats, emulsifiers, flavorings, dyes, and preservatives are added. Many of them can sit on shelves without refrigeration for months. Processed cheeses include Velveeta, American cheese, and even boxed macaroni and cheese dinners.

But processed cheese isn't only made by Americans. French children love La Vache Qui Rit (which translates to "The cow who laughs"), which was invented in 1921. A red cow with a grin appears on the packaging.

Cheese spreads can also be considered processed cheese, but that's more of a gray area, as many specialty or artisan cheese producers also make cheese spreads. Another gray area is cream cheese. Cream cheese is cheese, but several stabilizers like guar gum are added so that it doesn't break down into liquids and solids. The most famous brand of cream cheese is Philadelphia Cream Cheese.

A Cut Above

Cream cheese was first invented in 1872 by William Lawrence, an American dairy farmer. It was given the brand name of Philadelphia in 1880 because Philadelphia was considered to be a haven for good food.

The Least You Need to Know

◆ Cheese can be classified by milk or origin, but it is most commonly classified by texture or rind.

◆ The most common classifications for cheese are fresh, bloomy rind, washed rind, semi-soft, firm, hard, and blue.

◆ Processed cheese is derived from real cheese, but it isn't quite cheese.

◆ The Romans perfected and then spread more modern methods of cheesemaking.

Part 2

Old World Favorites

If you haven't been nibbling on a bit of cheese as you've read along with this book, this is the time to start. By now, we've explored what goes into cheese—what it is, what its history was, what milks go into it, and what the various types of cheese are. We can attend a cocktail party, and we can dissect the basics of what's on a cheese plate, knowing roughly what we might be tasting.

But now it's time to get into the big cheeses that influence all the other cheeses—the European greats, as well as the lesser-known beauties that have shaped dairy history. This part will take you through the individual cheese histories of Europe, explore what each country has contributed to the world of cheese, and discuss their main cheeses. By the time you finish reading, I hope you'll be very hungry.

WE'D BOTH LIKE A DOUBLE ORDER OF MACARONI AND CHEESE, BUT HOLD THE MACARONI!

French Cheeses

In This Chapter

- The history of cheese in France
- The name controlled cheeses in France
- The various cheesemaking regions of France
- French cheeses of note
- The role of cheese within French culture

No one enjoys cheese like the French do. In fact, to truly know cheese, you have to go to France. Although plenty of countries produce good cheese, and plenty of countries eat a lot of cheese, no one does it like the French do.

The French compete with the Greeks in terms of who eats the most cheese per person. A typical French person, on average, eats more than 50 pounds of cheese every year; the average Greek person eats a few pounds more. But the two differ in one key way: in Greece, almost all the cheese consumed is feta; the French consume a variety of cheese. The French also are one of the top producers of cheese, just behind the United States and Germany, and just ahead of Italy. And France is also the biggest exporter of cheese, in monetary terms.

But what takes France to a level above practically every other country in the world is the depth and the breadth of its cheeses. Charles de Gaulle once said of his beloved France, "How can you govern a country that has 246 varieties of cheese?"

And since the days of de Gaulle, that number has gone way up. Depending on who you talk to and which expert you consult, France has anywhere from 400 to 750 different types of cheese. From fresh to aged, soft to hard, raw to pasteurized, artisan to processed, there's more than a cheese for every day of the year, not to mention a cheese for every mood and every occasion.

In France, cheese is not just a meal or part of a meal, it is an experience in and of itself. Though not worshipped, cheese is nonetheless sacred and revered, and French cheese is often considered the standard against which all other cheeses are measured.

The History of French Cheese

Though it's not arguable that the French took cheese to new levels, what is debatable is how much the old Gauls were influenced by those invading Romans in the art of cheesemaking. What is known is that the ancient Gauls did make cheese, and the Romans did invade Gaul. One supposes that the Romans likely introduced the Gauls to the art of making harder, rennet-curdled cheeses because that's what they did throughout the rest of Europe.

What is also not completely known is which of France's venerable cheeses is the oldest. However, two of the oldest are Roquefort and Cantal. Both date back to the time of the Gauls, and Roquefort, in fact, may have been referenced by the Roman historian Pliny the Elder in 79 C.E., when he wrote of a cheese from the mountainous region of France near the Mediterranean. Prehistoric colanders to drain cheese have also been found in that region of Rouergue (part of Languedoc).

But this cheese that Pliny wrote about may have instead been Cantal, which is made in the nearby Auvergne region in the Cantal Mountains. In any case, by the eighth century, Charlemagne was enjoying Roquefort, and Roquefort shows up in monastery records in 1070 (another, oft-cited date of Roquefort's beginning). Roquefort has also been written about by other notable writers, including Brillat-Savarin, Colette, and Casanova; and during feudal times it was used to pay rent and cover debts.

After the Roman Empire fell, monks preserved and further developed cheesemaking in France. Monks helped farmers with agricultural production, and they taught them how to properly age cheese. The monks also developed different ripening and aging traditions of cheesemaking. One of the first cheeses created by monks, in an abbey in

Thierache in 960, was Maroilles, a washed rind. Other Trappist cheeses like Munster, Pont L'Eveque, and Epoisses followed.

A Cut Above

> Maroilles was called "the miracle of Maroilles," and it was favored especially by royalty, including several French kings. A similar cheese to Maroilles is called le Dauphin. When Louis XIV went to visit the region where Maroilles was produced, his hosts gave him a Maroilles that had been flavored with fresh herbs. Louis's entourage really enjoyed it, including his heir, the Dauphin, so Dauphin is now shaped like a dolphin, too.

Different cheeses evolved according to the different milks available, and varying cheesemaking traditions took root. In the Loire Valley, for example, a lot of goat's milk cheeses developed, whereas cows flourished in Normandy.

Other famous French cheeses were developed, including Brie or Brie de Meaux, which dates back to at least the twelfth century. In fact, Blanche of Navarre, countess of Champagne, sent several wheels of Brie to Philippe Auguste (Philippe II) to serve to the women he was courting.

Cheesemaking became more organized, too. By the thirteenth century, in Déservilliers, the first known cheese cooperative was formed. It was created by dairy women who were looking to increase their revenues from their milk production.

By the fifteenth century, cheese was even called by its modern French name—fromage. It originated from the early French word *forma*, which became formage, which became fourmage, and then fourmaigne before finally the French settled on fromage. In 1666, the first legal document related to cheese was issued in Toulouse, and it concerned Roquefort and its aging.

France's most popular cheese, Camembert, made its debut in the 1500s or 1600s. But popular legend dates the cheese to the 1790s. The story goes that it was created by Marie Harel, a French farmer, who was hiding a young priest from Brie who was on the run during the French Revolution. Supposedly, in return for shelter, he lent some of his cheesemaking knowledge to Harel, who then created Camembert. Though this is the popular story, older records date Camembert back to 1680, or even further, to 1569. But what is known for sure about Camembert is that when railroads became more widespread—in the 1850s—Camembert was on them. Camembert traveled more frequently after 1890 when Eugene Ridel, an engineer, invented the wooden box with which it's now so closely associated.

The 1800s also saw the experiments of a certain French scientist whose work would revolutionize and change cheese production the world over. In 1857, Louis Pasteur, chemist and biologist, invented the process of pasteurization—to kill germs with heat. Pasteur was working with the process of fermentation as it related to beer and wine making, but soon, others saw how his work related to milk. What makes this more than a bit ironic is that the greatest of France's cheeses are made with *lait cru* or raw milk. "A Frenchman invented the process that ruined most of the world's cheese, but it took the ingenuity of the U.S. Food & Drug Administration to mandate pasteurization of just about everything," bemoaned Steven A. Shaw in an article published on Salon.com (January 2000).

The 1800s and the 1900s also saw the start of factory cheese production. The way it worked in France was that the dairy farmers of a region would take their milk to a central cheesemaker, who would make the cheese. Then the cheese would be aged by an affineur or a professional who would age the cheeses correctly. One of those affineurs was Jules Bel, who started the Bel company in 1865 in Orgelet, in the Jura region of France. Bel would age the local wheels of Comté in the old wine cellars of a former convent. But it wasn't Jules who was the innovator of the Bel family. It was his son, Leon.

Leon wondered what to do with the leftovers of unsold Comté and Emmentaler. Instead of letting them go to waste, he developed a melting or processed cheese. In 1921, Leon registered a trademark for the cheese, La Vache Qui Rit, or Laughing Cow cheese. An early advertiser on radio, Bel also took the unheard of step of setting up a separate publicity department in 1926. In the 1930s, he started taking the cheese abroad; but instead of marketing it as La Vache Qui Rit, it became Laughing Cow cheese.

The 1930s also saw the invention of another famous cheese. Henri Androuet created Brillat-Savarin, a triple crème bloomy rind cheese that he named after the eighteenth-century French gastronome Anthelme Brillat-Savarin, who once said "Tell me what you eat, and I will tell you what you are."

Name Controlled Cheeses and the Debate over Raw Milk

Factory production of cheese continued to grow in the twentieth century. Around the same time, France started taking steps to protect its national dairy and other food treasures. The first cheese to receive any legal protection was Roquefort, which received its recognized Appellation d'Origine in 1925. In 1953, the French passed a law that more strictly defined what cheese was, but the more formal Appellation d'Origine Contrôlée or AOC designation system, which identified the cheeses and strictly controlled their production, wasn't established until 1979 and 1980.

The AOC system not only identifies cheeses and makes sure that other cheeses do not share the same names, but it also strictly outlines how these cheeses can be made. The cheeses that have AOC designation include Abondance, Banon, Beaufort, Bleu d'Auvergne, Bleu de Gex-Haut-Jura, Bleu des Causses, Bleu du Vercors Sassenage, Brie de Meaux, Brie de Melun, Brocciu, Cabecou du Perigourd, Camembert de Normandie, Cantal, Chabichou du Poitou, Chaource, Chevraillon, Chevrotin des Aravis, Comté, Crottin de Chavignol, Epoisses de Bourgogne, Fourme d'Ambert, Fourme de Montbrison, Langres, Laguiole, Livarot, Maconnais, Maroilles, Mont d'Or or Vacherin du Haut-Doubs, Morbier, Munster, Neufchatel, Ossau-Iraty Brebis Pyrenees, Pelardon, Picodon, Pont-l'Eveque, Pouligny-Saint-Pierre, Reblochon, Rocamadour, Roquefort, Sainte-Maure de Touraine, Saint-Nectaire, Salers, Selles-sur-Cher, Tomme de Savoie or Tomme des Bauges, and Valencay.

In addition to adding cheeses to the list, in recent years the biggest debate in France over cheese is over pasteurization. Large French cheese and dairy companies have been pushing to have all cheese made from pasteurized milk. For example, in early 2007, one large cooperative, Isigny-Sainte-Mere asked the National Institute for Origin and Quality to change the rules that govern the AOC label for Camembert, to allow them to make Camembert de Normandie from pasteurized milk. The request came, in part, from globalization expansion pushes. There was a public outcry, but it hasn't yet been completely resolved. It's interesting to note, however, that only 7 percent of French cheeses eaten in France are unpasteurized, compared with the 50 percent just 30 years ago.

While the French industrial side of cheese-making explores the possibility of pasteurizing all cheeses, many American artisans are going the opposite route: these cheesemakers would like to have the rules changed in the United States to allow the production of raw milk cheeses that are aged less than 60 days.

A Cut Above

To improve the popularity of lait cru cheeses, there's been a calendar published with scantily clad women posing with raw milk cheeses. The calendar is sponsored by France's regional cheese association, and the cheeses are posed with the sexy women in the months in which they are traditionally produced.

The Cheesemaking Regions of France

A country the size of Texas, France has enough mountains, hilly pastures, and river tributaries to provide a diverse terrain from which a delicious variety of cheeses evolved. France has 22 provinces, and almost all of them make cheese. But it gets a bit complicated when you consider that these provinces can further be divided into different agricultural and political regions. To cut through some of the confusion, we'll start with the provinces, and then break them down into the regions and note the cheeses that are made there.

The provinces are Normandy, or rather Upper Normandy and Lower Normandy; Brittany, Nord-Pas-De-Calais, Picardy, Champagne-Ardenne, Ile-de-France, Alsace, Lorraine, Pays de la Loire, Poitou-Charentes, Centre, Burgundy, Franche-Comté, Rhone-Alps, Midi-Pyrenees, Aquitaine, Auvergne, Corsica, Languedoc-Roussillon, Provence-Alpes-Côte d'Azur, and Limousin.

The Rhone-Alps can be broken down into the cheese regions of Haute-Savoie and Savoie. Aquitaine can be broken down into a couple of regions, including Perigord and Pays Basque or Basque Country. The Midi-Pyrenees can be called Quercy. It's important to know these regions within the provinces because sometimes cheese will be identified with them.

Normandy is one of France's most important cheesemaking regions. This region, besides being home to the D-Day beaches, boasts lush farmland, rich soil, and Norman cows, whose milk is world-renowned. It produces the only authentic Camembert, Camembert de Normandie (France's most widely copied cheese), as well as Pont L'Eveque, Brillat-Savarin, and Livarot. It is also home to some amazing varieties of apples, apple orchards, and Calvados, a distilled cider that actually pairs quite well with the region's cheeses.

Nearby Brittany is France's maritime province, but besides fish and seafaring ways, this province also is home to two Trappist cheeses, Port-du-Salut and Saint-Paulin.

Picardy and Nord-Pas-de-Calais (also known as Flanders) border Belgium and the English Channel, but they also make some pretty stinky cheeses—Gris de Lille and Maroilles—as well as one of the few annatto-colored cheeses in France, Mimolette.

Champagne-Ardenne is not only the region of the world's most celebrated bubbly, but its chalky soil is home to the fabulous bloomy rind Chaource. Ile-de-France, home to Paris, is also home to Brie, both Brie de Meaux and Brie de Melun, as well as the bloomy Coulommiers. Brie de Meaux is actually from the outskirts of Paris in the Seine Et Marne.

A Cut Above

At the end of the Napoleonic Wars in 1815, at the Congress of Vienna, a French statesman, Talleyrand, organized a competition for the best cheese in the world, and Brie was named *le roi du fromage*, or the "king of cheese." Although Brie took that honor, to this day, if you ask a cheese expert what the king of cheese is, Roquefort is crowned.

Alsace and Lorraine are separate provinces, but people usually refer to these heavily German-influenced regions as the Alsace-Lorraine. At various points in history it was a part of Germany and the Austro-Hungarian Empire, but ever since the two world wars, it's been a part of France. Lush green pastures make for extraordinarily silky milk that becomes the highly aromatic Munster.

The Loire River and its tributaries traverse through Pays de la Loire, Poitou-Charentes, and Centre, and these valleys are home not only to some spectacular white wines (Vouvray, Sancerre), but also some of the world's best chevres. The goats here produce some pretty notable cheeses, including the Selles-sur-Cher and Valencay. This region is also home to an amazing, cave-aged, bloomy rind cow's milk cheese called Cure Nantais.

The rocky soil of Burgundy isn't only home to famous vineyards; it's also birthplace of the famous Epoisses de Bourgogne and to some fresh chevres, including Montrachet, which is often exported to the United States.

That it borders Switzerland might have something to do with the mountain cheeses produced in Franche-Comté. In fact, this region has argued with Switzerland over the right to call their Gruyère, Gruyère. Instead, Franche-Comté calls its Gruyère, Comté or Gruyère de Comté. This mountainous area also makes a French Emmentaler, as well as ash-layered Morbier.

The Rhone-Alps borders Switzerland and Italy, boasting lush Alpine pastures, and it is home to the Alpine Beaufort, Tomme de Savoie and Reblochon.

Aquitaine, along with the nearby Limousin and Midi-Pyrenees, is home to some artisan goat's milk cheeses, much of which is just sold and consumed within the region. Aquitaine is also home to Perigord truffles and the wonderful Bordeaux wine region.

Auvergne is home to some mountain regions and some amazing cheeses including Saint-Nectaire, Fourme d'Ambert, and Cantal de Salers. Nearby, in the Languedoc-Roussillon region, specifically in the area called Rouergue, you'll find the caves of Cambalou, which age Roquefort. You'll also find two noteworthy cow's milk blues, Bleu des Causses and Bleu d'Auvergne.

Provence-Alps-Côte-d'Azur is considered to be a gourmet's delight, with its fresh herbs, olive trees, delicious fruit orchards, and fabulous fishing. It is also home to some great grazing lands for goats and sheep, which provide the milk for the chestnut leaf-wrapped Banon and the Picodon.

Lastly, there is the Pays Basque or Basque Country and the island of Corsica. This craggy mountain country isn't only home to one of the most ancient peoples in the world—the Basque—but also some amazing sheep's milk cheeses. The Basque, who speak their own language, Euskari, make *brebis* or sheep's milk cheese, including the famed Ossau-Iraty Brebis Pyrenees. Corsica, like Basque Country, specializes in sheep's milk cheeses, the most famous of which is Brindamour.

From Brie to Z: The Great Cheeses of France

With hundreds of cheeses to choose from, France is a cheese lovers' paradise—a paradise filled with everything from the delicate to the pungent, from the soft to the hard, and everything in between. This is hardly a complete list, but it provides a good introduction to the wonderful cheeses that France offers.

Brie

Perhaps the best place to start is with Brie. In France, there are really two types of Bries—Brie de Meaux and Brie de Melun. Brie de Meaux is the Brie that you're probably most familiar with. But real Brie de Meaux is made from unpasteurized milk and seldom aged the required 60 days to ship to the United States. Real Brie de Meaux is soft, creamy, and bursting with earthy flavor.

Brie de Melun is similar to Brie de Meaux, but it is aged differently—no rennet is used to coagulate the milk—and it has a saltier, sharper taste. A sort of pasteurized version of Brie de Meaux is called Fromage de Meaux. Also in the Brie family is Coulommiers, which is smaller than a Brie but also quite delicious.

Double and Triple Crème Bloomy Rinds

Then, of course, there are the double and triple crème bloomy rinds. Brillat-Savarin is a particularly luscious triple crème cheese that practically melts in your mouth. Explorateur is another rich triple crème, and it was invented in the 1950s and named for the first American satellite.

Camembert is sometimes lumped together with Brie, as it also has a bloomy rind, but Camembert is an entirely different animal. Real Camembert is the raw milk Camembert de Normandie. This bloomy rind cheese has a voluptuous nature with a mushroom aroma. It's utterly sexy and delicious. Because of this, it is widely copied the world over, but the copies pale in comparison to the original.

Chaource is a creamy, bloomy rind that has a tart and salty flavor with a bit of a red-colored rind. It's buttery and fruity, and worth trying.

Goat's Milk Cheeses

Moving from the bloomy rinds into the goat's milk cheeses, there are the Banon, the Selles-sur-Cher, and the Valencay, not to mention good old plain fresh chevre. Banon takes its name from a town in Provence. It can come young or more aged, but it is wrapped with chestnut leaves, and it has a soft, tart, nutty flavor.

Selles-sur-Cher is a goat's milk cheese that is dusted in edible ash, and the combination creates a tart and delicious cheese. Valencay is also dusted in charcoal, but it comes in a signature pyramid shape.

Washed Rind Cheeses

Some people avoid goat's milk cheeses because they taste strong or "goaty," and these people probably should avoid washed rinds at all cost. But true caseophiles adore a washed rind, and the French, of course, are masters at producing these pungent beauties. Washed rind cheeses, when young, tend to be firmer, but the longer they age, the creamier and tastier their interiors become. Epoisses de Bourgogne is a classic washed rind—tangy and moist when young but bursting with flavor, aroma, and cream when aged.

Livarot is a firmer washed rind, and because it is no longer made in monasteries but factories, its pungency is less powerful, but it still has a bite. Pont L'Eveque is one of the oldest washed rinds around, with a springy texture, a robust flavor, and a slight sweetness. It's a well-known and well-made cheese.

True Munster cheese isn't like the mild versions sliced up in a deli here. A real French Munster has a sweet, savory, and almost yeasty flavor. It also is quite aromatic, and one variation of it is called Munster au Cumin, which is Munster with cumin spice mixed in.

Reblochon is a washed rind developed in response to taxation. Because farmers had to turn over their milk to the lord in the region, they sometimes didn't milk their cows as "fully" as they could. That way, the second milking was richer and lusher, providing the basis for this unctuous cheese. Reblochon has a delicious, complex flavor and a definite aroma.

Saint-Nectaire, described by some as similar to Reblochon, is creamy, with some holes and a pale pink rind. Traditionally, it was aged on a bed of straw, and good versions of it should have a distinctively strong, tangy flavor.

Blue Cheeses

Blue cheeses are always in a class of their own, and Roquefort is in a class by itself. This sheep's milk blue is known as the "King of Cheeses" for good reason—it's simply one of the best cheeses on the planet.

It's been aged in the limestone caves of Cambalou for centuries, and the traditional way of introducing the cheese's mold was to place loaves of rye bread next to the wheels of cheese in the caves. Then, when they were good and moldy, they'd be ground up into a powder, which was then sprinkled into the curds when the cheese was being made.

A good Roquefort has crumbly paste for a texture, green blue veins of color, and a rich, peppery, yet metallic tang, with a little bit of sweetness and a definite saltiness. If you want authentic Roquefort, the label should have a red sheep seal; other Roqueforts are imposters, so this is really the only sure way to get real Roquefort.

A Cut Above

Legend has it that Roquefort was first created by accident. A lovesick young shepherd forgot his lunch of bread and cheese in a cave when he went to cavort with his lovely shepherdess. When he returned a month later, he saw that his snack was covered in mold, but his hunger got the better of him so he tried it, discovering that it was good indeed.

Although Roquefort is the most famous French blue, there are other wonderful blue cheeses. Fourme d'Ambert is a cow's milk blue that is less piquant than Roquefort. It's creamy and earthy, with a subtle complexity.

Bleu d'Auvergne is a buttery yet sharp blue, and some say it resembles Roquefort. But it is a much more approachable cheese than Roquefort for nonblue cheese lovers.

Bleu des Causses, like Bleu D'Auvergne, is also made in the Auvergne region, and it, too, is made from cow's milk. But Bleu des Causses is aged in limestone caves, and it is spicier than Bleu d'Auvergne.

Firm Cheeses

Firm French cheeses generally are a bit more approachable than the blues. They're also similar to Swiss cheeses, so people might also have a point of reference when trying them. But they are quite distinct from Swiss cheeses, with their own unique flavors.

Comté or Comté de Gruyère is one of the most famous French mountain cheeses. Made in huge wheels, it is wonderful cheese, with a firm texture and a fruity sweetness, yet a slightly spicy bite. It is a bit firmer and nuttier than Swiss Gruyère. Comté is graded on a scale of 1 to 20; the best receive 14 or more points and have a green stamp on them. Comté is also the most popular cheese to eat within France.

Beaufort is similar to Comté, but it has a higher fat content and is considered "the prince of Gruyères." It gets its rich, delicious flavor from the milk of Tarentaise cows, who graze in mountain pastures on flowers, grasses, and herbs.

Tomme de Savoie is made from the same milk as Beaufort, but it is made in the winter instead of the summer. It has an unusual-looking, grayish-brown rind, but it has a firm texture and a sweet, delicious taste.

Morbier is another mountain cheese, but it is semi-soft and has a layer of edible ash in the middle. Traditionally, the first layer was made with the morning's milking, then a layer of ash went on top of the curds, and then it was topped with curds from the evening's milking. Originally, this ash often came from oak charcoal, as is the tradition of cheeses from France's Loire Valley. Today, a recognized food-grade activated charcoal ash is used and is generally tasteless. Morbier is a good melting cheese.

> ### A Cut Above
> One of the best American artisan cheeses started out with a Beaufort recipe—Pleasant Ridge Reserve. Cheesemaker Mike Gingrich knew he wanted to make a Beaufort-style cheese, and he tried out eight different Beaufort recipes before creating his American original.

Cantal, a hard mountain cheese, is also one of France's oldest cheeses. This ancient cheese was originally produced by pressing it into wooden cylinders called le formage.

It is named for the Cantal mountain range, and the older the cheese is, the more flavorful it becomes. In general, it has a tangy, buttery taste. In recent years it has been manufactured mostly with pasteurized milk, but there are still some raw milk versions, which have a greater depth of flavor. A similar cheese to Cantal that's also made in the Auvergne region is Salers.

Ossau-Iraty-Brebis Pyrenees, often just referred to as brebis, is a delicious firm cheese made from sheep's milk. Basque shepherds move their Manech sheep from different pastures seasonally, and the resulting cheese is savory, flavor-packed, and one of a kind. It has a nutty, olivey flavor and a moist or oily texture.

Of France's harder cheeses, none other has the distinctive coloring of Mimolette. Mimolette is the French version of Edam. This tangy, fruity, and nutty cheese has a bright, orange color. Though it is colored with annatto like cheddar, it does not taste like cheddar at all.

Port-du-Salut is not a hard cheese, but it must be mentioned because it's a very big import in the United States. It has Trappist origins, but it is not a stinky washed rind; today, its orange rind comes from annatto. It is semi-soft, sweet, and very mild.

Modern Cheeses

Even more approachable than Port-du-Salut are Boursin and La Vache Qui Rit, two modern cheeses. Boursin is a delicious, creamy fresh cow's milk cheese that was created in 1957. A fresh cheese similar to cream cheese, it is sweet and easy on the tongue, and it often comes mixed with garlic and herbs or peppercorns. It is made without rennet, and only a starter culture is used. It's very approachable and is used frequently in cooking. Chefs sometimes stuff it in pasta, mix it in sauces, and serve it over warm, toasty crusts of bread.

A Cut Above

Boursin was the first cheese advertised on television in France. Its tag line, *"du pain, du vin, du Boursin,"* (the bread, the wine, the Boursin) is a catchphrase in French pop culture.

Although some chefs adore Boursin, few show respect toward La Vache Qui Rit or Laughing Cow cheese. Nonetheless, this processed cheese is popular the world over. In each country, it is sold in that country's native tongue. La Vache Qui Rit also is sold as La Vaca Que Rie, Den Leende Ko, Vesela Krava, and A Vaca Que Ri. Its red, smiling cow with earrings is an internationally known trademark.

French Culture and French Cheese

In France, cheese is served at any time of day, but more often than not it is served at dinner, in a separate course. At any formal French dinner, there will be a separate cheese course with anywhere from one to three different cheeses presented, perhaps with a bit of fruit.

Cheese is also often eaten in place of dessert, and indeed, some of the luscious, flavor-packed cheeses are desserts in and of themselves, especially when paired with a sweet French dessert wine.

In many places in France, cheese is not stored in the refrigerator and instead is kept in special cheese boxes that preserve the cheese and help it to continue to age until it is devoured.

> **A Cut Above**
>
> Colette, the occasionally scandalous twentieth-century French novelist, adored cheese. "If I had a son who was ready to marry, I would tell him, 'Beware of girls who don't like wine, truffles, cheese, or music.'" Enough said.

Cheese also plays a role in French cuisine, but not to the extent it does in Italian cooking. Mornay or cheese sauces, cheese soufflés, and cheese salads are all a part of French cuisine. Different cheeses are served regionally throughout the country.

Despite their reverence for cheese, the French do not eat as much raw milk cheese as they used to. Besides the push for pasteurization of some traditional raw milk cheeses, big dairy companies are homogenizing some of the great French cheeses. Most good cheesemongers try to steer clear of some of the big company versions of Roquefort, for example, and instead seek out the more artisan versions of the cheese.

The Least You Need to Know

- The French have been making great cheese for thousands of years, and two of the oldest cheeses are Cantal and Roquefort.

- There are 46 name controlled French cheeses, and anywhere from 400 to more than 750 varieties of French cheese.

- France has 22 different provinces, and they all make cheese. Normandy is probably the most famous because of its varieties, including Camembert, which is the world's most copied French cheese.

- France makes some of the world's best cheeses, including Brie de Meaux, Brillat-Savarin, and dozens and dozens of others.

Chapter 6

Italian Cheeses

In This Chapter

◆ The history of cheese in Italy

◆ The name controlled cheeses in Italy

◆ The various cheesemaking regions of Italy

◆ Italian cheeses of note

◆ Italian cuisine and cheese

Cheese lovers around the world owe a debt to those conquering Romans. Though the first cheesemakers in the world are believed to have been nomadic tribes in Asia or the Middle East, it was the Romans who took fermented milk products to new heights. The Italians, in turn, took what the Romans did and improved upon their techniques, and today, Italy produces hundreds of varieties of cheese in both farmstead and factory environs.

Though a lot of Italian cheeses have historic roots, some are modern creations. Because the Italians place such a high value on their cheeses, several of them, as well as the standards for making them, are protected under law and can only be made in certain regions and under very specific conditions. Most regions in Italy also boast specialty cheeses that are only made and sometimes only available locally.

And though cheese is enjoyed as a separate course like it is in France, many cheeses are created for use in cooking. Think of ricotta-filled pasta pillows, mozzarella-topped pizza, and grated Pecorino Romano sprinkled over soup. What would Italian cuisine be without its fine, fine cheeses?

Roman 'O Cheese—Italian Cheese History

How about those Romans? Until they came, saw, and conquered the world as they knew it, cheese was a peasant farmer's or shepherd's endeavor, a haphazard operation with inconsistent results. The Romans, with their imperial efficiency, not only set standards for cheesemaking that kept their armies fed (cheese was part of a soldier's stipend), but also spread their dairy knowledge and cheesemaking techniques to the areas now known as Switzerland and Great Britain, among other places.

But the cheeses that the Romans perfected go back even further in history. The Etruscans, who lived in Italy before the Romans took over, are believed to have been some of the first creators of harder grating cheeses. Cheesemaking, in all its tasty glory, was detailed in both written word and oral tradition. One particularly detailed treatise on dairy fermentation instructs cheesemakers to follow these basic instructions:

> *Heat the cheese milk to a warm temperature. Add animal or plant rennet to the milk. Remove free whey and press with weights. Place fresh cheese in a cool area and salt surfaces. Periodically brush and work cheese surface. Allow cheese to ripen.*

"This extraordinary document … looks as if it had been written yesterday," said the French microbiologist and dairy expert Germain Mocquot. But that document was actually written more than 2,000 years ago by the Roman writer Lucius Columella, a former soldier turned farmer who completed a 12-volume treatise on Roman agriculture called *De Re Rustica*.

Other Roman writers who scribed about cheese include Pliny the Elder, who described a cheese that eventually became the forerunner of Pecorino Romano. And when Mount Vesuvius erupted and destroyed Pompeii in 79 C.E., it actually preserved some ancient cheeses, showing off how modern those old cheeses really were (but you probably wouldn't want to gnaw on them).

Though the Romans and their vast empire fell to various barbarian forces, their cheeses and cheesemaking techniques persisted and continued to evolve.

A Cut Above

Invasions led to some very specific cheesemaking processes—burying or hiding cheese from those pesky barbarians. Farmers would wrap their cheese wheels in cloth and bury them in the ground, allowing the cheese to ripen while preventing it from being stolen. Thus, the tradition of *formaggi di fossi* or "cheese of holes" was born, and it continues to this day, though there's no longer any threat of invasion—except by hungry tourists.

Cheesemaking continued in the Middle Ages and evolved in Italy as in many other European countries largely due to the influence and preservation of monks. Grana Padano was created in the Abbey of Chiaravalle in Lombardy by the Cistercian monks, who helped foster agriculture in the region. The birth date of this popular grating cheese is 1135, the year the monks built the abbey.

By the end of the nineteenth century, cheesemaking was flourishing in Italy. In fact, some Italian cheeses were regularly being exported to other countries. Italian unification in 1870 contributed to the birth and growth of larger dairies that processed hundreds of gallons of milk every day. This production continued in the twentieth century, and after World War II, farms and cheesemaking continued to flourish.

But cheesemaking also flourished in other countries, and several countries began making Italian-style cheeses and calling them by Italian names. In 1951, the Stresa Convention, held in the northern Italian town of Stresa, stopped this practice in Europe.

Controlled Name Cheeses or the D.O.C. Cheeses

The Stresa Convention was all about cheese and protecting cheese. This convention involved Italy, France, Austria, Denmark, Norway, Sweden, and Switzerland, and it set up precise regulations and rules regarding the designation of cheeses, as well as their defining characteristics.

The result was that a cheese labeled Gorgonzola had to come from Lombardy, be manufactured the way Gorgonzola traditionally has been made in Italy, and had to taste, well, like Gorgonzola. A Gorgonzola-like cheese made in Norway could not be called Gorgonzola.

In 1955, to further control the name of Italian cheeses, the Italian government set up the D.O.C. mark or the Denominazione di Origine Controllata. According to *The D.O.C. Cheeses of Italy: A Great Heritage* (1992), "Cheese is a visiting card the past generations present their grand and great-grandchildren, the family book in which the ancestors' memories are kept. To recognize a denomination of origin means to grant the people of an area a patent of nobility."

Twenty-six different cheeses have such a patent and are protected under the D.O.C. seal, including Asiago, Bra, Caciocavallo, Canestrato Pugliese, Casciotta d'Urbino, Castelmagno, Fiore Sardo, Fontina d'Aosta, Formai de Mut, Gorgonzola, Grana Padano, Montasio, Mozzarella di bufala, Murazzano, Parmigiano-Reggiano, Pecorino Romano, Pecorino Sardo, Pecorino Siciliano, Pecorino Toscano, Pressato, Provolone, Ragusano, Raschera, Robiola di Roccaverano, Taleggio, and Toma.

Say Cheese

Pecorino is the generic Italian word for sheep's milk cheese. Caprino refers to goat's milk cheese. In Italy, sheep's milk cheese is more common than goat's milk cheese.

While some of these cheeses are superlative—Parmigiano-Reggiano is considered by many cheese lovers to be one of the best cheeses, if not *the* best cheese, in the world—some are not as beloved, and some are very similar to each other. *Pecorino* Sardo, Pecorino Siciliano, Pecorino Toscano, and Pecorino Romano are all hard sheep's milk cheeses.

The most noteworthy of the D.O.C.–branded Italian cheeses will be discussed in great detail later in this chapter.

Bel Paese: Italy's Cheesemaking Regions

Dante referred to Italy as *Bel Paese* or "beautiful country," and with its gorgeous pastures, rugged mountains, and idyllic seasides, it's no wonder he found Italy so beautiful. Italy is also a beautiful country for cheese. In fact, Italy ranks third in Europe, behind France and Germany, in cheesemaking production, and it has not only exported tasty creations such as Parmigiano-Reggiano and Pecorino Romano, but it has exported its cheesemakers, too. Today, mozzarella is the number-one cheese produced in the United States, and Italy exports more cheese to the United States than France does.

Today, Italian cheesemaking techniques range from small farmhouse operations to large, modern factories, and more than 400 different kinds of cheeses are produced in Italy. But though many of its great cheeses are known beyond its borders—provolone or Gorgonzola, anyone?—many are not—Bra or Crescenza, anyone? In fact, many Italian cheeses are so local that they are hard to find outside of the regions in which they are made.

Cheesemaking is an endeavor throughout Italy, but some regions produce more cheese than others, and some produce more important cheeses than others. Knowing a little bit about each of these regions will help you understand the cheeses they make and how the unique terroir of each region contributes to the cheeses.

Italy is a very regional country. People don't say they're from Italy—they're from Tuscany or Sicily. And when you go to Italy, except for some ubiquitous cheeses like mozzarella, which you will find everywhere, a lot of cheeses remain strictly local affairs. A cheese store in Tuscany, for example, will be dominated by various local pecorinos—Pecorino Toscano (sheep's milk cheese made in Tuscany), Pecorino di Fossi (sheep's milk cheese aged in holes in the ground in Tuscany), and Pecorino di Grotto (sheep's milk cheese aged in caves in Tuscany).

Cheese-Making Regions

Perhaps the two most important cheesemaking regions are Piedmont and Lombardy in the north of Italy. In Italian, Piedmont means pied of the monte, or foot of the mountain, and Piedmont lies right at the foot of mountains bordering Switzerland and France. It is a fertile agricultural region that not only produces some big Italian red wines like Barolo and Barbaresco, it also produces several varieties of rice, the famed white truffles or tartufi bianchi, and orchard upon orchard of peaches, pears, and apples. This rustic beauty also boasts a bounty of cheeses, including the original fontina or Fontina d'Aosta, as well as Caprini, Toma, Bra, and tons of others.

Moving west of Piedmont and into Lombardy, you'll enter another bountiful region of cheese. Bordering the Swiss Alps, this northern region is not only a scenic beauty, it is also lushly fertile with plenty of fields for cows to graze in. It also boasts a singularly famous city—Milan.

Just as some of the most sophisticated clothes come from this region, so do some of the classiest cheeses, including Taleggio, Gorgonzola, Stracchino di Crescenza, mascarpone, and ricotta, among dozens of others. In fact, picking a favorite cheese from Lombardy is sort of akin to picking a favorite pair of shoes out in Milan—all are delightful and distinct. But all that glitters is not golden, and all that's cheesy is not necessarily dairy-licious. Lombardy also produces the singularly modern creation Bel Paese.

Continue east along the northern border of Italy, and you'll encounter the Venteto and Friuli–Venezia Giulia regions, which include the Dolomite mountain range. Here, you'll also be able to traverse the canals of Venice, and if you head northwest of Venice, you'll also enjoy Asiago.

Head south and you'll find yourself in Emilia-Romagna, Italy's most important food region, home to prosciutto di Parma, the fine wheat that goes into Italy's famed pastas and breads, not to mention fields of tomatoes, orchards of cherries, and of course the two cities of Parma and Reggio, which lend their names to Italy's most beloved cheese, Parmigiano-Reggiano. Another fine cheese you'll encounter in the region is Grano Padano, also a great grater (pun intended).

Go south of Emilia-Romagna and head for the sun—the Tuscan sun. Beautiful beaches, lush hillsides, and craggy mountains give this region geographical diversity, as well as make it the perfect place to grow olives and grapes (think Chianti here). Its hilly landscape also makes more sense to pasture sheep than cows, and the main cheese is Pecorino Toscano.

Continue southward and the fertile pastures give way to rougher terrain. Though some cows do graze in Apulia, Lazio, and Campania, with their milk going into Provolone production, the sheep and goats rule the roost. Pecorino, in all of its lovely forms, can be found, including the most famous, Pecorino Romano.

The more southern regions of Italy are also home to another dairy mammal, the water buffalo. Since 200 C.E., water buffalo have made their home in Italy, producing the finest fresh mozzarella in the world Though water buffalo were killed by Nazis during the 1940s, after World War II herds were replenished by animals from India.

A Cut Above

Parmigiano-Reggiano, the famous cheese that has spawned countless inferior Parmesan imitators, is made in Reggio, not Parma. But because Parma is the region's center of commerce, the city lent its name to the cheese.

Say Cheese

Despite its origins in Lazio, which is within spitting distance of Rome, most of what is labeled as Pecorino Romano is actually made on the island of Sardinia. For authentic Pecorino Romano, seek out cheese that is labeled "Genuino Pecorino Romano."

Like much of southern Italy, the islands of Sicily and Sardinia have more rugged environs that are less hospitable to cows and more welcoming to sheep, though Sicily does boast some bovine beauties. These are also lands of pecorinos, but you can find some mozzarella here, too.

Buono Formaggi from Italy

You could eat a different Italian cheese every day and still have more to try after a year, but there are definitely some Italian cheeses you should try first. Some cheeses are readily available in the United States, others are a bit harder to come by. So in alphabetical presentation, here are some of the great, delicious, or noteworthy cheeses of Italy:

Asiago or Asiago d'Allevo is one of those D.O.C. cheeses. Made from cow's milk in Veneto, at the edge of the Dolomite Mountains, this cheese is named for the village of Asiago. In Italy, it comes in two versions—a younger, lightly pressed or *pressato* version made with whole milk, and an aged, skimmed milk version. The pressato is only available in Italy, and it is a delicately sweet cheese. The other importable version comes in three different ages—young or *fresco*, which is aged up to two months; *mezzano* (medium), which is aged up to five months; and *vecchio*, or old, which is aged at least nine months and typically more than a year. The aged version is filled with small holes, boasting a granular texture and a fruity, lightly sharp taste. Bel Paese is a modern concoction, created in 1929 by the Galbani company. A soft and mild cheese made in Lombardy, its flavor pales in comparison to other regional delicacies, but it remains popular nonetheless.

A Cut Above

Bel Paese is not only made in Italy; a version of it is licensed and made in the United States. It comes in larger waxed rind wheels or small, gold-colored tin-foil wrapped versions. The tin-foil versions remind me of Laughing Cow Cheese, with perhaps a bit more of a provolone aroma.

The immature might titter at the name, but D.O.C.–certified Bra cheese is a singularly delicious, if piquant, firm cheese. Yellow in color, this cow's milk cheese is made in the Alpine valleys of Piedmont, and it comes in two versions: the young is aged 45 days; the old, three to six months.

Butter and cheese go together like nothing else in this southern Italian dairy creation. Burrini cheese is made in Puglia and also on the island of Sicily, and it is a small, pear-shaped cheese. What's most unusual about it is that the cheese curds are molded around a pat of butter so that when you smoosh the cheese into a slice of hearty bread, you can spread both the cheese and the butter into it.

One of the more popular goat's milk cheeses in Italy is Caprini, which means "little goats." Made in Piedmont, this cheese is sweet, fresh, and tart—everything you'd want a goat's milk cheese to be.

Crescenza or Stracchino di Crescenza is one of those utterly spreadable and addictive cheeses. Made in Lombardy of raw cow's milk, this decadent cheese is usually high in fat, and it's almost like a cream cheese. It's unctuous, with a fruity, tart flavor, and its name comes from *stracca*, which means "tired." Cows used to be herded from the Alps to the lowlands in autumn and then back again in springtime. The cows were "tired," but they gave good milk, higher in butterfat.

A Cut Above

Crescenza is imported by some specialty stores, but it's harder to come by than some other fine cheeses. However, there are two decent American (with Italian roots) cheese companies that make it: Bellwether Farms in California and BelGioioso Cheese Company in Wisconsin.

Fiore Sardo means "flower of Sardinia," and this firm, D.O.C. cheese is piquant, with a rich taste and underlying sweetness. Made in Sardinia from sheep's milk, it is also known as Pecorino Sardo, and in Sardinia it is also sometimes known as Fiore Sardegna and Moliterno.

Fontina D'Aosta is the only real fontina. Not that the other fontinas are bad—they're just not quite the same. This D.O.C.–marked cow's milk cheese is made in Piedmont, and it is a classic firm cheese, packed with a few small holes and a lot of flavor. Light- and straw-colored, it has an earthy tang, and it's been made since at least the eleventh century, when it was known in the Valle D'Aosta just as caseus or cow's milk cheese. Extremely meltable, it is an ingredient in fonduta or Italian fondue.

Stinky Cheese

Beware of other Italian imports labeled Fontinella, Fontella, or Fontal. Those are fontina-like cheeses, but they're not the real Fontina D'Aosta. Swedish fontinas are also delicious, but again, they're not the real thing. Also, there's a glut of cheese labeled Sardo that is not real Fiore Sardo or Pecorino Sardo; instead they are cow's milk cheeses and far from the real thing.

Gorgonzola is one of those blues that make you sing the blues if you can't get enough of it. This delicious D.O.C. cheese has a greenish-blue mold, and it's been made in Lombardy for centuries. It's been made there so long that there are a couple of legends that explain its origin. In one, an innkeeper discovered that some young cheeses he had placed in his cellar had developed a bluish tinge; though unsure of their taste, he nonetheless served it to his customers, who clamored for more. Another legend (it might sound familiar) has it that a young man distracted by his lover had left cheese curd in a damp cellar by mistake. Whatever the actual origin, this D.O.C.–protected cheese boasts a sharp, spicy tang and a creamy texture.

Gorgonzola comes in two basic varieties—*piccante*, or sharp, and *dolce*, or sweet. Sweet Gorgonzola is often known as Dolcelatte. For an even more decadent treat, try Dolcelatte Torta, which consists of layers of sweet Gorgonzola interspersed with cream. Dolcelatte Torta is sometimes labeled in the United States as Gorgonzola Torta.

Grana Padano is a D.O.C.–protected cheese that is one of the most popular hard cheeses in Italy. Some of it is imported to the United States and called "Parmesan," but it is not the same as Parmigiano-Reggiano. Similar to Parmigiano-Reggiano but a bit milder, this cow's milk cheese is fruity and sweet, and it is made in Piedmont and Lombardy.

Even if you don't know the name, you've probably had a form of mascarpone cheese. If you've ever had tiramisu, which means "pick me up," you've had this creamy cow's milk treat. Sort of like a thick whipped cream, Mascarpone was invented in the 1500s in Lombardy, and its name might have come from the Spanish phrase *mas que bueno* or "better than good," which is what a visiting Spanish noble might have said to a cheese-maker upon tasting it. This decadent cheese is lush, with about as much butterfat, about 75 percent, as cream can have without becoming butter. A rare form of mascarpone is Mascarpone di bufala, which is made with water buffalo milk in Campania.

Mozzarella is one of the most popular cheeses on the planet, simply because pizza has become a universally popular dish. But there's really only one mozzarella worth talking about: Mozzarella di bufala. This fresh, *pasta filata–style* cheese is made from the milk of water buffaloes. It has a fresh, milky, sweet taste, and its curd offers a naturally stringy, springy texture. In Italy, it is often known as *il fiore di latte* or "the flower of milk," and traditionally it is made outside of Naples, in Campania. Small balls of mozzarella are known as *boconccini*, and smoked mozzarella is known as *mozzarella affumicata*, and if it is smoked intensely, it is called *scamorza*. The more rubbery, block version we're familiar with on most pizzas is known as *pizzaiola* in Italy.

Say Cheese

Pasta filata is the process of dipping curd into hot water, which causes the curds to release more whey, and then the cheese is stretched and kneaded. This process is used to make mozzarella, provolone, and string cheese.

Parmigiano-Reggiano is perhaps the most beloved and well known of any Italian cheese. One of the most strictly regulated cheeses in Italy, this cheese can only be made between April 15 and November 11, ensuring that the milk comes from bovines that graze on fresh grass rather than silage or hay. Yellow in color with a distinctive granular and hard texture, this cheese is sweet, fruity, and packed with flavor.

It must be aged for at least 14 months, and it can be aged up to four years. Three-year-old Parmigiano-Reggiano is known as *stravechio*, while four-year-old Parmigiano-Reggiano is called *stravechione*. The older the cheese, the more golden it will become. Not only does it make an incredible meal by itself, but when it is grated over pasta, pizza, or other dishes, its sublime flavor enhances. The Italians love it so much that when you get down to its inedible rind, they throw it in soup for flavoring (but they don't eat it).

The American Romano cheese is inspired by the better Pecorino Romano, which traditionally is made outside of Rome. This pungent and hard sheep's milk cheese is probably the best pecorino of the bunch. Used often for grating over pasta and other dishes, this cheese gives an extra oomph of flavor, but it can also be enjoyed on its own. Its special taste comes, in part, from the fact that it is only made between November and late June when sheep graze on natural pastures. Similar to Pecorino Romano is Pecorino Toscano, a sheep's milk cheese made in Tuscany. It is made in smaller wheels than Pecorino Romano and it is intense, but not as strong as Pecorino Romano.

What would a good Italian deli sandwich be without provolone cheese? In Italy, it comes in two forms—young or *dolce*, which is aged for a couple of months, and *piquante* or spicy, which is aged for six months or longer and rubbed with rennet to add an additional kick of flavor. This D.O.C. cheese has little holes in it, and its name comes from the word *prova*, which means "globe-shaped" in a southern Italian dialect.

Most commonly used as pasta filling in the United States, ricotta is an unusual cheese, as it is traditionally made with leftover whey. The whey is reheated, which brings out the remaining curds, and in fact, *ricotta* means "recooked." It can be made from a variety of milks, and in Italy it is often made with sheep's milk and water buffalo's milk, but in the United States it's made with cow's milk. This sweet, billowy cheese has a smooth taste and rather delicate flavor.

One of the stinkiest and most amazing cheeses you'll ever taste is Taleggio. This Lombardian, D.O.C.–protected cheese comes in 8-inch squares. Made from raw cow's milk, it is a washed rind cheese with a slightly yellow color, offering a depth of flavor and a strong but not unpleasant aroma.

Toma is a traditional Piedmont cheese, formed into a round or a *toma* (similar to *tomme* in French). These soft-ripened cheeses offer a delicious flavor, a sometimes mushroomy taste. They are similar to a Paglia-style cheese.

One of the best ways to experience Italian cheese is to taste it at an authentic farmhouse producer. In Italy, *agriturismo* sites or farms that do double duty as bed and breakfasts, are becoming popular. While many of them feature wine, vegetable growing, or olive oil groves, one where you can experience fine cheese is Fattoria La Parrina in Tuscany. This darling farm not only makes good wines, cheesemaker Philippe Trillaud makes a plethora of great cheeses from cow's milk, sheep's milk, and goat's milk. Two of Trillaud's best cheeses are Rosa di Maremma, a Brie-like cheese made from sheep's milk, and Guttus, an original blue cheese that is named for the Etruscan term for "the best."

> **A Cut Above**
>
> Perhaps the most unusual use of Taleggio I've ever encountered is when it is paired with chocolate. A Chicago chocolatier, Vosges, uses Taleggio in a truffle called "The Rooster." The sublime creation tastes better than most chocolate-flavored cheesecakes.

Italian Cuisine and Cheese

You can't talk about Italian cheese and not talk about Italian cuisine. The two are deeply intertwined if not inseparable. Every cheese mentioned in this chapter can be used in cooking. Many give character, taste, and depth to Italian dishes, and indeed, they have become known throughout the world simply because they are used so frequently in cooking. For example, though Parmigiano-Reggiano can be savored alone, most people know it as a condiment to pasta.

While we wholeheartedly agree that pasta with marinara sauce just tastes better with freshly grated cheese, we would also like to suggest that the next time you purchase some fine Italian cheese, savor it by itself, and do add it to a cheese plate if you are so inclined. These delicious cheeses will take on a whole new meaning and, in some cases, might even taste like new cheeses to you, if you savor them by themselves.

The Least You Need to Know

- ◆ The Romans not only built empires, they set a foundation for the world of cheese as we know it, especially Italian cheese.

- ◆ There are 26 Italian cheeses that are name protected, and more than 400 different Italian cheeses in total.

- ◆ The different regions of Italy, from the northern Alps to the southern boot, offer distinct terroirs for cheese production, but the two most famous regions for cheese are Piedmont and Lombardy.

- ◆ Italian cheeses are among the world's best, including Parmigiano-Reggiano, Pecorino Romano, and Gorgonzola.

- ◆ Italian food and Italian cheese go together like peanut butter and jelly, but do try some well-known Italian cheeses by themselves.

Swiss Cheeses

In This Chapter

- ◆ The history of Swiss cheesemaking
- ◆ The cows and mountains of Swiss cheese
- ◆ What causes the holes of Swiss cheese
- ◆ The cheeses of Switzerland
- ◆ The cultural phenomenon, Swiss fondue

It's not a big country, and it doesn't produce vast varieties of cheese, but there's no denying that Switzerland is one of the world's cheese power-houses. Switzerland has a long, long history of cheese and dairy, and it has preserved its traditions extremely well. In fact, one of its traditional cheeses spawned a whole category of cheeses named after the country: Swiss cheese, of course!

What's amazing is that only 25 percent of Swiss land is suitable for grazing, yet this small and extremely mountainous country has incredible dairy out-put. But leave it to the industrious Swiss to turn a possible negative into a positive tradition. Today, dairy and cheesemaking remains a vital and thriv-ing part of the Swiss economy. And that's a good thing for cheese lovers everywhere.

Swiss Cheesemaking: A Brief History

It's hard to say exactly when cheesemaking began in Switzerland. What is known is that this land, originally known as Helvetia, was home to a Celtic tribe that invaded the southern part of France (known as Gaul at that time) in 58 B.C.E. Like so many other unruly tribes of the era, they got put back in their places by the Romans.

The Romans, of course, brought their cheesemaking techniques, but some evidence suggests that Swiss cheesemaking dates back even further. Archeological evidence of cheesemaking—milk-curdling vessels—has been found around the shores of Lake Neuchâtel, possibly dating back to 5000 B.C.E. Those early Swiss folk who made cheese were known as the Sennen or mountain people. Today, the term refers to people who have the best mountain pastures.

The earliest written mention of Swiss cheese, however, was by Roman historian Pliny the Elder, who referred to it as "caseus helviticus" in the first century. Caseus helviticus was also sometimes called "caseus alpinus." Exactly what type of Swiss cheese Pliny was referring to isn't known. Some think he may have been referring to Sbrinz, a very hard grating cheese similar to Parmigiano-Reggiano. What is easily deducted is that the hard cheese he referred to was probably not the kind of Swiss cheeses that are around today. Nonetheless, caseus helviticus was probably a forerunner of the Swiss cheeses of today.

After the Romans left Helvetia, the land was invaded in the fifth century by Germanic tribes who ruled the area until three of the area's cantons (the Swiss version of provinces) rebelled in 1291, overthrowing their foreign rulers. Around the same time that rebel forces were setting the groundwork for today's Swiss federation, the cheese that's known the world over as "Swiss cheese" made its first recorded appearance in the Emme River valley: Emmentaler or Emmenthaler cheese. It was first written down in records in 1293, but it was first (at least in written works) called by its name in 1542.

Its smaller-holed cousin, Gruyère, makes a slightly earlier historic appearance: in 1115, Gruyère is paid as a tax or tithe by local farmers to the monks of Rougement Abbey. Appenzeller, another famous Swiss cheese, is believed to date back even earlier, to the eighth or ninth century. And Fribourgeois can be traced back to 1448, when it was served to an Austrian duchess.

Besides making great cheese through the ages, the Swiss have been selling great cheese and exporting it to other countries since at least the 1700s and probably earlier. One reason for their success at exporting is that their cheeses kept for longer periods, because the Swiss discovered that the bigger the wheels, the hardier the cheeses would be. The Swiss not only exported cheese, they also exported their able cheesemakers, who helped set up creameries in many regions around the world, including Russia, Scandinavia, and the United States.

A Cut Above

Throughout the Middle Ages, cheese was a sign of social standing. The age and quality of cheese in a family's cellar revealed how prosperous a family was. In one Swiss tradition, a big wheel of cheese would be purchased at the birth of a child and then served at his or her baptism, wedding, and funeral. Even though these hardy cheeses last a good long time, it's dubious whether a wheel could be kept for decades, but it makes for a good story, illustrating how important cheese is to the Swiss.

Wheels of Emmentaler are weighed before they are shipped out of Switzerland.

(Roth Kase)

To keep up with the demand for their great cheeses, the Swiss developed dairy cooperatives, and then, in 1815, they set up the very first cheese factory. Today, Swiss cheesemaking remains a cooperative endeavor with mainly smaller farms, and Swiss government regulations set up to keep its beautiful pasturelands pristine.

Like other European countries, the Swiss government also regulates the name of special Swiss cheeses, including: Appenzeller, Emmentaler, Gruyère, raclette cheeses (Bagnes, Conches, Gomser, Orsières), Saanen, Sapsago, Sbrinz, Spalen, Swiss Tilsit, Tête de Moine, Vacherin Fribourgeois, and Vacherin Mont D'Or.

Of Cows and Mountains

Why, in general, does Swiss cheese made in other countries not taste as good as real Swiss cheese? Two words: mountain pastures. In such a small country, with only 25 percent of its land suitable for pasture, innovation and ingenuity were required to make cheese at all, let alone make great quantities of superlative cheeses.

In the spring and summer months, Swiss farmers, the Sennen, would take their cattle up into the lush, green mountain pastures of the Alps. There, the farmers would live in little huts and their cattle would feast on the fresh clover and grasses that only grew in the mountains. These special plants caused the cows to produce lusher, richer in butterfat, milk, which in turn produced lusher, richer, more flavorful cheeses.

In fact, while up in the mountains, the farmers would make big wheels of cheese in giant copper kettles. The cheeses had to be hard and sturdy enough to be transported for sale in the lowlands. Before the weather turned bad and winter set in, the farmers would take their herds down the mountains to the lowland areas. Today, Swiss cheese is still made in copper kettles, but it is made in factories, not out in the open on hillsides. The copper is important, purists will tell you, because its ionization helps activate the enzymes in the cheese in a way that stainless steel does not.

A Cut Above

The changing of the seasons is always a big to-do. Cattle that move from the lowlands to alpine pastures are dressed up with flowers and paraded through town before they get to feast on their favorite grazing lands. The lead cow, the Herrkuh, has the loudest and snazziest bell of all the cattle, which is attached by a beautiful decorative collar.

Under Swiss law, farmers cannot feed their cattle one of the most common forms of cow food: silage, or animal feed produced by fermenting foraging plants in a silo. Strict governmental controls also make sure that recipes and production standards are uniform and uniformly adhered to. That's also particularly important because most mountain cheeses are made from raw, not pasteurized, milk. Because the best Swiss cheese is aged out—for a minimum of 4 months (which is what's often exported to the United States), and often for 10 months or longer. The longer a Swiss cheese is aged, the better and more complex flavor it will have.

Barrels of cheese are wheeled out before they get shipped to the United States.

(Roth Kase)

Swiss cheese also gets its depth of flavor from the cows that produce the milk. The particular Swiss prefer certain breeds of cattle to others, including the Braunvieh or Brown Swiss, a breed that dates back several centuries; Simmental; Fribourg; and Eringer. Each breed produces a very high-quality kind of milk.

Hole-y Cheese

The appearance of several Swiss cheeses is so unique that Swiss cheese is often considered a genre of its own. The holes of Swiss cheese make it easily recognizable and have spawned so many pale imitators and "Swiss cheese" creations.

Those holes are more properly referred to as "eyes," and they are caused not by man but by bacterial action. The eyes are formed by propionic acid bacteria, which produces carbon dioxide after eating the lactose in the cheese. For proper eye development, the cheese must be carefully aged. A good cheesemaker can check on the eye development just by touch—a wheel of cheese with proper eye development will sound different when thumped than a wheel of cheese with deformed eyes.

Improper handling of the cheese can result in defective eyes. If there are no eyes, the cheese is considered blind. If the eyes aren't lustrous, they're called dull or dead eyes. If they're less than 1 centimeter in diameter, they're small eyes. Too many eyes means that they're overset, and an extreme amount of eyes are called cabbage eyes. Too few eyes is a condition called underset. And blowholes are very large eyes—13 centimeters or more in diameter. In extreme cases, there might just be one giant blowhole in the middle of the cheese.

Swiss cheesemakers, being an exacting sort, will settle for nothing less than well-developed eyes. Any bad cheese is simply thrown out. Less than perfect is not tolerated—at least when it comes to cheese.

Sometimes moisture naturally accumulates in the holes, and when you cut into a wheel, the cheese "weeps." This is a natural occurrence, and some cheesemakers call that moisture "tears of joy."

A Cut Above

Swiss cheese and its holes have been the subject of songs, movies, and general pop culture references. In one film, Charlie Chaplin plays a waiter who tries to satisfy a diner's demand for Swiss cheese by boring holes into a hunk of cheddar. More recently, in Japanese anime, singer/voice actress Mary Elizabeth McGlynn sings a song called "I Want Love" with the lyrics: "And this Swiss cheese heart knows, only kindness can fill its holes."

The Great Cheeses of Switzerland

When you talk about Swiss cheese, you can't not talk about Emmentaler, also known as Emmental or Emmenthaler. This ancient cheese is to Swiss cheese what Waterford crystal is to glass: it's really the best. Once you try real Emmentaler, you can't eat the processed, fake Swiss cheese you once munched on.

Real Emmentaler is made in giant wheels of 100 to 200 pounds, and it is one of the world's largest cheeses. In Switzerland, Emmentaler accounts for half of all the country's cheese production, and 70 percent of that is exported.

And, yes, it has holes in it—holes that are typically no bigger than the size of quarters but no smaller than the size of nickels. It has a sweet, nutty taste and a firm texture. The older it gets, the sharper and deeper its flavor becomes. It is typically exported to the United States at 4 months of age, but a 10- or 12-month wheel tastes better. The French make a great Emmentaler called Emmentaler français grand cru in the Franche-Comté and Savoie regions using raw milk, but there are pasteurized milk versions of French Emmentaler coming out of Normandy and Brittany.

If you're buying imported Emmentaler and you want to make sure it is from Switzerland; check the rind to see if it is stamped, in red, with the word "Switzerland." Germans, Norwegians, and even Argentineans make versions of imported Emmentaler. Only one American cheesemaker makes traditional, big wheel Emmentaler, and that's Bruce Workman of Edelweiss Townhall Creamery in Wisconsin; his Green County version is incredibly good.

The second most popular Swiss cheese is Gruyère. Gruyère is similar to Emmentaler, but its wheels are only half as big (about 50–100 pounds). Made in the Swiss canton of Fribourg, in the area around the town of Gruyère, Gruyère is in the same family of cheeses as Emmentaler, but it has a more intense flavor that comes from the aging and the washing of the wheels of cheese. Like Emmentaler, it has holes, but whereas Emmentaler can be released at just three or four months of age, Gruyère is aged for at least six months and sometimes up to three years.

Gruyère has a darker yellow color than Emmentaler, and it has a fruity yet nutty flavor that lingers in your mouth. It is also a superb melting cheese, being the preferred cheese for au gratin onion soups and croque monsieur sandwiches. It is also the basis for any good Swiss fondue. The French also make a version of it called Gruyère de Comte. A very good American Gruyère is made by the Swiss family, Wisconsin-based company Roth Kase.

An interesting trend is happening with both Emmentaler and Gruyère. Several Swiss cheese companies, including the largest, Emmi, are aging these cheeses in caves for an extra long period of time. The cave-aged versions of both Emmentaler and Gruyère cost more than regular versions.

If you buy your Swiss cheeses from a reputable dealer, then you would probably not notice a big difference in the flavor. But if you buy your Swiss cheeses from a larger grocery store, these cave-aged versions will taste noticeably different. The reason is, despite the legendary standards of Swiss quality, in the last few years, some companies are making blocks instead of wheels of Emmentaler and Gruyère cheeses, and they're selling them sealed in plastic to be imported in the United States. With the cave-aged versions, even if they're sealed in plastic, they have more flavor because of their extra aging, and they are not going to be as damaged as lesser cheeses would be.

Appenzeller, sometimes called Appenzell, is another lovely Swiss cheese. Originating in the Appenzell region of Switzerland, this cheese usually has a few small holes scattered in it, and its orangey-yellow rind gets its warm color from being washed in wine and spices. It has a more piquant or spicy flavor than either Emmentaler or Gruyère, but it has fruity undertones, too. Like Gruyère, it melts well, and it can add a certain zestiness to fondues and other dishes that require melted cheese.

The raclette cheeses—Bagnes, Conches, Gomser, and Orsières—are created just for raclette, a dish made of scraped cheese. Raclette comes from the French verb *racler*, which means "to scrape," and that's just what you do with raclette cheeses—you heat up slices, and then you scrape them over potatoes, pickles, and bread. The Swiss even have special raclette machines in which to melt the cheese. They have strong, fruity flavors and a real creaminess that gets accentuated when it is melted. The cheeses are sometimes called Raclette de Valais, because that is the canton in which they are made.

Fribourgeois, also known as Vacherin Fribourgeois, is similar to Gruyère, but it is a smaller, nutty cheese with lots of little holes in it. It has a great, smooth flavor, and it is a good cheese for munching on.

It shouldn't be confused with Vacherin Mont D'Or, which is one of the few soft cheeses of Switzerland. This cheese has an herbal, woodsy sort of flavor, and it ripens in about a month to six weeks. Its rind also is encircled with a thin strip of bark.

Perhaps the opposite of Vacherin Mont D'Or are the hard, hard cheeses of Switzerland—the Sbrinz, Saanen, and Spalen. Sbrinz could have been the cheese the Romans referred to as caseus helviticus. It is similar to Parmigiano-Reggiano, but it has a milder taste. Aged for two years, Sbrinz has an amber color and a nutty, delicious flavor. In fact, at a public tasting at the 1998 Slow Foods Convention, it beat out Parmigiano-Reggiano. Saanen and Spalen are smaller than Sbrinz, but very similar in taste and grateability.

A Cut Above

Because it can be aged for several years, Saanen used to be a part of a young woman's dowry when she got married.

Sapsago is one of the most unusual cheeses of Switzerland, and in a sense it was the world's first processed cheese, made hundreds and hundreds of years ago by monks. First, skimmed milk is turned into curd and completely dried. Then that cheese is ground up and mixed with fenugreek and a wild Swiss clover, which give it a pale green color. That mixture is pressed into cone-shaped molds, and the cones are meant to be grated over food or mixed into butter or cream cheese. It has a very strong and definitely herbal taste, and a little of it goes a long way.

Tête de Moine literally means "monk's head." It also understandably is a cheese that was first made by monks in an abbey near the town of Bellelay, which is by the Jura mountains. It has a sharp, strong flavor and is simultaneously sweet yet beefy. The French make a version of Tête de Moine called Girollin, but it's not quite as strongly flavored as the Swiss original. What makes it unusual is not just its shape—round and drumlike, weighing about one and a half pounds—but how it is served. In Switzerland, it is sliced horizontally, not vertically, using a special tool called a *girolle*. The *girolle* is inserted in the top of the cheese, and then it shaves the cheese from the top down.

Swiss Tilsit or Tilsiter dates back only to the 1800s when Swiss cheesemakers borrowed the German recipe, which the Germans had taken from Dutch cheese-makers who were trying to make Gouda in East Prussia. In any case, Swiss Tilsit is a great cheese. Similar to Appenzeller, it is a bit earthier in taste. It originally was called Royalp, but now it is just known as Tilsit.

Say Cheese _____

A **girolle** is a special Swiss apparatus used to shave off slices of Tête de Moine cheese. It looks almost like a hand crank, and when you turn it, it will slice off a neat little ruffle of cheese.

Swiss Fondue

Cheese is so important in Switzerland that one of its national dishes is made just from cheese. Fondue is a meltably delicious dish, with a long history in Switzerland. Like many ethnic dishes, it was first developed out of necessity. Swiss herders—the Sennen—used what they had on hand—bread, wine, and cheese—to feed themselves in cold winters. It was made with leftover scraps of cheese, and older bread tasted better when dipped in this concoction. Over time, this dish came down from the mountains and ended up on the tables of noblemen. And somehow, it ended up with the French name of fondue, coming from the verb *fondre*, which means "to melt."

Each region of Switzerland makes a slightly different version of fondue, using different cheeses, using or not using cherry brandy, and thickened with flour or corn meal, or not. (See Chapter 25 for recipes for fondue.)

The French gastronome Jean Brillat-Savarin is credited with spreading fondue to the rest of the world. After escaping the French Revolution, he made his way to the United States, where he spent two years teaching music and language lessons, and he also authored three books on food that are still used in culinary schools today.

What's interesting to note, however, is that Brillat-Savarin's fondue is different from traditional Swiss fondues in that it incorporates cream and eggs. The Swiss fondue craze of the 1970s in the United States dates back to the late 1950s, when jetsetters headed to Switzerland to ski. Not only did they ski, they ate fondue, and it became a cultural phenomenon.

The Least You Need to Know

◆ Though small in size, Switzerland is a giant in cheeses, making some of the largest and most important cheeses in the world.

◆ Almost all Swiss cheeses are hard, mountain cheeses made from the raw milk of cows pastured in the Alps.

◆ The two most important Swiss cheeses are Emmentaler and Gruyère; Emmentaler is the cheese that most people recognize as "Swiss cheese."

◆ The holes in Swiss cheese are caused by carbon dioxide, a by-product of bacteria eating milk sugars.

◆ Fondue is a dish created by Swiss herdsmen.

Chapter 8

Cheeses of the British Isles

In This Chapter

- The historical origin of cheesemaking in the British Isles
- A historical account of cheesemaking in Ireland
- How cheddar became great and also how it became generic
- The cheeses of England, Ireland, Wales, and Scotland

With its lush, green pastures, heavy rainfall, and great soil, it's not surprising that cows like it in the British Isles. Great Britain and Ireland were destined for cheesemaking—the climate and geography contribute to a nearly perfect environment.

And cheese has been around in the British Isles for probably the better part of 2,000 years. Though it goes way back in history, it wasn't until about 100 C.E. that the Brits and then later the Irish, the Scots, and the Welsh started making their signature hard cheeses. That was when the Romans came to town, building roads and making cheese. Those old Brits took to cheese like a fish does to water, and the rest, they say, is history, an interesting history that continues today in both factories and small farmhouses. British and Irish cheeses continue to evolve and amaze, with old traditions being revived and new legacies beginning.

The History of Cheese in the British Isles

No one knows exactly when cheesemaking began in the British Isles, but cheesemaking implements dating back to the Iron Age have been found in scattered sites in Britain. The tradition of British cheesemaking as we know it only dates back to the first century C.E. after the Romans took over.

Like so many other European peoples, the old Angles and Saxons were introduced to rennet-based cheesemaking by the Romans, who took the soft, fresh cheeses that were common and showed how to age them and turn them into hardier masterpieces. The Romans are believed to have created the first Cheshire cheese, the oldest cheese with a proper name in Great Britain.

After the Romans left the isles, the cheeses and cheesemaking techniques they established had taken root and begun to evolve on their own. When Christianity began to spread to the islands, monasteries were built and that's where the next wave of English cheesemaking took hold. One of the earliest mentions of cheese was in the Domesday Book, written at the end of the eleventh century. More monks came to make cheese in 1066 when William the Conqueror arrived. Besides conquering, William had dairy on the brain, and he brought along Cistercian monks from Burgundy who helped the shepherds in the Yorkshire Dales make cheese from sheep's milk.

Perhaps the most famous cheese in the world, cheddar, dates back to at least this time. In 1170, King Henry II is recorded as purchasing 10,240 pounds worth, after declaring that cheddar was the best cheese in England.

Monasteries continued their association with all things dairy until Henry VIII decided he wanted to divorce his wife. When the pope wouldn't let him, he decided that there wasn't enough room on the islands for him and Catholicism. Because the monasteries were being shuttered, the monks left to find employment at local farms, where their cheesemaking prowess was put to good use.

Cheese was made from the milk of sheep, goats, and cows, but by the sixteenth century, cow's milk became the milk of choice for cheese. Because the Brits prized their cream and butter, most hard cheese at that time was made from skim milk. Firm cheeses made from creamier milks were more palatable, and fresh cheese was a delicacy reserved for only the richest of the rich.

Cheeses made in the Middle Ages in England were described by Andrew Boorde in 1542 as "green cheese, soft cheese, hard cheese, and spermyse cheese." Cheese deemed green was not called that because of its color, but rather because it was young.

Spermyse cheese was made with curds and the "juice of herbs," which suggests that it was made not with rennet but possibly with plant coagulants. One particular plant known as Lady's Bedstraw was also referred to as the Cheese Rennet Plant because of its coagulating nature.

Fortunately for us, those bitterly hard cheeses improved, and by the sixteenth century they had started to evolve into something similar to the cheeses we associate with Great Britain today. Double and Single Gloucester are believed to have originated in Gloucestershire from the milk of the Old Gloucester cattle.

 **A Cut Above**

Some hard cheeses of that era, particularly those from Suffolk and Essex, were deemed extremely bad, so bad that a nasty little jingle in which they described themselves as such: "Those that made me were uncivil, For they made me harder than the devil. Knives won't cut me, fire won't sweat me, Dogs bark at me but can't eat me."

The farmhouse tradition of making great hard cheeses had begun, and the very best farmhouse cheeses were starting to get purchased at country markets in the regions where they were made and then resold by merchants in areas that didn't have such good cheese. By the end of the 1600s, cheese merchants in London had set up an unofficial guild and begun to ship good cheese over long distances by sea. By this time, nearly every county in the country was making cheese.

The 1700s saw the debut of what many consider to be the king of British cheese: Stilton. This honorable blue dates back to at least the 1700s, with its earliest written reference occurring in a letter by William Stukeley dated 1722. The cheese could have been created by Elizabeth Scarbrow, housekeeper of the Ashby family in Leicestershire. Other accounts say that a blue-veined, cow's milk cream cheese was produced by farmers in Wymondham.

Though Stilton's exact origins aren't known, it takes its name from the village of Stilton, a stagecoach town about 80 miles north of London. Travelers headed toward Scotland and other northern destinations would make their first stop in Stilton. Convenient to the local farms in the area that made the cheese, Stilton became the market for this blue-veined beauty. A Wymondham cheesemaker, Frances Pawlett, is credited with setting the quality standards for Stilton. She and her husband set up the first marketing cooperative for the cheese in the area, and with the help of the owner of the Bell Inn in Stilton, the Stilton trade began to grow and expand.

Stilton has always been a difficult cheese to make, a sentiment voiced 200 years ago by Mrs. Musson, a Stilton cheesemaker who said, "Stiltons, with the exception that they make no noise, are more trouble than babies."

A Cut Above

Despite its name, Stilton has never been made in the village of Stilton. It's also interesting to note that while cheddar takes its name from Cheddar, cheddar is no longer made in Cheddar.

As the British began exploring and conquering much of the known world, they took their cheeses with them. The British Navy, in 1739, took Cheshire with them as their cheese of choice, and the colonists in the New World—the pilgrims on the *Mayflower*, for example—took cheese as a necessity.

The mid-1800s were not exactly prime years for British cheese. In 1860, there was a great cattle plague, and thousands of cows had to be killed. Around that time, American cheddar began being imported and then industrialization came to the dairy industry. Pasteurization began being used in cheese and dairy operations. These sweeping changes led to the quiet deaths of some farmhouse cheeses. World War I impacted English cheese even more. Shortages and rationing took a toll, and cheesemaking standards began to slip, as it became a method of preserving milk rather than continuing tradition.

In 1933, the government set up the Milk Marketing Board to control milk sales and set cheese standards. Those standards were both good and bad, as government employees didn't understand the variable nature of traditional cheesemaking techniques. Many cheesemakers stopped making cheese. Big factories were built, taking in surplus milks, and farmhouse cheeses fell by the wayside.

In 1954, rationing was finally lifted, and traditionalists could return to their cheesemaking ways. That set up two segments of cheesemaking—the big factories and small farmhouses. The farmhouse cheeses experienced a revival in the 1980s, and by 1994, the Milk Marketing Board was completely disbanded, allowing farmers to market their milk to whomever they wanted. Many farmhouse cheesemakers returned to old, time-honored standards and traditions, and others are developing new and innovative cheeses. Though most cheeses today are made from cow's milk, there are some British goat's milk and sheep's milk cheeses, too.

The History of Cheesemaking in Ireland

The history of cheese in Ireland is similar to that of Great Britain, but a bit different. It is believed that the Celts of Ireland were first taught cheesemaking by Viking invaders, and then, of course, the Romans played their role. Christianity took hold in Ireland, but Henry VIII's expulsion of the Catholic Church did *not* affect Ireland, nor did it affect the monasteries or the monks who helped the country's agricultural ways, including those of cheesemaking.

Like the rest of the British Isles, Ireland has had a farmhouse cheese history, but unlike the rest of the isles, that history persevered over time. For one thing, Irish butter was king of the dairy products, and cheese, produced mainly in farmhouses, was good, but not nearly as known or sought after as the creamy, delicious Irish butters. For another, factories didn't take over farmhouse production in the late nineteenth and early twentieth century the way it did in Great Britain.

Though the Irish made a mix of fresh and aged cheeses, cheddar-style cheeses were among the most popular. In the 1970s, Irish traditions changed. The Slow Food movement took hold, and in Ireland, that meant going back to traditional ales and bread-making traditions, and for some it also meant rediscovering old, traditional cheeses.

A group of Irish cheesemakers formed the CAIS, the Irish Farmhouse Cheesemakers Association in 1983. When they started, the CAIS wanted to ensure professional cheesemaking standards and hygiene, but they also wanted to ensure that the farmhouse cheeses themselves had strict standards. The milk for the cheeses had to come from one source or a very limited number of local sources; the cheeses had to be handcrafted on small-scale production; and only raw milk could be used.

Not only did the innovative cheesemakers spread the word of their exceptional cheeses throughout Ireland, the news began to spread throughout the world. That can be seen in the one standard that they've adapted from their original set of rules: pasteurized milk can be used in some cheeses. (Especially the ones exported to the United States.)

A Cut Above

Besides producing great cheese, the Irish have produced some giants in the fields of literature and music, and they have had a word or two to say about Irish cheese. James Joyce, who said "A corpse is meat gone bad. Well, and what's cheese? Corpse of milk." (*Ulysses*, 1922) "The Waterford Boys," a traditional Irish song, includes one line about cheese: "In tavern I rolled, in the landlord he strolled, 'Good morrow,' says he and says I, 'If you please, will you give a bed and then bring me some bread and a bottle of porter and a small piece of cheese?' My bread and cheese ended, I then condescended to take my repose, sure I bad him good night."

Further expanding the market and promoting Irish cheeses were the brothers Sheridan—Seamus and Kevin. These two foodie siblings started selling delectable farmhouse cheeses from their stall in the Galway Saturday market in 1995, thus founding Sheridans Cheesemongers, which today has two shops, one in Galway and the other in Dublin. The Sheridan brothers and others like them continue to promote Irish farmhouse cheeses, and these true artisanal originals are now found the world over.

A Word or Two About Cheddar

Say what you will about British cheese, there's not a cheese that's been more copied, emulated, and changed than good old English cheddar. It is also one of the world's few cheeses that has never been protected, and thus, it is cheddar, not Cheddar. Cheddar is, in fact, the most widely made cheese in the world, though mozzarella, with the popularity of pizza, is gaining.

Because it is so widely manufactured, many people think they know what it is, but real cheddar is a fine dairy creation, and traditional, cloth-bound cheddar is, indeed, another thing entirely. Cheddar cheese gets its name from both a place and a process. Cheddar is made by the process of *cheddaring* or cutting the cheese into curds, then pushing the curds into piles that stick to each other and become slabs, and then the slabs get piled on top of one another. That process presses the whey out. There is also, however, a town of Cheddar in Somerset, and also in Somerset are the Cheddar Gorge caves. While cheddar is no longer produced in Cheddar, it is still produced in Somerset, as well as Devon and Dorset.

Traditional cheddar is cloth-bound, a hard, white cheese with little calcium crystals that crunch in the mouth. Some cheddars—and other cheeses—get their color from *annatto* seeds, or crushed red seeds from the achiote tree, a natural food coloring.

> **Say Cheese**
>
> **Cheddaring** is the process of cutting, slabbing, and piling curds to create cheddar. **Annatto** is a South American red seed from the achiote tree that is used to color cheddar and other cheeses.

Traditional English cheddar is not colored with annatto, but annatto is used to color Red Leicester. Real English cheddar is also not formed in bricks or block shapes, but rather tall wheels. It is not only made in England, but the Scots and the Irish also produce some delicious wheels of traditional cheddar. Though the block-formed, milder, orange-colored derivatives are most common in the United States, good cheddar makers can be found in Wisconsin,

California, and Vermont. They can also be found in Canada, Australia, and New Zealand, and even South Africa makes cheddar.

A Cut Above

Cheddar has been taken on expeditions to Antarctica with the British Captain Robert Falcon Scott in 1901, and it was also taken to the North Pole with Wisconsin explorer Eric Larsen in 2006. But perhaps the most interesting cheddar story involves Queen Victoria. In honor of her wedding to Prince Albert in 1840, a mammoth, 1,250-pound cheddar was created. After receiving such a gracious gift from cheesemakers, she sent the wheel on a tour of England and then after its tour was done, she didn't want it back.

The Great Cheeses of the British Isles

When you're talking about the cheeses made in the British Isles, you're talking about a lot of cheese, much of it extremely good. Some of the great cheeses are steeped in centuries of tradition, others are quite new, created within the last couple of decades. But whether they're old treasures or new delights, they all have that signature of being crafted from some very, very good milk.

English cheddar is in a class by itself. Besides being cloth-bound, it has a different taste from most cheddars made in the United States. Typically, a true English cheddar is aged for about a year or two, but it isn't often aged out to seven or 10 years like some fine American cheddars are. It has the same crystalline crunch you'd expect from a cheddar, but it won't be orange and annatto-color. It will be ivory or cream-color, and it will have that signature tang of a cheddar, but not sharp or mouth-puckering. There's almost a nuttiness to it, and it is deliciously complex, but not overwhelming.

Stilton is not only the king of English cheese, it's also known as king of the blues. This honorable blue is aged for a month before it is pierced (poked with holes so that blue veins can better develop), and it has a mineral yet nutty taste that mingles well with fruits and strong wines; it has traditionally been served with a tawny port. In fact, in older times, it used to be pierced with knitting needles and had port poured over it.

Cheshire, like English cheddar, is a cloth-bound hard cheese made from raw cow's milk. And although it could be considered a cousin of cheddar, Cheshire is its own cheese. It has more moisture than most hard cheeses, and it can be white or "red." Red Cheshire is colored with annatto, and it has more of an orange than red sheen to it. It boasts a mild, salty taste, with a citrusy aftertaste. It is also the traditional cheese used in Welsh Rarebit, which is almost like a beer and milk fondue poured over bread (more on rarebit in Chapter 25).

Caerphilly is a hard Welsh cheese, one of the original English crumblies, or hard cheeses that crumble easily. It was often taken by Welsh miners into the coal mines as a snack. It was first made in Caerphilly in the 1830s. Though World War II stopped production in Wales, Caerphilly continued to be made in England, and today, production has resumed in Wales. It's one of those rediscovered farmhouse cheeses, and it boasts a salty, creamy nature with just the right amount of tang.

A Cut Above

My favorite mention of Caerphilly is by John Cleese in the wonderful Monty Python "cheese shop" skit. Cleese plays an erudite customer who desires cheese. The shop owner, played by Michael Palin, amiably tries to serve Cleese, but every time Cleese inquires about a cheese, Palin doesn't have it. Cleese mentions every cheese known to man, including some that don't exist (Venezuelan beaver cheese), but, alas, Palin doesn't have any of them.

Double and Single Gloucester are hard, buttery cheeses. The single version is made with skimmed milk from the evening's milking combined with the next morning's whole milk. Double Gloucester is made with the whole milk from two milkings. Both cheeses are hard, delicious cheeses sometimes colored with annatto. More mild than cheddar, with a buttery sweetness, both cheeses are quite delicious. Huntsman cheese is a layered cheese made up of Double Gloucester and Stilton.

Derby is a traditional English cheese with the dubious distinction of being the first cheese in England to be made in a factory. Sort of like a softer, creamier, buttery cheddar, Derby has in recent years experienced a resurgence. It also comes in the Sage Derby variety, which has real bits of the herb mixed into its creamy paste.

Dunlap is a famous Scottish cheese that ceased production in the 1950s, but it has been revived in recent years by some farmhouse producers. This hard cheese is mild and buttery with just a hint of acid. It was actually once made on the farms of Robert Burns, the poet.

Another recently revived cheese is Crowdie, which is believed to be Scotland's oldest cheese, introduced by the Vikings. Whereas Dunlap is aged, Crowdie is fresh and soft. Both are wonderful cheeses and well worth trying.

Yet another revived, traditional Scottish cheese is Caboc. Legend has it that it was created by Mariota de Ile, daughter of a fifteenth-century MacDonald lord. Mariota had been endangered by being kidnapped by the Campbell clan, so she escaped to Ireland. There she learned how to make cheese, and when she returned to Scotland, she made Caboc. In the twentieth century, it had declined in popularity until an artisan cheesemaker revived it in 1962. Caboc is a double-cream cheese covered in oatmeal.

Lancashire is a golden-hued cheese that kept mill workers well fed during the Industrial Revolution. It is a hard cheese that boasts a moist, crumbly texture and a delicious buttery yet tangy taste. Today, you can find both farmhouse and factory versions.

Red Leicester was first made when there was a surplus of milk from Stilton making. Carrot juice was originally added for color; today, annatto colors it. It has an almost chewy texture with a light, sweet smell and mild taste.

Wensleydale is the most famed of all the dale cheeses made in Yorkshire. Some farmhouse versions are made with sheep's milk, but most versions are of the cow's milk variety. Its history goes back to those Cistercian monks who hooked a ride with William the Conqueror back in the eleventh century. In recent years, it can be seen in the Wallace and Gromit movies, and it is the cheese that Wallace refers to when he says "Cheese, Gromit?" Crumbly yet moist, it has an almost honey taste with the right amount of tang.

Though most of the British and Scottish cheeses you will see imported are firm or hard cheeses, Ireland's farmhouse producers make a wide variety of delicious styles.

One of the best Irish cheeses is Cashel Blue, made in the Tipperary region by Louis and Jane Grubb, descendents of butter makers who were expelled from England in the seventeenth century. Cashel Blue is a firm and moist blue with a tangy taste. The longer it ages, the creamier and more piquant it becomes.

Milleens is an Irish semi-soft, washed rind cheese that has a subtle, sweet taste. Created by Veronica Steele, one of the foremothers of the modern Irish farmhouse cheese movement, this cheese varies with the seasons, depending on what the cows have been munching on. It's one of those delicious, mildly stinky cheeses that boasts a whole lot of flavor. Steele and her husband and son make the cheese, and Steele has passed on her cheesemaking knowledge to several other cheesemakers.

Another washed rind is Gubbeen, which is made by Tom and Gina Fergusson (Gina was taught by Steele). It is an earthy-tasting cheese with a light-pink washed rind. It tastes of mushrooms and nuts. Like many artisan cheesemakers, the Fergussons are particular about their cows and how they are raised, and about their cheese, which is so much the better for consumers.

The Irish produce a lot of cheddars, and some of the best Irish cheddars are flavored with stout or wine. A lot of Irish cheddar is made by Kerrygold, a company served by dairy farm cooperatives and established by the Irish Dairy Association. It is the largest exporter of Irish cheese and butter. Two of its most popular cheeses are Blarney Castle, a mild, Gouda-like cheese, and Dubliner, which is similar, but stronger than the typical cheddar. Both are good cheeses, and they're available in a lot of regular grocery stores in the United States, which is not surprising since Kerrygold exports to 80 different countries.

The Least You Need to Know

- ◆ Though about the size of New England, Great Britain and Ireland are two powerhouses in cheese.

- ◆ British cheese dates back thousands of years, but the kind of British cheese that we're familiar with started with the Romans, who taught the Angles and the Saxons how to use rennet.

- ◆ The British cheeses cheddar and Stilton are two of the most well-known cheeses in the world.

- ◆ Cheddar is the world's most popular cheese, but real English cheddar is a white, cloth-bound cheese with less sharpness than the orange, supermarket varieties.

- ◆ Ireland's cheese history is mostly of a farmhouse nature, and although it almost died out, it has been revived in the last three decades and is a force to be reckoned with.

Chapter 9

Spanish and Portuguese Cheeses

In This Chapter

- ◆ Spanish cheesemaking: a unique history and geography
- ◆ Discovering Spain's numerous (100 plus) cheeses
- ◆ The history of cheesemaking and the distinctive cheeses of Portugal

The ruggedly beautiful Iberian Peninsula is home to more than 100 different cheeses. Indeed, some of the world's best cheeses can be found in Spain and Portugal. These two countries have long traditions of making cheese, and both have some singularly distinct cheeses and cheesemaking techniques. Spain has a history of combining different milks in cheeses, while cheesemakers in Portugal have often used plant coagulants instead of rennet to curdle milk.

Despite their innovative techniques and long history, though, much of Spain and Portugal's dairy goodness is not that well known. Fortunately for us, more and more of the beautiful cheeses of the Iberian Peninsula are becoming readily available and promoted here.

The History and Geography of Spanish Cheese

With a staggering array of more than 100 different and distinct cheeses, Spain is definitely a cheese lover's land. To understand Spain's cheeses, it helps to understand a bit of its history. Before the Romans even conquered Rome, Spain had been conquered and settled by the Phoenicians, the Carthaginians, and the Greeks, all of whom had spent extensive time in Spain. Then the Romans came along and built their roads and aqueducts (you can still see an immense one in Segovia), and they also brought along their foods, specifically olives, which they planted across the vast countryside. The Moors also spent a lot of time in Spain—700 years—and their influence can be seen in the spices—saffron, cumin, and cinnamon—as well as citrus fruits used in Spanish cooking to this day.

Throw into this mix the Celts, who settled in Galicia in northwest Spain; the Basque people, who settled along the Pyrenees in Pais Vasco; and the Catalans, who settled along northeast Spain in Catalonia. Galicia is decidedly Spanish today, but the Catalans and the Basques speak different languages. Catalan is a Romance language, but Basque is an ancient tongue, its origins basically unknown, and different from any other language on the planet, with its almost unpronounceable consonants. Then just for more fun, add the Spanish conquistadors, who explored the new world—North and South America—and brought back a variety of interesting plants and foods like chocolate, tomatoes, peppers, and so on.

This means that, culturally speaking, Spain has a variety of influences, and its geography adds to its uniqueness. The Iberian Peninsula connects the Atlantic Ocean with the Mediterranean Sea in southwestern Europe, making it a very coastal region. Spain is also the third largest country in Europe. It has a lot of mountains, and the climate is a bit drier than the rest of Europe. But it also has great soil, which led to great—and diverse—agriculture.

Now, what does this have to do with cuisine, or more specifically, cheese? Everything. The imprints of these various peoples and geographic considerations can be tasted in the cheeses. While different ethnic groups conquered and settled Spain, their various traditions were filtered and then passed down by farmers and shepherds.

Shepherds, in fact, are believed to be the first cheesemakers in Spain, and their hands really imprinted Spanish cheese. Other European cheesemaking traditions were preserved and handed down in the Middle Ages by monks in monasteries, but, although Spanish monks took their country's cheesemaking skills to California, it was the shepherds who developed and preserved cheesemaking within Spain. During the Middle

Ages, shepherds also made pilgrimages throughout the peninsula, which helped develop cheesemaking traditions throughout Spain. One of the most important pilgrimages that shepherds (and lots of other people) made during the Middle Ages was St. James Way or el Camino de Santiago, which ends in Santiago de Compostela in Galicia, where it is believed that the remains of the apostle of Saint James are buried.

Mixed-milk cheeses can be found throughout the country, but the predominant milk of each area is the base of its regional cheeses. In general, cattle were kept along the north, where Spain's lushest pastures can be found. Cow's milk cheesemaking developed along the coast from Galicia to the Basque country, as well as along the northern mountain ranges, the Cantabric Mountains and the Pyrenees. Some cows can also be found in the Canary Islands and the Balearic Islands (Mallorca, Menorca, and Ibiza).

Sheep's milk cheeses were developed more inland, where grazing lands were rougher for cattle, from the north in Cantabria and Basque country down to the meseta or rolling plateaus of Castilla-Leon, Castilla La Mancha, Aragon, and Extremadura. Sheep's milk cheeses can also be found on Mallorca, one of Spain's islands. Goat's milk cheeses are found along the Mediterranean coast, from Catalonia to Andalusia, along with Extremadura, as well as on both the Canary Islands and the Balearic Islands.

Though the shepherds preserved and spread cheesemaking during the Middle Ages and beyond, in modern times the Spanish government took over the preservation of recipes, techniques, and even names of traditional cheeses. Spain came into cheese protection a bit late, as France, Italy, and Switzerland already had laws in place for decades. The first modern step came in 1981 when the government set up protection laws. These new laws determined which cheeses would be name controlled with protection of origin designations Denominacion de Origen Protegida, or D.O.P., or in the United States simply D.O.

The first cheese to be approved and name controlled was Roncal in 1981, and new cheeses are still being added to the list. Right now, there are more than a dozen or so such cheeses, including Cabrales, Cantabria, Idiazabal, La Serena, L'Alt Urgell, Mahon, Majorero, Manchego, Murcia al Vino, Nata de Cantabria, Quesos de Liebana

> **A Cut Above**
>
> In Spain, goats are often referred to as "the poor man's cow." In centuries past, it wasn't uncommon to see shepherds with their flocks of goats traversing small Spanish towns. As they went through town, the shepherd and his family would occasionally stop to milk the goats, right in the street, for customers. Leftover milk then was turned into fresh cheese.

(Ahumado de Aliva, Pido, Picon, and Quesuco), Palmero, Roncal, Tetilla, Torta de Casar, Valdeon, and Zamorano. What's interesting is that the majority of the cheeses on Spain's list are sheep's milk, goat's milk, or mixed-milk cheeses, rather than cow's milk cheeses.

Spanish Cheeses

In 1988, the Spanish government commissioned a survey to catalogue every Spanish cheese to make sure that Spanish dairy heritage would not be lost. More than 80 cheeses were discovered in that initial survey, and today it's been determined that there are more than 100 different Spanish cheeses. That means that after France and Italy, Spain produces the largest variety of cheeses in Europe.

The most popular cheese in Spain—and the most well-known cheese outside the country—is Manchego. Created in the La Mancha region, the land of Don Quixote, this firm sheep's milk cheese boasts an aromatic flavor, an ivory color with little, irregular holes. It has a mild, nutty taste, and it is typically pasteurized, though some of the rarer forms come from raw milk. It can be aged from two months to two years. The two-month version is called *fresco* (young), to the one-year-old *curado* (cured) to the two-year-old *anejo* or *viejo* (old). It also can be sold *en aceite* or rubbed in extra virgin olive oil. As it ages, the flavor becomes more intense, and it is often served with *jamon serrano* (serrano ham) as part of a *tapas* (appetizer) meal. It goes amazingly well with strong Spanish red wines like rioja, and it also is traditionally served with quince paste.

A Cut Above

Don Quixote didn't dine on Manchego, but he did eat cheese, and there was a particularly memorable incident in Miguel de Cervantes's book *Don Quixote* (1605) involving the Man of La Mancha, his trusty sidekick, Sancho Panza, and a helmet full of cheese. Sancho had purchased some cheese curds from some shepherds, and he didn't know where to put them so he put them in Don Quixote's helmet. Of course, Don Quixote put the helmet on with the cheese in it. After the cheese squished and leaked onto his face, Quixote said "What's this? I think my head is softening, or my brains are melting, or I am sweating from head to foot!"

Another quite popular cheese in Spain is Cabrales, an unusual blue cheese. Made of a mix of cow's milk, sheep's milk, and goat's milk, Cabrales has a distinctly fruity yet spicy flavor. It is ripened in natural limestone caves in Asturias, and unlike other blue cheeses, it is so blue that it's almost purple. Cabrales is similar to Picon or Picos de Europa, which is made in Cantabria.

Perhaps the spiciest Spanish cheese, Afuega'L Pitu, earned its name honestly. Translated in the Asturian dialect of Spanish, it means "fire in the throat." And that's what this spicy, paprika-rubbed cow's milk cheese does when you eat it—its spicy heat engulfs your senses.

Garrotxa is a Catalan cheese made from goat's milk. This cheese is one of the most unusual goat's milk cheeses, with a gray rind and a firm texture. One of Spain's newer cheeses, it boasts an herbal yet nutty flavor, and it's become quite popular in recent years.

Idiazabal is one of Pais Vasco's best dairy creations. This raw sheep's milk cheese has been made for centuries in the high mountain pastures, traditionally sold in the fall after the shepherds moved their flocks to lower pastures. It has a smoky flavor; it was traditionally smoked because shepherds aged it in the stone chimneys of their small houses. The cheese also boasts a sweet, buttery taste, a pale yellow color, and some tiny holes.

Mahon, made in Minorca, is one of the island cow's milk cheeses. As Spain's second most popular cheese, it is similar in taste and texture to Parmigiano-Reggiano, but unlike that Italian cheese, it has a bright orange rind. The rind achieves its signature color because the cheese is rubbed in paprika, oil, and butter. It can be served fresh or within 10 days, or it can be aged up to 10 months.

Queso de Murcia al Vino is a sort of modern twist on a traditional goat's milk cheese from southeast Spain. Queso de Murcia is just a smooth yet spongy fresh goat's milk cheese. In 1986, the local government challenged cheesemakers to make their cheese more distinctive—and have a longer shelf life—and in return, they would give this queso a regional commercial status (sort of like the local D.O.P. stamp of approval). The cheesemakers decided to wash the cheese with local red wine, and the wine washed cheese was a great success. It's no wonder: the wine gave the milder cheese a dramatic burgundy color and a fruity flavor.

Mixed milks mingle in both Quesuco and Ahumado de Aliva. Quesuco has a mix of goat's, cow's, and sheep's milks; Ahumado is the smoked version of the same cheese. They are nutty, delicious cheeses that age out rather well.

Roncal is a mountain cheese that was honored with the distinction of becoming the very first D.O.P.–designated cheese. But its history goes back to the 1200s, when the local government set regulations for sheep in the area. The sheep hung out in alpine pastures from July until September and then moved to winter grazing grounds from October until May. Because of this change of scenery, the milk produced has a quite delicious flavor, and the resulting cheese is pungent, sweet, and almost herbaceous.

A Cut Above

La Serena is a Spanish sheep's milk cheese, but there's a similarly named California cheese called Serena. Made by the Three Sisters Farmstead, Serena is an Italian-style cow's milk cheese. It's a great cheese, but completely different from La Serena.

Queso de la Serena is one of Spain's great sheep's milk cheeses. Made from raw milk, it's made in Extremadura. Two qualities make this cheese unusual. It is made only from the milk of merino sheep, an ancient Spanish breed, and the curds are created not with rennet but with cardoon thistle. The semi-soft cheese has almost a buttery texture, but a strong yet sweet flavor. Torta del Casar is another merino sheep's milk cheese made in Extremadura, but the Torta is a bit more salty. The traditional way to eat the Torta is to cut open the top of the rind and scoop out the gooey good stuff inside.

Cheeses in Spain not only have some unusual flavors, but two of them have a most unusual shape—Tetilla and San Simon. These two cow's milk cheeses from Galicia are the kind of cheeses that an adolescent male might find amusing because they are curved, well, like a woman's breast. *Tetilla* even means "nipple" or "teat." Tetilla is a semi-soft cheese that has a mild and tangy flavor. San Simon is smoked and sort of like a smoky mozzarella.

Zamorano is not only one of the few cheeses that start with the last letter of the alphabet, but it is a delicious, firm sheep's milk cheese first created by wandering shepherds in the Castilla-Leon region of Spain. It is similar to Manchego, but many consider its flavor to be superior, with a tart yet nutty taste.

Portugal and Its Cheeses

Unlike Spain, which was invaded and conquered by different tribes throughout the ages, Portugal was protected from invasions by the Atlantic Ocean to the west and rough mountains to the east. That means that the Portuguese people developed a culture independent from such outside influences—with one exception: the Romans did conquer them, and brought their cheesemaking techniques with them.

Cheesemaking in Portugal started in the north of the country, near the Montes Herminios mountain range, and it began with sheep. Shepherds then crisscrossed the country in search of better pastures and milder climates in winter. Until the

1950s, cheesemaking in Portugal was much as it had been throughout the centuries—restricted to farms and accomplished by shepherds or cheesemakers called *roupeiros*. In the 1950s, however, cheesemaking moved to small village creameries, run by roupeiros. The roupeiros usually inherited their positions and carefully guarded their recipes.

Then, after watching the Spanish begin to protect their cheeses, the Portuguese government decided to protect their country's best cheeses, giving them a D.O.P. or designation of protected origin status. The first five cheeses to be given such protection were Serra da Estrela, Serpa, Beira Baixa, Azeitao, and Sao Jorge. More recent additions include Cabra Transmontano, Castelo Branco, Evora, Nisa, Pico, Mestico de Tolosa, Rabacal, and Terrincho.

Like Spain's, Portuguese cheeses are made from the milk of cows, goats, sheep, or sometimes a blend of one or two. Several of Portugal's cheeses are made not with rennet but cardoon thistle. Its cheeses are less well known than Spain's, but because most of its cheeses remain small in production scale, they are very good indeed.

> **A Cut Above**
>
> The cardoon thistle—or purple thistle flower—is used in almost all Portuguese cheeses instead of rennet. The pistil of the flower is cut and then dried out in the sun for three weeks, then it is crushed in water, the water is filtered, and the resulting solution is added to cheese to curdle it.

Serra da Estrela is often called "the king of Portuguese cheese." Dating back centuries, this sheep's milk cheese is made in the mountain range of the same name in the Beira region. This tangy sheep's milk cheese can be eaten young—after two or three weeks of aging—but its flavor intensifies and becomes sharper if it is aged for a few months. Instead of rennet, thistle is used to curdle it.

Another very popular Portuguese cheese is Serpa, a creamy sheep's milk cheese made in the Baixo Alentejo region. Like Serra, thistle is used for curdling. Serpa has a light orange rind that gets its color from being rubbed with olive oil and paprika. It becomes tangy and sharper as it ages, but young it has a rather buttery flavor.

Sao Jorge is a cow's milk cheese that is made on the Sao Jorge Island, part of the Azores Islands. It dates back to the fifteenth century, when Flemish settlers brought over cows from the mainland to help them become self-sufficient. Because the Azores were often a stop for seafarers on their way to the New World, such a cheese became a staple of life. Sao Jorge looks similar to Gouda, but it has more of a cheddarlike taste, and as it ages, it becomes a good grating cheese.

Azeitao is a great raw sheep's milk cheese made near the Arrabida Mountains. Like other Portuguese cheeses, thistle is used in place of rennet. It has a smooth texture and a strong, earthy aroma. It is a semi-soft cheese, but at room temperature, it becomes unctuous.

Evora is a firm sheep's milk cheese that is made in the Alentejo region of Portugal. It has a fruity and salty taste but an acidic finish. The longer it is aged, the more "sheepy" its taste becomes.

Portuguese cheese, though typically produced in small volumes, is of high quality, and you can expect more and more Portuguese cheese to be exported to the United States in the coming years.

The Least You Need to Know

- With more than 100 different types of cheese, Spain is an important cheese-producing country.

- Spain has an unusual cheesemaking history, having been invaded and conquered by various peoples; therefore, its cheeses are often a bit more unusual than the rest of Europe.

- Manchego is the most popular Spanish cheese, but other important Spanish cheeses include Mahon, Cabrales, and Idiazabal.

- Spain makes cow's milk, sheep's milk, and goat's milk cheeses, and sometimes mixes all three into single varieties of cheese.

- Both Spain and Portugal, but especially Portugal, make nonrennet cheeses that instead use thistle to curdle the milk. The two most important Portuguese cheeses are Serra da Estrela and Serpa.

10

Scandinavian and Baltic Cheeses

In This Chapter

◆ Learn the history and cheeses of Denmark

◆ Explore the Viking origins of cheesemaking in Norway

◆ Study Swedish cheeses and their historical beginning

◆ Unique Finnish cheeses and their origin

◆ The historical beginning of cheesemaking in the Baltic states and some traditional cheeses

You might not think that a region filled with rugged mountains and dense forests so close to the Arctic Circle would have much to do with dairy or cheese, but dairying has long been an honored tradition in Scandinavia, in the lands where the Vikings once ruled and stormed the seas.

In fact, in many cases, the Vikings initially started cheesemaking in Denmark, Norway, Sweden, and Finland. Swiss, French, and German traditions also played a role in the development of the cheeses in these lands. Some of the well-known cheeses are adaptations of other European favorites, but there are distinctive Scandinavian cheeses and traditions, too.

Today, Scandinavian countries not only make a lot of cheese, they export great quantities, especially to the United States. Popular exports include Jarlsburg, Havarti, and Danish Blue or Danablu. Cheeses in Scandinavia are made primarily from cow's milk and goat's milk, but some are made with reindeer's milk. Many of the cheeses of this region are milder than those in southern Europe, and because of their cooler climates, firm and hard cheeses tend to be more popular.

The Baltic states of Estonia, Latvia, and Lithuania are geographically and culinarily distinct from the Scandinavian countries, but they do have some cheesemaking ties. In fact, some of the largest dairy factories in the Baltic are owned by Scandinavian companies. Like Scandinavia, the cheeses of the Baltic states tend to be a bit milder on the palate than those of other regions in Europe.

Denmark and Its Cheeses

Denmark's cheesemaking roots may go back to 3000 B.C.E., with the production of acid or nonrennet cheese. Some archaeological evidence even shows that the earliest Danes started burning down forests and cultivating livestock in 4000 B.C.E. But cheese really didn't become a commodity until the age of the Vikings, from about 500 C.E. onward. The Vikings kept cows, and milk, butter, and cheesemaking followed.

With its temperate climate and good rainfall, combined with lush meadows, cattle have found more than suitable living arrangements in Denmark. The oldest document on cheese dates back to 1232, indicating that cheese was used as a form of currency to pay taxes to the church and king.

Denmark has always been a center of trade, and many of its cheeses are derivatives from cheeses in Germany and Holland. Others are similar to Swiss varieties, for good reason: in the early part of the nineteenth century, a Danish king wanted to add to his country's cheesemaking repertoire, so he invited a Swiss cheesemaker to come and teach the local farmers his methods. The result of his visit is Samso, a sort of pale and milder version of the very Swiss Emmentaler. Softer than a true Swiss, this cheese has tiny holes and a buttery taste while young that grows more pungent with age.

Samso is perhaps the most popular cheese within Denmark, and several other Danish cheeses can be considered derivative cheeses, including Danbo, which often has added caraway seeds. (In the United States, Danbo is sometimes called Christian IX or King Christian cheese.) Other similar cheeses within the "bo" family include Elbo and Tybo, as well as Fynbo and Maribo, which are similar to Gouda.

Samso might be the most popular cheese within Denmark, but Havarti certainly is its most popular export. This cheese was invented by a nineteenth-century Danish entrepreneur named Hanne Nielsen. Seeking to improve her country's cheeses, Nielsen traveled and experimented to come up with new Danish cheeses. Havarti was her greatest success, and it gets its name from the farm where she created it. This creamy, firm cheese has tiny holes and a light yellow color. It is often flavored with herbs like dill or caraway seeds, and it has a pleasant taste. It can have a dry or a washed rind; washed rind versions have a stronger flavor. Sometimes extra cream is added to it as well. It's frequently served on sandwiches.

A Cut Above

Because many Danish cheeses are similar to other European cheeses, their names were changed in 1951 at the Stresa Convention. Cheese names like Roquefort and Gorgonzola were protected by their countries of origin, so Danish Schweizer or Swiss became Samso.

Esrom is another mild Danish cheese, made from an old recipe that the Danish Cheese Institute rediscovered in 1951 and named for a monastery where it may have originated. It's a semi-soft cheese with small, irregularly shaped holes. It has a sweet but often pungent taste, especially the longer it ages. Sometimes it is flavored with garlic, onion, or pepper.

But not all the cheeses made in Denmark are mild. In fact, Denmark is known for its Danish blues, the most prominent of which is, in fact, called Danish Blue or Danablu. This cheese was invented in the early twentieth century by Marius Boel, who wanted to create a blue cheese that was similar to Roquefort. Although Boel started with this French cheese as a model, the resulting Danish Blue is entirely different. Danish Blue is a salty, very white cheese with a creamy feel and a sharp-edged (some say metallic) flavor.

Another Danish blue cheese is Bla Castello or Blue Castello, which was developed in the 1960s. It has an almost Brie-like texture and it is enriched with cream. Mildly spicy, it's a lighter blue than Danablu.

Previously known as Danish Gorgonzola, Mycella was renamed in 1951, taking its name from the mold that colors it: *penicillium mycellium*. It's a rather mild blue.

Another Danish interpretation cheese is Danish Fontina, which is much different from both Italian and Swedish styles of this cheese. This firm cheese has a stronger odor, but a mild, nutty, sweet flavor.

Several Danish cheeses are made and exported by Arla Foods, including Esrom, Danbo, Havarti, and Danish Fontina. Arla Foods is the world's largest producer of organic milk.

A Cut Above

There aren't a whole lot of Danish authors waxing poetic about cheese, but a certain famous writer of fairy tales used this dairy product as a plot point. Hans Christian Anderson wrote about cheese in his tale "The Goblin and the Grocer," sometimes called "The Goblin and the Huckster" (1853). A student goes to buy some cheese, noticing that it is wrapped in a page from a book of literature. Instead of buying the cheese, he buys the entire book, eating plain bread and butter for dinner instead.

Norwegian Jarlsberg and Other Norsk Favorites

Norway doesn't have a lot of grazing land, but cattle farming and dairying dates back several thousand years in the land the Vikings chose as their home base. For many years, butter was considered the most valuable dairy product, and it was sometimes used as a type of currency. Many cheeses were created from the leftovers of butter or soured, skimmed milk. The resulting cheeses were more acidic in nature, and initially didn't have any curdling from rennet. The Viking sailors used these acidic cheeses as nourishment on their long voyages at sea.

One of the oldest Norwegian cheeses that probably went along on Viking voyages is appropriately named *Gammalost*, or "old cheese." Gammalost isn't named for its ancient history (though it's been written about since 1100), but rather for its aged taste and appearance. This extremely robust and aromatic cheese is not a long-aged cheese, but its rind develops a green-brown mold and looks older than it really is. It was traditionally wrapped in straw soaked in gin and juniper berries, which also added to its distinctive flavor. It's a very low-fat cheese and is seldom exported. Today, it's produced commercially by the TINE Dairy in Vik, Norway.

The modern dairy industry in Norway traces its roots back to the nineteenth century, when dairy cooperatives were formed and the government brought in Swiss cheese-makers to teach them more about cheesemaking and using rennet. Norway's most famous cheese, Jarlsberg, was developed around this time.

Jarlsberg was actually created by a pioneering dairyman named Anders Larsen Bakke. He developed the cheese in the village of Vale, about 50 miles south of Oslo. The cheese was named for the county "Jarlsberg & Larviks Amt" (the county was renamed Vestfold later on). It was first recorded in the county's annual report in 1855. The cheese fell out of favor in the early twentieth century, but in the 1950s, a dairy science student, Per Sakshaug, at the Agricultural University of Norway wrote his thesis on this cheese from Vestfold. His paper intrigued Professor Ole Martin Ystgaard, who began experimenting with recipes and production methods of Emmentaler and Gouda to see if he could re-create this old cheese, achieving success in 1956.

Exportation of this yellow, smooth, Swiss-like cheese began in 1961. Jarlsberg's pleasant, nutty taste and irregularly sized holes make it a very popular cheese in the United States, and it's used frequently in cooking, especially for sandwiches and fondues. The biggest exporter of Jarlsberg is the TINE dairy cooperative, which is also Norway's largest food producer.

A Cut Above

Jarlsberg's popularity has attracted the attention of Hollywood, making an appearance on both *The Sopranos* and in the Meryl Streep movie *The Devil Wears Prada*. In fact, the cheese shows up in two scenes between Anne Hathaway's character and her boyfriend, played by Adrian Grenier. Just as Hathaway is about to throw away her grilled cheese sandwich, Grenier stops her, saying "Give that to me. That's like 10 bucks' worth of Jarlsberg in there."

One of the most unusual and easily recognizable Norwegian cheeses is Gjetost. This dark, caramel-looking cheese was first created in the 1800s by Anne Hov, a farmer's wife. Hov took a popular local cheese made of pressed whey and added cream to it. This cheese sold more than her regular cheese and developed a great following. In fact, it reportedly saved the Gudbrandsdalen Valley from financial ruin in the 1880s.

Gjetost traditionally was made just from goat's milk, but today it's often made from a mixture of cow's and goat's milks. It gets its signature brown color from milk sugars that caramelize during production. Ski Queen Gjetost is made from both cow's and goat's milks, and Ekte Gjetost is made just from goat's milk. It has a smooth, almost fudgy texture, and a sweet, distinctive taste. It's a common snack food for Scandinavian skiers, and it's also often served as a breakfast food.

The imprint of two crossed keys is on Nokkelost cheese. (*Nokkel* means "key" in Norwegian.) Nokkelost is actually a derivative of a Dutch cheese called Leiden, which is named after the Dutch city of the same name, which also has two crossed keys on its emblem. This firm, cow's milk cheese is flavored with cumin, cloves, and caraway seeds, and because of its cumin flavor, it also known as Kuminost. Kraft once sold an American version of this cheese in the 1960s, calling it Caraway cheese, and some advertisements touted "A Taste of Scandinavia in Every Slice."

Slices of Scandinavia can also be found in Ridder cheese. Originally, this cheese was invented by a Swedish cheesemaker, but it spread to Norway, where its buttery taste remains very popular. Ridder means "knight" in Norwegian, and just as one might expect, this firm, washed rind cheese can have strong aromas. Wisconsin's Roth Kase makes an American version of this cheese called Knightsvale.

> **A Cut Above**
>
> Cutting Norwegian cheeses is relatively easy, thanks to the cheese plane, an invention by Thor Bjørklund in 1925 that was first manufactured by his firm, Bjørklund and Sons. In 2005, that same firm created the first nonstick cheese plane.

Swedish Cheeses and Their Origins

Originally, cheesemaking traditions were believed to have been introduced into Sweden by traveling tribes from the east. The first cheeses made in Sweden were made from goat's milk, as cow's milk was reserved for butter production. In the Middle Ages, monks furthered the cheesemaking traditions in Sweden, and a document dating to 1555 describes how they made large, open-eyed cheeses. Just as both Norway and Denmark were influenced by Swiss cheesemakers, so, too, was Sweden. In 1786, Erik Ruuth, a Swedish count, invited a Swiss cheesemaker to visit his manor in Marsvinsholm. A few years later, Swiss styles of cheese began showing up.

One Swiss style of cheese popular in Sweden is called Greve. Developed in 1964 by the Ornskoldsvik dairy, it's sort of like a milder Emmentaler, with a sweet, nutty flavor and large holes. It is typically aged for only 10 months.

Another popular Swedish cheese is called Svecia, from the Latin word for Sweden, *Suecia*. This firm, light yellow cheese, though a twentieth-century creation, is based on the kind of traditional Swedish cheeses that have been made in smaller villages since the thirteenth century. For a long time, these cheeses were named after the villages in which they were made, but in 1920, they became the common name for all locally produced cheeses. Svecia is available in different sizes and ages, and it typically has small holes and a pleasant acid taste that becomes more spicy as it ages. Sometimes these cheeses have cloves, cumin, or caraway seeds mixed in for extra flavoring.

Similar to Svecia is the Herrgard or "manor house" cheese. This cheese was created in the late 1800s to serve as a replacement for imported Gruyère. Herrgardost (Herrgard cheese) boasts a firm texture, good melting ability, small round holes, and a mild, nutty taste.

Created a little bit before Herrgard is the Västerbotten cheese, one of those beautiful culinary mistakes. Dairymaid Eleonora Lindstrom was making a local cheese, but interruptions left her to alternately heat and then stir the curd. This extra long stirring time created a very different cheese than the one she was supposed to make, but fortunately for her, the new cheese had an appealing flavor. Västerbotten is salty and a little bit fruity, with a grainy texture and irregularly shaped eyes. It is considered by many to be Sweden's most famous cheese.

A Cut Above

There is an annual scholarship competition for culinary students to create the best modern dish using Västerbotten cheese as an ingredient. There's also a tourist Cheese House visitors center in Burtrask, Sweden, the birthplace of Västerbotten.

Västerbotten has remained purely traditional, but one traditional cheese, Prastost, has taken an absolutely modern incarnation. Prastost literally means "priest cheese," and it's often just referred to as Prast. Its roots date back to the sixteenth century, when farmers would give their tax payments or tithes to the church in the form of cheese. It's a sweet, sharp-tasting firm cheese, filled with irregular holes, and sometimes it is washed in spirits like whisky or vodka. When it's washed with whisky it's called Saaland Pfarr, but the vodka versions, which are made only with Absolut vodka, are called VODCheese.

Two other popular Swedish cheeses are Graddost, a creamy cheese created in 1961 that is similar to Havarti, and Hushallsost, known in Sweden as farmer's cheese. Hushallsost is made with whole milk, and it's been around for more than seven centuries.

Swedish Fontina also needs to be mentioned. Different from both the Italian and the Danish versions, this sweet, creamy, and easily meltable cheese is much milder tasting than the original Italian version.

Finland and Its Distinct Cheeses

With one third of its territory located within the Arctic Circle, Finland is a land of beautiful, vast forests, lakes, and long winters. But despite the seasonal challenges, dairy farming is not only an important form of agriculture, it is the biggest agricultural industry in the country. Cows are the main dairy animals, but reindeer are also prized for their milk.

Finland's cheesemaking traditions date to around the Middle Ages. Cheeses were used to celebrate festivals, pay taxes, and so on. Like other Scandinavian countries, Swiss cheesemakers helped develop Finnish cheesemaking. In 1856, Swiss cheesemaker Rudolph Klossner made the first Finnish version of Emmentaler, which has become known as Finnish Swiss and today is made by Valio, the country's largest cheesemaker, under the brand Finlandia.

Finnish Swiss is made with pasteurized milk, whereas traditional Emmentaler is made with raw milk. The cheese has a milder Swiss taste. Similar to Finnish Swiss is Lappi cheese, a pleasant, firmer cheese with smaller holes. It was developed in the Lapland region of Finland.

The Finns also make a blue cheese called Aura in Aanekoski. This cow's milk blue takes its name from the nearby Aura River. It comes in two different ages—a younger version that is aged for 6 weeks and an older version aged for 12 weeks. When it's imported, it is sold under the name Midnight Blue.

Finland is also the birthplace of one of the most unusual cheeses on the planet, Juustoleipa, also known as *leipajuusto* or *narskujuusto*. Juustoleipa means "bread cheese," and if you've ever seen a slice of juusto, it looks almost like a piece of bread. Its distinctive brown crust comes from the process: after the curds are drained and pressed, they are then toasted on a fire, which gives the cheese its distinctive appearance. Juustoleipa has a sweet, creamy taste and an almost chewy texture. Unlike other cheeses, if you toast it over a fire, it doesn't get all melty and gooey, so it's often served warm. It was created so that it could be stored for a long time; then, when people were ready to serve it, they'd heat it on a fire before eating. Today, Finns enjoy eating this cheese by dunking it in coffee, pouring cream and sprinkling sugar over it, or serving it with jam, especially cloudberry jam.

Juustoleipa is also distinctive in that it traditionally was made from either reindeer's milk or from a cow's beestings—the rich milk from a cow who recently had given birth to a calf. It's not a commonly imported cheese, but a few domestic versions are crafted in Wisconsin.

Another cheese that sometimes is made from the milk of reindeer is Munajuusto or Ilves. This farmhouse cheese was made not only of milk, but also eggs added to the milk. Ilves, which is the factory-made version of the cheese, comes in a pale yellow disk with a lightly browned crust.

A local version of cottage cheese called Raejuusto, made with cow's milk, is served on its own, sprinkled over soups and salads, or mixed with cucumber, olive oil, and black pepper.

The Finns also enjoy a local processed cheese made by Valio, called Viola. It's a spreadable, creamy cheese often served on sandwiches for lunch.

The Baltic States and Their Cheeses

Cheesemaking and dairy farming have been around for centuries in the Baltic states. In Lithuania, there's evidence that milk and dairy products have been made for more than 1,000 years. Cattle have been bred in Estonia since about 1000 B.C.E., and cheese, in fact, was used to pay the rent in 1569. In Latvia, traditional Latvian cheese was first written about in the 1500s.

Though cheesemaking and dairying have been around for centuries in the Baltic states, this region doesn't have too many original cheeses. As in Scandinavia, Switzerland exported its technology to cheesemakers here in the eighteenth century, who made styles of cheese similar to Swiss, Gouda, Edam, and Limburger.

The traditional cheeses of the Baltics were sour milk or curd cheese. Soured milk, which happened through the aid of lactic acid bacteria with no use of rennet, was then cooked and the resulting curds were pressed, and the cheese was either served fresh or dried. Today, some of those cheeses are sold under the brands Janis, Baltukas, Sventinis, and Birute, and sometimes caraway seeds, poppy seeds, onion, garlic, fruits, and jams are added for flavor.

Both traditional soured milk cheeses and the other European-style cheeses were being manufactured at dairies before World War II. The Second World War left the Baltic countries under Soviet occupation, and Soviet rule forced consolidation of the dairy industry. After these countries regained their independence, the cheese and dairy industry expanded and improved, and other companies, including Finland's Valio, have invested in Baltic dairy plants.

Today, Lithuanian companies produce Gouda, mozzarella, Brie, and other European cheeses.

The Least You Need to Know

◆ The roots of cheesemaking in Denmark, Norway, Sweden, and Finland go back to the days of the Vikings. Many cheeses started out as imitations of other European cheeses, but evolved into their own distinct variations.

◆ Samso is the most popular cheese within Denmark, but the most popular exports are Havarti and Danish Blue or Danablu.

◆ Jarlsburg is the most popular exported Norwegian cheese, but another distinctive Norsk cheese is Gjetost, a dark, caramel-colored cheese made from whey.

◆ Västerbotten is Sweden's most popular traditional cheese, while Prastost or "priest cheese" now has an Absolut vodka–laced version called VODCheese.

◆ Finland's cheesemakers make one of the most unusual cheeses ever, Juustoleipa, which is made from reindeer's milk.

◆ The Baltic countries traditionally made soured milk cheese, and today they make versions of other European standards.

Chapter 11

Cheeses from the Rest of Europe

In This Chapter

- ◆ The interesting background of Dutch cheeses and some popular samples
- ◆ The historical beginning of cheesemaking and a sampling of cheeses from Germany and Austria
- ◆ Belgian cheeses and their history
- ◆ Eastern European cheeses and an historical account of their origins

Think of Holland, and the image of wooden shoes might pop into your head. Ponder Germany, and beer might come to mind. Muse about Belgium, and you think of chocolate. When you think about these countries, cheese probably isn't the first product that comes to mind. But though neither the Netherlands, Germany, nor Belgium are instantly associated with cheese, each of these countries does have a rich and varied dairy tradition. Not only that, but each of these countries produces a *lot* of cheese—Germany and Holland, for example, are two of the world's largest cheese and dairy producers, and Belgium makes more than 250 different kinds of cheese. The fact is, these countries produce some absolutely fantastic—and occasionally world-renowned—cheeses. Gouda or Munster, anyone?

Holland, Germany, and Belgium all boast a distinct and varied dairy history. They also each boast some very rich pasturelands and a climate that cows tend to like. So it's not surprising that the fine cheeses that come out of these European countries tend to be made from cow's milk. Cows also provide the main source of milk for most cheeses produced in Austria and Eastern European countries. Austrian cheeses tend to be similar to those of Germany. Eastern European countries do have a dairy tradition, but several traditional cheeses had an interruption or change in production under Soviet rule in the twentieth century. But with the end of the Eastern bloc era, they are catching up in production.

Gooda Cheese—Holland's Great Cheeses

If you're talking about Dutch history or economy, forget the wooden clogs and tulips. Cheese and dairy have been near or at the center of Dutch life for centuries, and no wonder. Its lush, fertile pastures were and remain the perfect setting to raise cattle.

Archaeological evidence in the city of Friesland in north Holland even suggests that cheese has been made in the Netherlands since at least the second century B.C.E.; other historical records date Dutch cheesemaking back to around 400 C.E. The most prolific milking cattle—the Holstein, also known as the Friesian, hails from Friesland, Holland, and it is believed to have been bred for about 2,000 years.

No matter when cheesemaking started in Holland, it is undisputed that the Dutch perfected it during the Middle Ages. Cattle-raising methods improved and so did cheesemaking. As early as 1100, Dutch barges paid tolls to Koblenz, Germany, in cheese, and old bills in the city of Rotterdam reveal that it was a valid profession to be a *caescoper* or cheesemonger. The cheese industry really started to rev up, though, in the 1300s when the first cheese and dairy markets in Holland were established. Farmers would take their dairy products, including cheese, to be publicly traded and weighed, and giant scales were set up in the middle of town to weigh giant wheels of cheese. Cheese weigh-houses, where cheese was weighed and certified, became an important center of trading activity.

An intricate process of buying and selling ensued on a weekly basis in these towns, with farmers offering up their cheeses to the highest bidders. In fact, a specific form of haggling known as "cheese bashing" developed. Buyers would bang the palms of their hands against the cheese to check the size of the holes in the cheese, and they kept up the banging until a price was agreed upon. Cheese weigh-houses are now tourist attractions, and in the summer months, cheese markets are held for visitors to enjoy.

With all this banging and selling going on domestically, it's not surprising that the Dutch took cheese-selling to the next level and started exporting it. By the 1500s and 1600s, cheese was being exported on a rather large scale; in 1649, the port city of Edam, where Edam cheese was made, exported 1 million pounds of cheese. The Italian historian Lodovico Guicciardi, after visiting Holland, wrote that the Dutch cheese and butter were worth as much as imported spices.

Spices, through the founding of the Dutch East India Company in 1621, in fact, were added to Dutch cheeses. By the middle of the 1600s, the Dutch were exporting Gouda and Edam to almost every country in Europe, and by the time Louis XIV took the throne in France, the French had banned the import of Dutch cheeses because of the cost. (French cheesemakers began developing their own versions of Dutch cheese, and Mimolette was created.) Cheese was so popular that many artists included it as a subject, and even the great Rembrandt did a portrait of it.

A Cut Above

Cheese was so popular that there's even a Dutch folk tale called "The Boy Who Wanted More Cheese," about a little boy who loved cheese so much that the fairies were able to get him to go off on a fantastical, middle-of-the-night cheese binge.

Dairying began to become more modern in the nineteenth century, when cheesemaking moved from farms to creameries or small factories. In 1883, the first creamery, New Life, was established south of Den Helder in north Holland; and also in 1883, the first dairy cooperative was set up in Friesland. Today, the Netherlands is the fifth largest producer of cheese, and it is the third largest exporter of cheese.

The vast majority of cheese produced—and exported—in the Netherlands is Gouda and Edam. Gouda, in fact, accounts for more than 50 percent of total Dutch cheese production. Gouda is an ancient cow's milk cheese, dating back to at least the sixth century, when it was first made in farms near the town of Gouda. Most of the Gouda that is imported in the United States is younger Gouda, which has a very mild taste. Young Gouda has a soft paste, a light yellow interior, large holes, and is usually covered with a red wax. As Gouda ages, its flavor develops and intensifies, becoming tangier and saltier; it also darkens and becomes harder. Gouda can be aged from a few months (the most common, young Gouda that most people are familiar with) to 18 months or even three years.

One type of aged Gouda is called Boerenkaas, made using raw milk and produced by hand in a farmhouse setting. Its name translates literally to "farmer cheese." A young Boerenkaas boasts fruity, light flavors, while an aged version has stronger aromas and tiny calcium crystals like those that develop in good Parmigiano-Reggiano.

A Cut Above

Not only is Edam shaped like a cannonball, but rounds of it were actually used in place of cannonballs in 1841, helping the Uruguayan fleet defeat the Argentinean navy.

Similar but distinct is Edam cheese, named after the port city north of Amsterdam, which comes in large, round globes or balls, and is made from partially skimmed milk. Like Gouda, most imported Edam is young, only a few months old. Edam can be aged for up to 10 months, and as it ages, its sweetness becomes nuttier.

The third most popular Dutch cheese is Leiden, also spelled Leyden and known as Leideskaas. Made in and around the university city of Leiden, this Gouda-like cheese is colored with annatto and spiced with cumin seeds before it is washed in brine. The aromatic cumin contrasts with the creamy, nutty flavor of the cheese. Similar to Leiden is Friesekaas, which is flavored with both cumin and cloves.

Another colorful cheese is called Commissiekaas or Dutch Mimolette. Commissiekaas is basically a mature Edam, colored with carrot juice. It is perhaps the closest cheese to mimic a pumpkin in color and shape.

Roomkaas is a cream-added cheese, similar to a Gouda. Still another cheese that has Gouda roots is Kernhem. Created just 25 years ago, a Dutch cheesemaker accidentally cured his Roomkaas at a temperature that was too high, and the cheese became gooey. But it tasted so good that they decided to make it again, and the name, Kernhem, which means "knife sticker," stuck. This cheese has a pronounced Gouda flavor and a distinctive texture.

German Cheeses and Deutsch Dairy Favorites

Like Holland, Germany boasts a superb dairy environment. With lowland plains, cattle have called Germany home for centuries. In fact, nonrennet cheeses are believed to have been made there for more than 1,000 years.

By 96 B.C.E., the Romans had conquered what is now southern Germany, so they almost certainly left their imprint on German cuisine; but the Germans didn't take lightly to colonization and invaded Rome right back. Cheese-wise, however, it is believed that Charlemagne had a bigger impact on Germany. In the eighth century the Franks spread their cheesemaking prowess, and German cheese and cuisine began to take shape.

Cheese became such an important part of the German diet that in the Middle Ages, there were two types of cheese made in castles: herrenkase was made for the nobility, while gesindekase was made for common folk. In 1341, German cheese trading was centered in the village of Liebenwerder, and it was renamed Kasemarkt or "cheese market."

German cheese development continued when the Bavarian noble Maximillian imported the skills of two Swiss cheesemakers in 1821, introducing the first Emmentaler to Germany. The late 1800s also led to the practice of approving ripening cellars called Garkeller, to improve production standards.

Today, cheesemaking is concentrated in the north and southeast of Germany, with Bavaria being Germany's most important dairy region, producing hundreds of different cheeses. Germany today makes about a third of all the cheese produced in Europe, exporting almost two million tons of it annually. But while cheesemaking is big business in Germany, most dairy farms only average about 50 cows. Modern Germany is known for producing some of the best cheesemaking equipment, and Germany also produces a fair amount of organic cheese.

German cheeses are typically very mild or rather strong in flavor, and many of them are semi-soft or firm in texture. Germany not only makes typical or traditional German cheeses, but it also manufactures French, Italian, Dutch, and other European varieties.

A Cut Above

In the German city of Nieheim, the "German Cheese Market" is held every other year, in even numbered years. It is a tourist event, which draws farmstead and artisanal cheesemakers from around the world.

One of the most notable German cheeses was created by those Swiss cheesemakers who came to Bavaria. Allgauer Emmentaler, a name-protected German cheese, is a raw cow's milk Swiss-style cheese with holes. It can only be made in certain southern Bavarian towns. Allgauer Emmentaler offers a sweet, fruity taste similar to regular Emmentaler cheese.

Algauer Bergkase is a traditional farmhouse cheese, and it simply means "mountain cheese." Germans describe it as the "baby brother" of Algauer Emmentaler. The best versions are made in small alpine farms during the late spring and summer. It has fewer and smaller holes than the German Emmentaler. Algauer Bergkase can be eaten as young as three months, but it can also be aged a year or a little longer.

Butterkase has a flavor that its name suggests—a buttery taste and color. It is a mild yet quite popular cheese, and it's also known as Damenkase or ladies' cheese. It's often served for breakfast or a snack.

A more modern cheese is Cambazola or Weiss-Blau Brie. Created in the 1970s, this cheese combines the soft, bloomy rind of a Camembert with the blue mold of a Gorgonzola. It's a creamy blue with a more delicate flavor than most other blues, and many people describe it as a blue cheese for people who don't like blue cheese.

A Cut Above

Limburger, which is also made by the Chalet Cheese Cooperative in Wisconsin, used to be the means to achieving practical jokes, especially on newlyweds. The joker would place a slice of this pungent cheese on top of the engine of another person's automobile; when they started their car, it would be filled with the scent of Limburger, an aroma that could linger for weeks.

Unlike Cambazola's mildness, the German Limburger is anything but mild. This is a cheese that gives strong German cheese its reputation. Created first by Trappist monks in Belgium, the Germans adopted this cheese and made it their own in the 1800s. This washed rind cheese has a reddish brown color on the outside and a creamy yellow interior. It is one of the strongest-smelling cheeses on the planet, and its taste can definitely be described as robust. Similar to Limburger is Romadur or Romadurkase. This is a milder washed rind, with a sweet-sour taste and a little bit of smoky flavor.

Munster is another strong German cheese, but not nearly as strong as Limburger. Made originally in the Munster Abbey in the Alsace region, this cheese started out as a French creation, but with that region being taken over by the Germans, then the French, and so on, it was adopted by the Germans, and today, it's made in both countries. It has a light orange washed rind and a mildly strong flavor. The American version is called Muenster.

Quark is perhaps the mildest—and most popular—German cheese. This fresh cheese, which simply means "curd" in German, dates back to the Iron Age, and it is sort of like a cross between yogurt and cottage cheese. It accounts for 40 percent of all cheese consumption within Germany, and the best quark is smooth and fresh tasting. Regular quark is made with skimmed milk, but other versions involve cream or buttermilk. Quark is used a lot in German cooking, especially desserts.

Another popular German cheese is Tilsit or Tilsiter, which was discovered by Dutch immigrants who were living in East Prussia. These immigrants were trying to make Gouda, but the affinage process didn't go as expected. This cheese is washed in brine, and it takes about six months for it to mature. Moist and creamy, it has a dry sort of fruitiness and a spicy nature. It is produced mainly in northern Germany today.

Different Types of Austrian Cheeses

Austrian cheeses and their history are very similar to German cheeses. Many cheeses made in Germany have an Austrian counterpart. Perhaps the most popular Austrian cheese is Austrian Emmenthaler, also called Austrian Swiss. It's not very different from German or Swiss Emmantaler. The Austrians also make an Austrian Gruyère, which is similar to the Swiss original.

There is also an Austrian Bergkase, and the only noticeable difference is that the Austrian version has smaller holes. Similar to Quark is the Austrian Topfen. Topfen is an Austrian staple, and it is creamy, fresh, and often flavored with paprika.

But there are a few Austrian originals, including Kugelkase. After basic curds are formed, pepper, caraway seeds, and paprika are mixed into the cheese, which is then rolled into balls, salted, and cured. It is a tasty, spicy, local specialty.

Another popular Austrian cheese is called Mondseer, which is made near Salzburg. This washed rind cheese has a strong aroma, small holes, and is similar to the Danish Esrom, except that it has a firmer texture.

Belgium: Small Country, Big Cheeses

Though a small country, Belgium is mighty in terms of its cheeses. Its cheesemaking history actually predates the Romans, and the Belgian people, or rather the Belgae, a Celtic tribe who settled there, had some rudimentary cheesemaking knowledge. The Romans, of course, introduced more modern cheesemaking techniques, but Charlemagne's building of abbeys set Belgium cheesemaking in motion. Charlemagne encouraged the building of 50 different monasteries, and the monks not only spread the word of God, but they spread the word of cheese, as they helped farmers with their agricultural skills.

Charlemagne himself set up his empire in the ninth century, with Aachen (a town in Germany near the border of Belgium) as his base of operations. There he had cellars dug to store and ripen cheese. Though his empire faded, Belgium at various times was taken over by the Austrians, the Spanish, and the Dutch, but continued to make cheese. Like their robust beers, many of Belgium's cheeses were made and developed at Trappist monasteries, including Limburger, which is more popularly produced in Germany.

Today, Belgium produces more than 250 varieties of cheese. Many of these cheeses are modern copies of old cheeses; in the 1960s, Belgian cheesemakers investigated historical cheeses and their recipes to preserve them.

Perhaps Belgium's most famed cheese, Herve, is an orangish, washed rind cheese with a rather pungent and yeasty aroma. It has a sweet, spicy taste. Some versions are made with double cream or raw milk.

An especially delicious Belgian cheese is the semi-soft Chimay. Washed in Chimay ale, this creamy, sweet cheese has a depth of flavor. It is actually one of our most favorite cheeses on the planet, and it's worth a try.

> **A Cut Above**
>
> One modern Belgian cheese is called Rubens. This chubby cheese, which is based on an old Belgian recipe, boasts a picture of the famed Flemish painter on the packaging. The Dutch have their painted cheese, too: an aged Gouda called Rembrandt.

Maredsous is another Trappist-style cheese, and it's made by the monks at the Maredsous Abbey. Shaped like a loaf, it is washed in brine, and it has a pale yellow interior. It is not as strong as Herve.

Princ'Jean is a triple cream cheese that is rather rich and luscious. There is a peppercorn version of it, too.

Wyendale is a soft and creamy yet nutty cheese with a buttery taste. It looks like it was handcrafted on a farmstead cheese operation, but it is actually made in a modern factory.

Some Delectible Eastern European Delights

Though it's not a hotbed of dairy operations, cheesemaking nonetheless remains an important part of Eastern European cuisine and culture. The first cheeses of Eastern Europe were probably made by the Slavs when they crossed into Romania and Bulgaria during the sixth century B.C.E. They made a fresh cheese that was similar to feta. The Romans made their impact on cheese, as did Turkish invaders. The borders of Eastern European countries were often overrun by invaders and conquerors, all of whom left their imprint on local cheeses.

After World War II, however, much of the region's local cheesemaking had been replaced by large and bland factories. In recent years, however, small cheese production has started up again, and cheesemaking should grow to new levels in terms of both quantity and quality.

A notable cheese of the Czech Republic is Abertam, a traditional farmhouse cheese. This sheep's milk cheese is robust, and is pressed into balls before being ripened for about two months.

Another sheep's milk cheese is called Brinza, an ancient cheese of Romania dating back to before the time of the Romans. It is a delicate, mild fresh cheese that is salted to be preserved in winter. Similar to Brinza is Bryndza, which is made in the Slovak Republic, but Bryndza is more like feta and is matured for a longer period of time than Brinza.

Damski is a specialty cow's milk cheese from Poland that is smoked over natural wood. It has a sweet flavor, and it is made in the Mragowo region of Poland.

Halloumi is a popular Romanian cheese that is made from stretched curds. It is a sheep's milk cheese that dates back to Roman times, but its exact origins are unclear, and today it is also made in Cyprus and Lebanon.

Liptoi is a Hungarian cheese sold in pots that is made from a mix of sheep's milk and cow's milk. Various spices are mixed into this fine, creamy cheese, and when spices are added, it's known as Liptauer.

Perhaps the most unusual Eastern European cheese is Ardalena, which is made from water buffalo's milk in Transylvania. This year-old aged cheese is used for cooking and snacking, and it has a tangy bite.

The Least You Need to Know

- The Netherlands, Germany, and Belgium are all big cheese-producing and -eating countries.

- Gouda and Edam account for most Dutch cheese that is produced.

- Germany produces a great quantity of cheese, the most popular of which is Quark.

- Belgium produces more than 250 different kinds of cheeses, and one of the best is Chimay.

- Eastern Europe produces a variety of cheeses, and since the dissolution of the Soviet bloc, it is growing in quality and quantity.

12

Greek, Balkan, and Middle Eastern Cheeses

In This Chapter

◆ Greece's long-time love affair with cheese and the various Greek favorites

◆ The Nomadic origins of Turkish cheesemaking and the most popular cheeses of Turkey

◆ Other notable Balkan cheeses

◆ Cheesemaking's early ties to the Middle East and some of the local residents' favorites

The Greeks love their cheese. In any survey or study of cheese eating, the Greeks come out on top as the largest consumers of cheese. And with such a long history of cheese—they are one of the first people to make and consume cheese—it's no wonder. Cheese, especially Greek cheese, is a wonderful thing. The ancient Greeks considered it one of the foods of the gods, and today, the most heavenly Greek cheese is feta. But not all Greek cheese is feta, and there are some other astounding Greek cheeses to be savored.

Nearby Turkey also has some wonderful cheeses to be tried. It is also worth noting that some Middle Eastern cheeses are similar to Turkish or Greek cheeses.

The History of Cheesemaking in Greece

The ancient Greeks loved their cheese, and they are very likely one of the very earliest peoples to make cheese. The Greeks loved cheese so much that they considered it a food of the gods, one they shared with humankind. In Greek mythology, the gods sent Aristaeus, son of Apollo and the shepherdess Cyrene, to teach the Greeks how to make cheese. This minor shepherding deity is also credited with teaching the Greeks how to make olive oil and gather honey, and he also taught them how to hunt and was considered one of the more benevolent deities.

Cheese also played a role in Homer's *Odyssey*, particularly in the scenes in Chapter 9 involving Polyphemus the Cyclops. Written around 700 B.C.E., Homer details how Polyphemus, who had a voracious appetite, kept himself well fed by raising sheep and making cheese. Odysseus and his men landed on his island and made an interesting discovery when they reached Polyphemus's cave. "He was out shepherding so we went inside and took stock of all that we could see. His cheese racks were loaded with cheeses, and he had more lambs and kids than his pens could hold … as for his dairy, all the vessels, bowls, and milk pails into which he milked, were swimming with whey … when they saw all this, my men begged me to let them first steal some cheeses."

Some believe that the cheese Polyphemus had been making in such vast quantities was feta, as he was using the milks of both goats and sheep for his cheese. Feta and Kaseri, two popular Greek cheeses, are believed to be among the oldest cheeses around, dating back thousands of years.

Other Greek writers who wrote of this noble food include Aristotle, Pythagoras, Varro, Euripides, and Aristophanes. Aristotle, in fact, believed that cheese helped digest other foods. He also believed new cheese was better than aged cheese, describing old cheese as "very naughty."

Naughty cheeses aside, cheese became and remains a very important part of the Greek diet, and even today, cheese is eaten at every meal. Because of the mountainous terrain, sheep and goats thrive better than cattle do, and cheeses like feta have thrived throughout the ages.

A Cut Above

Aristotle had a mixed bag of wise and weird observations about cheese and milk. In *History of Animals* (350 B.C.E.), he wrote, "Now, the camel's milk is the thinnest, and that of the human species next after it, and that of the donkey next again, but cow's milk is the thickest. As a general rule, milk is not found in the male of man or of any other animal, though from time to time it has been found in a male. Such occurrences, however, are regarded as supernatural and fraught with omen."

For most of Greece's history, cheesemaking remained a small-scale farming and shepherding activity. Change, however, began to come at the end of the nineteenth and beginning of the twentieth century, when cheese production moved from small farms and into small and then progressively larger factories. Like much of the rest of the world, the majority of Greek cheese is made in larger factories, but there are still some smaller, artisan cheeses that are absolutely exquisite.

Greek Cheeses

In Greece, the average person eats more than 50 pounds of cheese per year. In fact, that 7-ounce slab of feta that you might use for an entire Greek salad is just one serving of feta for one person in Greece. "Cheese is on the table all day long in Greece," says Sheri Cardoos, an importer of Greek cheeses. "There's feta in the morning, at lunch, and in the evening. Cheese is a pretty big staple in Greece."

As Cardoos mentioned, feta is the big cheese in Greece. Some 115,000 tons of feta is produced in Greece, and the majority of it—85 percent—is eaten in Greece. What's interesting to note is that although feta is an ancient Greek cheese, up until recent years, its name was not at all protected, and it has been adopted throughout much of Europe. In 2002, however, it received its long-due recognition in Europe that feta is only a cheese from Greece, as it received its protection of origin or D.O.P. status.

That status, however, was threatened, and it took a ruling by the European Union high court in 2005 to solidify feta's status as only being a Greek cheese. German and Danish producers had sought to have feta declared a generic name, saying that it wasn't where it was made but how that was important. But the Greeks argued that extensive grazing of local sheep and goats on the rough, mountainous terrain of Greece gives feta its special taste.

The European Court of Justice sided with the Greeks, saying that several Balkan countries have produced similarly brined cheese for a long time, but they don't call it feta. The court also noted that feta produced in countries other than Greece often incorporates Greek references on its packaging, trying to associate a cheese not made in Greece with Greek culture.

It's a good thing feta is protected, as Greek-made feta simply tastes better than most other varieties of this briny cheese. And though you've probably tasted feta on a Greek salad at a Greek diner in the United States, you probably haven't tasted feta. The biggest difference, besides country of origin, is the milk.

Most cheese marketed here as feta is made with cow's milk. Real Greek feta is made from a blend of sheep's milk and goat's milk, typically with an 80-20 ratio, with never more than 30 percent goat's milk. The sheep and the goats graze naturally, eating mountain grasses, clover, and the like, and that gives a layer of depth and nuance to the cheese. It is also whiter in color than the cow's milk versions.

Feta is a fresh cheese that, after the curds are pressed and cut, is brined in salt water for typically two months. Like its more generic counterparts, real feta has a crumbly texture, but real feta also has an innate creaminess to it, owing to the higher fat content of sheep's milk. It also has a tang, from the goat's milk, and good feta also has a sweet milky flavor. It also, naturally from the brine, is saltier than many other cheeses, but good feta is not overly salty.

Feta can also be barrel-aged for four months, one of the rarer forms of this cheese. It has a stronger and greater depth of flavor. And then there's also basket feta, made by molding the curds in handwoven baskets, which gives it a more unique shape and a creamier texture.

The French and the Bulgarians also make pretty good feta with sheep's milk, with French feta typically being on the creamier side and Bulgarian feta being on the stronger side.

A Cut Above

The Greeks make a cow's milk version of feta, but it's not called feta; it's called Telemes.

The next most popular Greek cheese is Kaseri. Like feta, Kaseri is made from a mix of sheep's milk and goat's milk, with the goat's milk not to exceed 20 percent. It's a firm cheese, aged for at least three months. Like mozzarella and provolone, Kaseri is a pasta filata or pulled curd cheese. It has a rich, buttery taste and is a great melting cheese.

Graviera cheese is a popular hard cheese that can be made from cow's milk, goat's milk, sheep's milk, or a mixture of the different milks. It has a slightly sweet taste and a delicate aroma. There are two main versions of Graviera—Graviera of Crete and Graviera of Naxos. The Cretian version is aged for five months and made with sheep's milk or sheep's milk and goat's milk. Graviera of Naxos is aged for only three months and can be made with cow's milk or a mixture of cow's milk, sheep's milk, and goat's milk. Both versions of Graviera are similar to Gruyère.

You might not know Kefalotiri by name, but you know it for the famous flaming cheese dish it is used in—*saganaki*. Kefalotiri is an ancient sheep's milk cheese, dating back to the Byzantine Empire. This firm cheese is fruity and pleasant, with a tangy finish and small holes. Besides saganaki, it's also used as a grating cheese and in cheese pastries.

A blend of Kefalotiri and Graviera is Kefalograviera. This hard sheep's milk cheese is sort of a cross between the two cheeses, and it can also be used for saganaki.

Like the Italians, the Greeks make a few whey-based cheeses, including Anthotiros, which is made from sheep's milk and goat's milk; Galotiri, which is made from sheep's milk, goat's milk, and/or cow's milk; Mizithra, which is made from sheep's milk and goat's milk; and Manouri, which is made from sheep's milk or goat's milk.

Manouri is considered the best whey cheese, as it has sheep's milk cream added to it. This fresh, soft cheese is sweet and milky, and it is often served for breakfast in Greece, topped with jam or honey.

Xynotyro, besides being one of the few cheeses that start with the letter X, is a sheep's milk and goat's milk blended-whey cheese that translates as "sour cheese." It leaves a sweet-sour taste on the tongue.

The History and Cheeses of Turkey

The ancestors of modern Turkey were nomadic tribes who traveled to the area from central Asia. Like other nomads, they were shepherds who traveled with their sheep, and they probably made some of the first cheeses around. One of the first written references to cheese in Turkey can be found in the eleventh-century Turkish dictionary, written by Mahmut of Kasgar, who perhaps wrote one of the most poetic descriptions of cheese, describing it as "sleeping milk." Cheese also played a role in the *Book of Dede Korkut*, a collection of Turkish legends that finally was written down in the twelfth and thirteenth centuries.

Say Cheese

The Turkish word for cheese is **peynir,** and it first appeared in *The Book of Dede Korkut*. Previously, cheese was called *udma* and *udhıtma*.

In the 1400s, cheese played such a prominent role in Turkish culture that it was given to Byzantine rulers as gifts. And in 1502, the Code of Law legalized the name of cheeses throughout the Ottoman Empire that were sold in Istanbul. Among those cheeses listed were Midili or Mytilene, Teleme (like the Greek Telemes), and Tulum.

Slowly, Turkish cheese has become modernized. The first pasteurized milk factory opened in 1975, and today cheese is made in modern factories, but some shepherds still make cheese using traditional methods that date back to nomadic times. Turkish cheese is made using cow's milk, sheep's milk, and goat's milk, and there are even fat-free Turkish cheeses.

The most popular Turkish cheese is Beyaz Peynir, a sheep's milk cheese very similar to feta. But unlike feta, Beyaz Peynir is curdled using a vegetable coagulant instead of rennet. It is aged in brine for about six months, and before serving it is often soaked in cold water or milk to remove some of the salt. It is produced in the Marema region of Turkey. It is an essential part of a Turkish breakfast, and it is also used as a filling in boreks, or pastries.

A Cut Above

There is a YouTube video called "bir dilim beyaz penir." This video is of a young man singing. The song translates to "A Slice of White Cheese." The title leads us to believe he just might be waxing poetic about cheese.

Another popular cheese is Kasar Peyniri, and there are two different varieties of this cheese: Eski Kasar (old kasar) and Taze Kasar (fresh kasar). It has a taste that is similar to Parmigiano-Reggiano, and it is generally produced with sheep's milk.

Some other popular Turkish cheeses are the Tulum or Tullumu varieties. Tullum cheese is made from sheep's milk or goat's milk, but it is cured in the stomach or skin of a goat. One Turkish writer described it as having a strong taste, "as such, it is not suitable for breakfast." It is a white-colored cheese with a crumbly texture.

Similar to the Greek Graviera, the Turks make Kars Gravyeri, a Turkish version of Gruyère. It is aged for at least 10 months, and it is made with cow's milk near the Anatolian city of Kars, which is known for its pastures and cattle.

Kars Peniri is sort of like a Turkish cream cheese, a more processed kind of cheese.

Mihalic Peynir is a hard, aged sheep's milk cheese often used for grating in place of Parmigiano-Reggiano. Like feta and Beyaz Peynir, it is preserved in brine.

The Cheeses of the Middle East

The very first cheeses were likely made in the Middle East by traveling nomads, and the earliest evidence of milk curdling can be found on Sumerian bas reliefs dating back thousands and thousands of years. The original cheeses of the region were probably fresh sheep's milk or goat's milk cheeses, and today, fresh sheep's milk and goat's milk cheeses are still quite popular.

Although Bedouin tribes may make cheese in the old nomadic fashion, most cheese made in the Middle East today is made in factories. Cheese is made in Lebanon, Syria, Israel, and Jordan, among other Middle Eastern countries, but the most important cheese-producing country in the Middle East is Cyprus, and its most important cheese is Halloumi.

Halloumi is often mistaken to be a Greek cheese, and indeed, many Greeks do enjoy it. But this pasta filata cheese is unique, as it is one of the rare cheeses that don't melt. Though it can be made with cow's milk, the best Halloumi is made with goat's milk or sheep's milk. It has a rubbery, but not too rubbery, texture, and it can be grilled. Traditionally, chopped fresh milk is added to the stretched curd cheese, and it should have a mild and slightly tangy flavor.

The Least You Need to Know

- The Greeks are one of the earliest peoples to ever make cheese, and today they eat more cheese than anyone else on the planet.

- The most important and most popular Greek cheese is feta, and real Greek feta is made with a mix of sheep's milk and goat's milk, not like the cow's milk versions of feta most commonly found in the United States.

- The most popular Turkish cheese is called Beyaz Peynir, and it is similar to feta, except it is not made with rennet.

- The most important Middle Eastern cheese is Halloumi, and it is made in Cyprus.

Part 3

American Artisans and Other New World Delights

We've covered the European greats—those cheeses that have shaped the dairy industry, the most popular imported cheeses, and the rare ones you should try if you ever get the chance. And although they're incredible and amazing cheeses, they're not the only game in town.

In fact, the most exciting developments in the world of cheese aren't happening in Europe—they're happening in the United States, Australia, New Zealand, and unusual places like South Africa. Most of the interesting cheeses in the world are coming from small, artisan producers in unexpected places.

And today, American cheese is much like American wine was 30 years ago—ready to take on and conquer the European greats. This part will explore that phenomenon—as well as a lot of other exciting developments in the world of cheese. Grab a slice of cheese and hunker down.

13

A Slice of History: American Cheese Basics

In This Chapter

◆ The history of cheesemaking in the United States

◆ The story of J.L. Kraft and the processed cheese revolution

◆ America's return to the basics of farmstead and artisan cheesemaking

For many years, American cheeses have been a bit like Rodney Dangerfield—they just didn't get any respect. A good example of this is in *The Concise Encyclopedia of Gastronomy*, published in the United States in 1981.

> *Compared to some European nations, Americans are not great cheese eaters, though during the last decade our cheese consumption has increased considerably. Neither do we have a great cheese-making tradition, nor any original American cheeses.*

That smug little passage was written by an American food writer, and although it was written a couple of decades ago, that unfortunate sentiment is still sometimes held by both Americans and Europeans today.

And nothing could be further from the truth. Americans love cheese, and Americans make great original cheeses—in fact, several American cheesemakers are besting Europeans in international competitions. It is true that most of America's tremendous cheese output is by large factories, and many cheeses on grocery store shelves happen to be bland or processed, but that is only a portion of the picture of American cheese. In the last 20 years, and especially in the last five, specialty and artisan cheese producers have grown in quantity, quality, and popularity. Small artisan producers make small batches of high-quality and often original cheeses in more than 30 different states. It's not well known, but the United States has cheese and dairy roots that go back as far as the country's history, throughout which Americans have developed fine original cheeses.

The Start of Cheesemaking in the United States

Records don't say whether Christopher Columbus took cheese on his voyages to the New World, but it's likely he and other European explorers did, because it was a good source of nutrition that traveled rather well. The first records of cheese were on the list of supplies the pilgrims took on the *Mayflower* in 1620, and both cattle and goats were brought on some of the first trips to the New World. In the earliest years, goats tended to be favored over cows because they needed less care, and they also were excellent at clearing land. By 1639, there were about 4,000 goats in the Massachusetts Bay Colony alone.

From the days of the first American settlements until the nineteenth century, most cheese and dairy production was done on family farms, typically by women. By the middle of the seventeenth century, goats were replaced by their bovine counterparts. Cows were more docile than goats (they wouldn't raid neighbors' gardens or fields), and they could also be used for milk and cheese, but they were also an excellent source of meat and leather, and they could plow fields. The first cows were the red cows of Devonshire, but because the early colonists were more keen on survival than on breeding stocks, the bovines were bred indiscriminately, and they were used for meat, dairy, and plowing. As a result, the cows were a little bit worse for the wear.

But despite these challenges, early American settlers did make cheese, most of it cheddar or cheddarlike, and by 1650, the colonies in New England had enough surplus of butter and cheese that they could trade some. Eventually, almost every farm had a family cow. Agricultural historian Howard Russell wrote, "In old, settled eastern Massachusetts there were, in 1767, about two cows for each five persons."

Gradually, more deliberate breeding started to happen in the late eighteenth century when gentlemen farmers began to improve breeds just for sport and show. Better breeding meant better milk, and by 1809, the first livestock improvement association, the Pennsylvania Society for Improving the Breed of Cattle, was formed.

With the growth of the new country, especially the bigger cities like New York, Philadelphia, and Boston—demand for more cheese and butter grew. Though dairying and cheesemaking continued to be a farmstead effort, production improved, and some farms became noted for their cheese, butter, or milk. As a result, the first epicenters for good dairy products developed. One of the most famous dairylands in the middle of the 1700s was Rhode Island. In fact, most good New England cheese was labeled "Rhode Island cheese" because Rhode Island was so revered for its cheese at that time. New York and Pennsylvania also became known for their dairy products, and by the middle of the 1800s, New York was the biggest dairy producing state.

A Cut Above

To celebrate Thomas Jefferson's election in 1801, a cheesemaker in Cheshire, Massachusetts, asked every farmer in the area to bring in a whole day's milking on July 20, 1801. All that milk (from 1,200 cows) was transformed into cheese and, using an oversize cider press, they made a 1,235-pound wheel of cheese, which was then taken to Jefferson in Washington.

The nineteenth century was a time of transition for America's dairy farms. The history of American cheese has a dual nature: on one hand, large factories, and on the other, small farmstead cheesemakers. Both have been extremely influential. The first big change came with Jesse Williams, a dairy farmer in Rome, New York, who had an entrepreneurial spirit. Williams was known for making good cheese, and in 1851 he decided to process the milk from one of his sons' farms with that from his own herd. Gradually, Williams started processing milk from other local dairy farms, and soon other enterprising dairymen began copying his efforts.

By 1880, when the very first cheese factories were opening in Europe, there were almost 4,000 cheese factories throughout the United States, which made 216 million pounds of cheese that year. By the turn of the twentieth century, farmstead cheesemaking had rapidly declined. Cheesemaking also started moving west in the nineteenth century, and by the twentieth century, Wisconsin had earned its state slogan as "America's Dairyland."

Technological developments and scientific advances also added to the dairy transformation. Pasteurization, cream separators, and the innovation of bottling milk all helped move milk and cheese production into centralized factories. In general, these weren't the big factories of today; milk still couldn't travel very far, and most creameries were small by today's standards. The United States also began to export some cheeses and butter.

Say Cheese _____

Filled cheese was unnaturally diluted cheese in which some of the milk was replaced with other fats like margarine or lard or some other vile substance.

But there was also was a darker side to America's dairy industry. Some farmers were less than scrupulous and, in order to make bigger profits, they would water their milk down with, well, water, and sometimes other substances. Some cheesemakers would also dilute their cheeses by replacing natural dairy fats with oils. Those cheeses were known as *filled cheese*. Public outrage and exposure by muckraking journalists ensued. By 1895, a law was passed that banned the practice of diluting cheese.

The 1800s also saw an influx of immigrant cheesemakers from across Europe. The first cheesemakers in the colonies were Englishmen (or women), but waves of immigrants came to the United States bringing cheesemakers from all different regions. Wisconsin, especially, became a destination for Swiss cheesemakers. By 1930, many of the most familiar European cheese varieties had some American counterparts being made.

Though most cheese made in the United States was cheddar, followed by Swiss and German styles, there also were a few American originals. Colby and Brick were created in Wisconsin; Jack or Monterey Jack was created in California; and Liederkranz, a Limburger-type cheese, was created in New York.

Around the turn of the twentieth century, a Canadian started wholesaling cheese in Chicago—and ended up changing cheese as we knew it.

Living the American Dream: The Story of J.L. Kraft

That Canadian was James L. Kraft, known as J.L. Kraft. In 1903, with just $65, this 29-year-old former grocery store clerk moved to Chicago and began selling cheese directly to grocers from a horse-drawn wagon. (His horse was named Paddy.) Kraft knew that the key to success would be supplying his customers with fresh and consistent-tasting cheese.

Kraft waited at the head of the line every day at the South Water Street Market in Chicago to make sure that he got the best cheese, and then he made personal calls to each of his grocers, who liked that he delivered the cheese so they didn't have to wait in line at the market. Eventually, he started packaging the cheese under his name, Kraft, and four of his brothers joined him in 1909 so they called their business J.L. Kraft & Bros.

But there were some problems inherent in the cheesemongering business. No matter how fresh or good the cheese was, natural cheese is a living food, so it ages, and in a short time could go from fresh to putrefied, meaning grocers lost money. Some wouldn't even sell it during the summer.

The name of the game was shelf life and consistency, so Kraft experimented to see if he could come up with a way to make cheese last longer. He might have been inspired by some Swiss cheesemakers who had preserved Gruyère in tins. In any case, Kraft eventually discovered that if you heat and stir cheese, add emulsifying salts, and then pour the mixture into a sterile container, when the cheese cooled it would again become solid.

In 1915, Kraft began selling 4-ounce tins of this processed cheese. That was the start of processed cheese, and in 1916 Kraft was issued a patent for the "Process of Sterilizing Cheese and an Improved Product Produced by Such Process." By 1917, Kraft was supplying tins of processed cheese to American armed forces in World War I.

That was the start of the processed cheese revolution. Kraft's inventors continued their experiments, and Kraft's sales and marketing force began spreading the word. In the 1920s, Kraft started selling cheese in London and Hamburg. In 1921, a new word was added to the American lexicon: American cheese. It first appeared in a patent Kraft applied for. The term American cheese was not included in a listing of "natural" or regular cheeses; it was used to refer to a processed cheese that included cheddar or colby as an ingredient. The 1920s also saw the Kraft processed cheese line expand: in 1928, they acquired a different processed cheese from Monroe, New York: Velveeta.

> **A Cut Above**
>
> Some emulsifiers that are typically used to create processed cheese include sodium phosphate, potassium phosphate, tartrate, or citrate, all of which are chemically enhanced salts. They keep the cheese's fat globules from separating when heated, which is why processed cheese melts better than normal cheese.

Velveeta was actually created by a Swiss immigrant and cheesemaker named Emil Frey. Frey had been experimenting with leftover whey, the big by-product of cheese-making, and he discovered that if you blend it with cheese, you get this silky smooth and very meltable food product.

A Cut Above

Velveeta is so synonymous with being cheesy that a band that plays '80s rock calls itself Velveeta. There also an alt-blues band that is named Velveeta Jones, and there's even a Velveeta Room comedy club. Kraft's innovative efforts, mergers, and advertising savvy worked: by 1930, more than 40 percent of all cheese consumed in the United States had the Kraft label.

Kraft purchased the Velveeta Cheese Company and began marketing the cheese. Three years after Kraft introduced Velveeta to its broad market, the American Medical Association gave this "pasteurized process cheese food" its seal of approval, making it the first cheese product to be thus christened.

Kraft didn't stop with Velveeta. In 1928, through a merger with the Phoenix Cheese Company in New York, Kraft acquired Philadelphia Cream Cheese. Cream cheese is another uniquely American cheese, and its history dates back to the end of the nineteenth century. It was invented by William Lawrence, a New York dairyman, in 1872. Lawrence made that cheese from not just milk, but also cream. The cheese received its city moniker from a New York cheese distributor who called it "Philadelphia" because the city was considered to be the home of high-quality food, thus any high-quality food was of "Philadelphia quality."

Besides taking on other innovative products, Kraft inventors kept working in food science to develop other products. In 1937, Kraft Macaroni and Cheese dinner was introduced; in 1950, Kraft Deluxe processed cheese slices; and in 1953, Cheez Whiz made its debut. (Almost 50 years later, author Joey Green penned *Clean Your Clothes with Cheez Whiz*, explaining how the product's natural enzymes cut through grease.)

Though American consumers readily accepted Kraft's newfangled products, not everyone was happy, and some producers of "natural" cheese sought to have the Kraft cheese products labeled "embalmed" or "renovated" cheese, because although the products start out as natural cheese, the salts and heating process changes a lot of what makes cheese cheese. The Federal government, however, decided on the more neutral "processed" label.

Plenty of other dairy companies, both here and abroad, took the success of Kraft and began to make processed cheese products of their own. Kraft, which is now owned by Altria Group, which also owns Philip Morris Companies, continues to make its best-selling products, which have evolved and grown into new products, including everything from SpongeBob Macaroni and Cheese to Cheez Whiz Light.

The American Cheese Society and the New Artisan Cheesemakers

Not everyone liked the processed cheese at the time it was introduced, and while plenty of cheese factories jumped on the bandwagon, some cheesemakers didn't succumb. The trend over the course of the twentieth century definitely was to get bigger and more consolidated. Plenty of small cheese plants merged or closed as transportation and technology improved, and although the number of cheese plants went down, the actual amounts of cheese increased.

Plenty of dairies and cheesemakers consolidated, increasing in size and output while often compromising quality, but not every cheesemaker thought bigger was necessarily better. Cheesemakers like Joe Widmer in Wisconsin and Ig Vella in California—like their fathers before them—kept making cheese the way they'd always made it: by hand and in small batches. Loyal local customers and mail order sidelines kept these cheese factories going.

In the 1960s and 1970s, the environmental movement got underway, and some people believed in getting "back to nature." Around the same time, fine cheeses from Europe began being imported on a larger scale than ever. By the late 1970s and early 1980s, some new specialty cheesemakers started getting into the business. Inspired, some of them even spent time in Europe apprenticing or exploring, and they began to make European-style cheeses. Chefs in big cities responded. Around the same time, some European dairy corporations started opening up shop in the United States.

The number of farmstead cheesemakers initially increased in the expected cheesemaking regions—Vermont, California, and Wisconsin—but it has spread to, as of the last count, 38 different states. These specialty and farmstead cheesemakers informally networked and helped each other out, and in 1983, a group of specialty cheesemakers banded together to form the American Cheese Society. This organization formed to uphold high standards for cheesemaking and to preserve the rich traditions of American cheesemaking.

Within the last decade, especially the last five years, the artisan and specialty cheese movement has grown dramatically. A good example of this can be seen in just the number of cheeses entered in the American Cheese Society's annual competition.

In 2005, a record of 749 cheeses were entered; in 2006, there were 941; and in 2007, there were 1,208 cheeses entered from 200 different cheesemakers, representing a 27 percent growth in just one year.

What the new artisan cheesemakers all bring to the table is a passion for fine cheese. What's also interesting is that many of them are creating distinctly American cheese— original cheeses that do not necessarily have any European counterparts—like Humboldt Fog, Red Hawk, Pleasant Ridge Reserve, and Driftless lavender and honey sheep's milk cheese.

A Cut Above

Many American cheese experts say that American specialty cheese is where American wines were 20 years ago; they're just beginning to be talked about and garnering the respect they deserve.

Though America grew over the twentieth century to become the largest cheesemaking country in the world (and also the largest importer of cheese in the world), American cheesemakers are finally beating European cheesemakers in international competitions. Some of the finest American cheeses are being exported, too.

The trend of specialty cheeses can also be seen on the large factory level, and some of the largest cheesemakers in the United States will likely get into specialty cheesemaking or at least market some of their products as such. More and more cheesemakers are also going organic, and many specialty cheesemakers insist upon having recombinant bovine growth hormone (rBGH)-free milk.

American cheese has sort of come full circle—it's gone back to being locally produced in small batches. In short, it's an exciting time for specialty cheese in the United States.

The Least You Need to Know

◆ Cheese came with the pilgrims on the *Mayflower*, and the first settlers made cheese from goats and cows, eventually using mainly cows because cows also doubled as draft animals.

◆ The world's first cheese factory opened in the middle of the nineteenth century in New York.

◆ Canadian immigrant J.L. Kraft revolutionized the cheese world with his processed cheese and built on that with Velveeta, Cheez Whiz, and Kraft Macaroni and Cheese.

◆ The "back-to-nature" movement of the 1960s started a resurgence of interest in traditional cheesemaking, and that interest has exploded over the last decade.

◆ Today, America's specialty cheesemakers can compete—and win—on an international level not only in besting European cheesemakers, but also in creating new and original American cheeses.

14

Wisconsin Cheese and America's Dairyland

In This Chapter

- ◆ How Wisconsin became known as America's Dairyland
- ◆ Exploring the history of the world's fifth largest cheesemaking region
- ◆ Beyond the cheddar wheel: Wisconsin's specialty cheesemaking prowess
- ◆ Pleasantly surprised: Pleasant Ridge Reserve and other big cheeses of Wisconsin

Cheese and Wisconsin have been pretty synonymous for more than 100 years, with cheese production dating back as much as 150 years. California may have overtaken Wisconsin in overall milk production more than a decade ago, but Wisconsin still upholds its title as the country's largest cheese-producing state. Wisconsin is, in fact, the fifth largest cheesemaking region in the world.

Wisconsin not only produces the greatest volume of cheese in the United States, but it also creates the biggest variety of cheeses. That's a part of the Wisconsin cheese story that not many people know. Wisconsin is the birthplace of several cheeses, both commodity and artisan, and there's a whole lot more than cheddar going on.

Welcome to America's Dairyland

Wisconsin became known as America's Dairyland in the 1930s, less than two decades after it rose to become the nation's largest dairy producer. Today, cheese is a $21 billion industry in Wisconsin. Wisconsin's state license plates proudly proclaim this "America's Dairyland." And with a production of about one third of the country's entire cheese output, it's no wonder. Cheese is the state's largest single industry, providing a greater economic impact than potatoes are to Idaho or oranges are to Florida.

Wisconsin dairy farms have an average herd size of 87, way below California's nearly 800 and even Vermont's 100. The state also counts about 1,300 cheesemakers working at about 115 cheese plants, from multi-million dollar corporations to itty-bitty guys making one cheese at a time on the borrowed equipment of other, generous cheesemakers' facilities.

A Cut Above

Wisconsin's license plates used to be even more dairy-centric. They used to be yellow in color, and they were known as "butter plates." Today, however, they're basic white. But the state Department of Motor Vehicles website invites new residents with this thought: "Welcome to Wisconsin, where it's the cheese, and so much more!"

Cheesemakers from all over the world come to the University of Wisconsin and the Center for Dairy Research to catch up on the latest dairy trends and technology. The state is also home to dozens of government and agricultural agencies, cheesemaking organizations, and even corporations that manufacture the accoutrements of cheese-making.

A Cut Above

If Wisconsin is number five, who are the top four cheese-producing regions? As of 2005 (the most recent data available), the top cheese-producing regions in the world are:

1. United States (excluding Wisconsin)—6.72 billion pounds
2. Germany—4.25 billion pounds
3. France—4.02 billion pounds
4. Italy—2.43 billion pounds
5. Wisconsin—2.40 billion pounds

America's Dairyland has been known not only for quantities of dairy goodness, but for quality. In 1921, it became the very first state to grade its cheese for quality. It also was the first state to require its cheesemakers to be licensed, and it is the only state to offer a "Master Cheesemaker" certification program.

A Cut Above

To become a master cheesemaker, a cheesemaker must have been making that cheese for a minimum of five years, and a cheesemaker can only apply for a master's certification in two cheeses at any one time. The certification process takes an additional three years to complete, with a formal judging of the cheesemaker's cheese at that time.

How Wisconsin Got Milk

Many dairy experts point to Anne Pickett as the "mother" of Wisconsin's cheese-making industry. Back in 1841, this entrepreneurial farmer's wife set up the state's first cheese factory by picking up milk from her neighbors and then adding it to the batches produced by her herd to make cheese. But the state's cheese industry really didn't get more professional until the 1870s, when dairy farming became more eco-nomically viable for farmers. The Wisconsin Dairymen's Association began in 1872, and the University of Wisconsin began offering its first cheesemaking classes a decade later. Around the same time, Swiss immigrants began setting up shop in the fertile hills of southwest Wisconsin's Green County.

Just as Wisconsin was growing into its dairy powers, two local cheesemakers invented two never-before-seen cheeses: colby and brick. Colby was invented in 1874 by Joseph Steinwand in the small Wisconsin town of Colby. Swiss immigrant John Jossi created brick in 1875 to satisfy the hearty appetites of the state's many German residents.

A Cut Above

Ever see those crazy Green Bay Packers fans don their "cheeseheads" as they cheer on Brett Favre? Well, though those foam hats might, upon first glance, appear to be cheddar, they actually have holes like Swiss. Foamation, the St. Francis, Wisconsin, company that makes them, specifically says that they are not supposed to represent any particular type of cheese.

Formal organizations such as the Wisconsin Dairymen's Association were necessary. Not only did they help professionalize the state's cheesemaking efforts, but they also set higher quality standards for both milk and cheese. It meant that farmers couldn't dilute their milk with water or dilute their cheese with other inferior fillings. The standards enabled Wisconsin to compete with New York State, which was the country's very first dairy-centric region. Competition was tough, as many cheese brokers in Chicago and other regions didn't want to buy cheese that was "produced out West," as it was deemed inferior to Eastern cheese.

Gradually, though, as Wisconsin's efforts persisted, cheesemaking began to flourish. The state's natural limestone water reserves, coupled with a geographical and climatological region conducive to growing alfalfa, clover, and grass, made dairying a natural and delicious fit. After the turn of the century, Wisconsin's dairy initiatives picked up steam and its reputation for fine cheese grew. By 1910, there were 1,928 cheese factories; by 1920, that number had grown to 2,771, and only three counties in the entire state had no cheese factories.

After the peak in actual factory numbers, Wisconsin's creameries began to consolidate as agriculture and transportation became more mechanized. But through all the changes, from horses to trucks, from cans to tanks, Wisconsin has remained the biggest cheese-producing state in the nation.

Master Cheesemaker Myron Olson shows off a block of his Baby Swiss.

(Jeanette Hurt)

Putting the Special into Specialty Cheese

In recent years, California has grown its cheesemaking operations, and it remains a real threat to usurp Wisconsin's production title. But California's 55-some cheese producers only make 250 different varieties of cheese, compared to Wisconsin's 115 creameries making 1,000 different dairy varieties.

That's right. While the state's dairy promotional materials only tout "more than 650" different varieties of cheese, Wisconsin's cheesemakers actually make around 1,000 different types of dairy products, and almost all of them are cheese. But because this number has especially increased over just the last decade or so, they do not advertise the actual number, for fear that people will think they're exaggerating.

But it's no exaggeration, and in fact, Wisconsin is the largest producer of specialty cheese in the United States. The National Agricultural Statistics Service reported that Wisconsin produced 387 million pounds of specialty cheese in 2006 alone. Cheddar and mozzarella remain the state's biggest commodity cheeses, but Wisconsin also makes blues, fetas, provolones, parmesans, asiagos, and several Hispanic varieties, not to mention numerous American originals. A handful of smaller cheesemakers craft fresh mozzarella, and many smaller cheesemakers produce not only the regular cheddars, but also flavored varieties, bandaged offerings, and the specialty versions that are aged anywhere from 1 to 10 years.

Many cheesemakers in Wisconsin who make cheddar also sell cheddar cheese curds, the state's unofficial snack food. Most cheese factories sell bags of fresh curds to customers and grocery stores. Some come flavored in garlic, Cajun seasonings, or herbs, and they're also served fried at restaurants and county fairs throughout the

Stinky Cheese

Most colbies on the supermarket shelves really aren't colby cheese at all. Lax regulations allow mild cheddars to masquerade as colbies (even shaped in longhorn form, which is the traditional colby shape). Real colby, however, can be determined by the presence of tiny holes that look almost like pin pricks. The faux colbies have none.

A Cut Above

You can always tell how fresh a curd is by its sound. If it audibly squeaks in your mouth, then it's really fresh. If fresh cheese curds aren't available, you can also get that squeaky melody by nuking the curds in the microwave before serving. It's not quite as good as fresh, but it's the next best thing.

state. People also use them to top pizzas, chilis, and soups, and, unlike their finished cheddar counterparts, they can be frozen because of their higher moisture content.

While there will always be a place for cheddar, mozzarella, and other commodity cheeses, the state's future lies in specialty and artisan cheese products. Today, 80 of the state's 115 cheese plants produce at least one type of specialty cheese, and all of the new cheese plants that are gearing up to go online with production are specialty or small- or medium-size producers.

Not Necessarily Big, but Tasty: Wisconsin's Must-Taste Cheeses

To say that it was hard to narrow down this section to some of the state's best cheeses is an understatement. When practically all of the cheesemakers in the fifth largest cheese-making region in the world make some sort of special or interesting cheese, picking and choosing among them is more than a tad difficult. We're quite sure we have missed some, and that new cheeses will be out between this writing and your reading.

That said, the following cheesemakers are all noteworthy, most on a global scale, because of the uniqueness of their operations, the quality of their cheese, or a combination of important factors. These are the cheeses that make you say "Ahh" when you taste them; the cheesemakers themselves make you go "Wow." Here, in alphabetical order, are 15 great cheese companies and their delicious cheeses.

BelGioioso Cheese Company's founding in 1979 by Italian native Errico Auricchio could be considered the start of the specialty cheese movement in Wisconsin. Auricchio, a fourth-generation cheesemaker who grew up outside of Naples, saw that there might be opportunities in the United States for Italian-style cheese made there rather than Italy.

Auricchio chose Wisconsin for its proximity to good dairy, and after purchasing an old cheddar factory in northeastern Wisconsin, he started making provolone, parmesan, and other Italian cheeses his employees had never even heard of. Today, he's grown the company to include additional factories, and he's known for making American Grana, an 18-month-old parmesan-type cheese, as well as several types of provolone and even gorgonzola. His cheeses, which have won numerous awards, are available throughout the United States.

If B is for BelGioioso, then C has to be for Sid Cook and Carr Valley Cheese. Cook, also a fourth-generation cheesemaker, has to be one of the most prolific and award-winning cheesemakers in not only the United States, but the world. This talented cheesemaker makes more than 60 different types of cheese and has won more than 150 different awards.

Though Cook makes a mean (and award-winning) array of cheddars, he's most known for his innovative work in mixed-milk cheeses—he makes cheeses out of cow's milk, goat's milk, sheep's milk, and blends of two or three. His most recognized mixed milk is the Gran Canaria, an aged blend of three milks affinaged with olive oil, which took Best of Show in the 2004 American Cheese Society competition.

A Cut Above

Buying specialty cheese by mail started with Ray Kubly. When he was a senior at the University of Wisconsin, a business professor made an off-hand remark that somebody should be selling Wisconsin's cheese by mail. Kubly was the first person to do that in 1926 when he sent out 50 packages of cheese by mail, and his company became The Swiss Colony, one of the largest direct-marketing companies in the world.

The Gran Canaria boasts a complex and fruity array of flavors, a perfect complement to a fine glass of wine. His triple crème Creama Kasa is buttery, smooth, and oh-so-creamy. Another American original is his Cocoa Cardona, a cocoa-rubbed firm cheese that is sweet enough to munch on for dessert or even drizzle with chocolate sauce. Benedictine is another original—a mix of sheep's, goat's, and cow's milks that is cured into a washed-rind wheel of intense flavors. Cook also opened up a new cooking school in Sauk City, Wisconsin, and brings in chefs from around the country who use his cheese.

Like Carr Valley, Cedar Grove Cheese is located in southwestern Wisconsin. But while this little factory makes some great flavored jacks and cheddars, along with a few sheep's milk specialties, the real innovation comes in how owner Bob Wills processes the wastewater that happens during the cheesemaking process. Instead of flushing it down the drain, it goes through a system of 10 tanks that naturally cleans the water using tropical plants, microbes, snails, and small wormlike creatures. This Living Machine™ treats the 7,000 or so gallons of wastewater that is produced every day, and after the machine cleans the water, it is released into a creek that feeds into the Wisconsin River Basin.

A Cut Above

Cedar Grove was the first creamery in the country to implement the Living Machine™ to treat wastewater. Although several other cheesemakers across the country have expressed interest in this mean, green cleaning machine, it remains the only cheese factory in the country to have such an ecological system in place.

Myron Olson uses a "trier" to test the ripeness of his Baby Swiss.

(Jeanette Hurt)

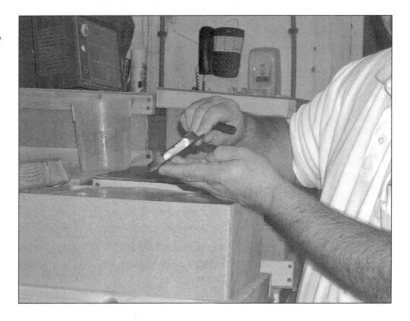

Though their cheddars and jacks are tasty, the sheep's milk cheeses Cedar Grove crafts for the Wisconsin Sheep Dairy Cooperative are not only award-winning, but quite palate-pleasing. Try the buttery and nutty Dante or the robust Mona. Both are American originals worth trying.

A Cut Above

Master cheesemaker Myron Olson is the only cheese-maker in the country who holds a special limburger license; back in the 1960s and '70s, Swiss cheese companies would make limburger in the off-season, thus glutting the market with stinky cheese. The government decided that limburger makers needed to have special licenses, and Olson was issued such a license.

Chalet Cheese Cooperative has been around for more than 100 years, but age alone isn't what makes it significant. At one time numerous cheese factories across the state and even the country made the stinky limburger cheese. Chalet alone still produces this washed rind favorite. This cheese cooperative also makes a tasty baby Swiss cheese.

Limburger, despite its stinky reputation, has a sweet, creamy taste, and if you're a little wary of trying it, start with a younger version. The younger the cheese, the less aromatic it is, and any version tastes especially good with a little honey mustard or combined with braunschweiger (liver sausage) and red onions. Chalet's baby Swiss is sweet, nutty, and so easy on the tongue; it's the perfect snacking cheese.

Bruce Workman's wheels of Emmentaler float in a brine solution for more than a week before they begin their year-long process of aging.

(Jeanette Hurt)

The Crave brothers didn't start out making cheese, they started out raising cows. But in the 1990s, they realized that in order to have a viable dairy farm they would have to do one of two things: grow bigger (which wouldn't have been good for the cows or for them), or get specialized. So they decided to make some cheese, and built a creamery right on their farm. Today, they not only make some of the freshest mozzarella and mascarpone cheeses around, they also make the delicious, soft-rind and flavorful Les Freres and the smaller but equally tasty Le Petit Frere, which features an illustration of youngest brother Mark and his show calf, Bubba. Both their mozzarella and mascarpone boast a sweet flavor and ultra creamy texture. Les Freres, although you can taste that it's made with the same great milk, is much more robust and earthy, but it's not overpowering, and has a clean finish.

Anne Topham started making fresh goat cheese shortly after Laura Chenel began making her cheese out in California. In fact, this founder of Fantôme Farm paid a visit out to Chenel's operations when she began building her creamery because when she started in 1984 there weren't any like-minded operations in Wisconsin for her to visit. Today, Anne milks her small herd and, with the help of her partner, Judy Borree, makes fresh and aged bloomy-rinded goat cheeses, selling most of them directly to consumers at the Dane County Farmer's Market in Madison. Her fresh goat cheese is divinely delicious, and if you buy it from her at the farmer's market, she can even tell you the names of the goats who made it. Her aged, bloomy-rinded goat's cheese is so decadently delicious that it's been served at the James Beard House.

Henning's Cheese makes big cheese. Gigantic cheese, in fact. This cheddar producer in eastern Wisconsin makes the biggest wheels of cheese in the country, upward of 12,000 pounds. These big wheels are sold to different grocery stores and specialty foods stores. They become display items and the store owners cut the cheeses for customers. Some of its cheeses, in fact, have been professionally carved with the images of sports teams or other decorative ideas.

A Cut Above

The Dane County Farmer's Market is the largest farmer's market in the country, and several local cheesemakers hawk their rinds there. It's held every Saturday in the summer in the Capitol Square. Off-season, it's held indoors.

Though master cheesemaker Kerry Henning is known for the big boys he creates, he's also won awards for his flavored cheddars, of which he makes almost a dozen. He's also been asked by some of his stores to come up with new flavors. From his fruity apple and cinnamon to his more traditional garlic and dill, Henning likes experimenting with taste.

Especially recommended are his tomato and basil (sort of like a Capri salad, except it's cheddar, not mozzarella), a savory and sweet combination of sun-dried tomatoes, minty basil, and mild cheddar goodness, and his newest flavor, cracked peppercorn white cheddar. The cracked peppercorn offers a bit of bite that contrasts nicely with the sweet cheese.

At Hidden Springs Creamery, Brenda Jensen uses draft horses to plow the farmland. Her sheep are tended organically, and she makes her award-winning fresh sheep's milk cheese, Driftless, in a small creamery right on the farm. Though she's only been making her cheese since 2006, she took first, second, and fifth place in her category at the U.S. Cheese Championships in 2007. Her lavender and honey Driftless just takes your breath away—so sweet, so creamy, so utterly dreamy. The plain and basil versions are also quite delicious, and she's been experimenting with some aged sheep's milk cheeses that should be on the market in 2008.

Tony and Julie Hook of Hook's Cheese have been making cheese for more than 20 years. Though they started with conventional cheeses like cheddar, colby, and jack, they have become known for several artisanal blues, as well as Sweet Constantine, an American original similar to parmesan except made with whole milk. Their aged cheddars have won several awards, too, and in 1982, Julie became the first female cheesemaker to win the coveted Best of Show at the World Cheese Championship for her colby.

These Wisconsin cows only eat sileage during winter months.

(Jeanette Hurt)

Julie's colby is a real colby, with pin-prick holes and a soft, mild flavor that manages to be mild but not bland. For those who like cheddar, though, there's nothing quite so sublime as their 7-year-old and 10-year-old versions—both have layers of depth, sweetness, and crystalline cheddar bite, a bite that isn't sharp from imbalance, but a bite of delicious, delicious flavor. Their blues also offer tang and sweetness, but they're not overpowering, and they're quite delicious. Especially recommended are Tilston Point, an English style inspired by actual English immigrants who settled in their area of Wisconsin, and Blue Paradise, a double-cream blue cheese that melts in your mouth.

A lot of cheesemakers say they cave-age their cheese, but their caves might be merely cellars. Not so at Love Tree Farms. Mary Falk and her husband Dave's fresh air aging cave overlooks one of the several ponds on their Grantsburg, Wisconsin, farm. Among their cheeses, perhaps the most famous is their signature, a delectable sheep's milk American original, Trade Lake Cedar, a natural rind cheese aged on cedar boughs—a fruity, nutty cheese with definite undertones of wood. Their Gabrielson Lake cheese is softer, more buttery, but equally delicious. Their Little Holmes is an unusual cheese— dusted with peppermint flakes and then aged before being wrapped in nettles soaked in vodka; Big Holmes and Sumac Holmes are extra-aged versions of this tasty cheese.

The goat cheese at Montchevré-Betin isn't imported from France, but cheesemaker Jean Rossard is. He and his able crew make logs and logs of fresh chevre, as well as aged crottins, crumbled goat goodies, and other blissful forms of goat cheese. As one of the larger goat cheese plants in Wisconsin, three shifts a day make the cheese, and if you've ever shopped at Trader Joe's, you've probably seen their cheese (but under a different label). Montchevre's soft logs and crottins are just delicious—with the right balance of tang and sweetness. Of the logs, a personal favorite are those Rossard's staff gently hand-rolls in peppercorns.

Montforte Cheese or Wisconsin Farmer's Union Specialty Cheese Co. doesn't have a romantic story. This little cheese company was started by the farmer's union as an investment that's paid great dividends. The company needed to put their money somewhere, and a blue cheese products company needed a more consistent source of great blue cheese. So they started up Montforte, which only makes two cheeses: blue and gorgonzola. Both their cheeses, however, started getting a lot of attention in 2006 when the gorgonzola won best gorgonzola in the world at the 2006 World Cheese Championship and the Montforte blue won first in its class in the 2006 American Cheese Society competition. Both the blue and the gorgonzola are some of the absolute finest specimens of their kind—tangy, sweet, and oh, so blue.

The Mount Sterling Cheese Cooperative is part of the reason Wisconsin is the largest producer of goat milk. In fact, its farmers only raise goats—and their goat milk goes into award-winning raw milk cheddar, flavored Monterey Jacks, and goat milk butter. The raw milk cheddar is aged for 60 days and is smoother than its cow-milk counterparts. Of the flavored jacks, do try the chive—it's crisp, summery, and sweet.

Pleasant Ridge Reserve is probably the most recognizable and award-winning cheese in Wisconsin, if not the country, and it is one of the most notable of the American originals. Made by Mike and Carol Gingrich and Dan and Jeanne Patenaude, this Beaufort-style Alpine cheese is a washed rind beauty. Made from its pasture-grazed herd of cows, this handcrafted cheese is aged in cellars to a perfection unseen in most cheeses. In fact, the first year they started making it, they won Best of Show at the American Cheese Society in 2001. They did it again in 2005, proving their win was no fluke. In fact, even among those who are import snobs, Pleasant Ridge is on their list of great cheeses. And every year, it keeps racking up the awards. This significant cheese boasts layers of flavors that change and grow in complexity over time. Nutty, with an underlying sweetness, this cheese offers some herbaceous qualities and a freshness that is undeniable. It's one of those cheeses that impresses again and again.

The Roth family history with cheese started more than 140 years ago in Switzerland. In 1991, Fermo Jaeckle and his cousins Felix and Ulrich Roth decided that instead of just exporting Gruyère and other varieties of Swiss cheese to the United States, why not make Swiss styles of cheese in the United States? Their ingenuity paid off. Today, they make dozens of styles of cheeses at their plant in Green County. Known for Gruyère, they also make fontina, Buttermilk Blue, and even a washed rind, low-calorie cheese called St. Otho's.

Their Roth's Private Reserve, an aromatic washed rind, Alpine-style cheese won first runner-up in the 2006 U.S. Cheese Championship. It's hard to find (but well worth it if you can track it down), boasting earthy aromas and lingering, palate-pleasing flavors. If you can't find it, its signature Gruyère is also incredibly tasty and just perfect for fondue. St. Otho's offers a great mouth-feel and a milder flavor than most washed rinds, but for a low-calorie cheese, it's amazingly different. The fontina is more of
a Swedish style, sweeter than Italian versions, while the Buttermilk Blue is a bitingly good blue cheese—it's strong and packed with flavor. And their Vintage Van Gogh is a sweet, nutty and easily munchable Gouda, a perfect dessert cheese.

The Least You Need to Know

- As the fifth largest cheesemaking region in the world, Wisconsin offers not only great volumes of cheese, but great variety.

- Wisconsin, in fact, makes more specialty cheese than any other state.

- Wisconsin's evolution as America's Dairyland developed because of a plethora of cheese organizations and strict cheese laws, which still make it a Mecca for cheesemaking today.

Chapter 15

California Cheese and Happy Cows

In This Chapter

- ◆ How California has grown into a dairy powerhouse
- ◆ The history of the second biggest cheese-producing state
- ◆ How California's diversity in people and terroir impacts its cheese-making
- ◆ Big farms, great cheeses

A funny series of commercials shows cows moving from the wintery, blustery Midwest to sunny California. They all end with the tagline, "Great cheese comes from happy cows. Happy cows come from California."

These clever commercials might upset dairy folk in other states (primarily Wisconsin), who say that their bovines are just as jolly, but there's no denying that they illustrate an important point: California has become a dairy and cheese powerhouse. With less than half of Wisconsin's number of cheese factories, California is poised to edge out the Dairy State for its cheese title. Visit any California dairy, and the excitement about becoming the country's largest cheese producer is so palpable you can almost touch it.

But the joy isn't just giddiness about producing the nation's greatest quantity of cheese. It's also about the quality, the fine farmhouse cheeses and American originals that are coming out of this far western state. It's also about trumpeting the diversity of the state's cheesemakers, whose dairy traditions can be traced back to the state's original Spanish missionaries.

Welcome to Where Happy Cows Live

When people think of agriculture and California, they often refer to the state's famous vineyards and wine regions. But dairy cows and milk production make up California's largest agricultural product, far surpassing grapes. Dairying has, in fact, always been a part of the state's agricultural heritage, and it's actually been around for as long as the grapes have been growing, tracing back its history more than 200 years.

This California cow suns itself happily.

(Marin French Cheese Company)

But dairy really came to the forefront in 1993, when California's milk production exceeded Wisconsin's. Not only has California maintained its milk crown since that pivotal year, but its cheese production has continued to grow, so much that it's nearing Wisconsin's overall production. Experts predict that within the next few years, California will be the largest producer of cheese in the country. Consider these surprising records: in 2006, California cheesemakers made a record 2.2 billion pounds of cheese—higher than 2005's record 2.1 billion pounds, and nearly double the 1.17 billion pounds produced in 1997.

Such large amounts of cheese are backed up by a lot of milk. In fact, California has an unprecedented amount of milk production, with a record high of 38.8 billion pounds in 2006, up 3.4 percent over 2005's incredible production level. Nearly half—48 percent—of California's milk becomes cheese. As such, California makes about 1 out of every 4 pounds of cheese in this country.

And one out of every six cows makes her happy home in California. Most Californian cows live in much bigger herds than those of Vermont or Wisconsin. The average herd size in California is 800, but cattle ranches can easily grow to house herds of 8,000 or even more. Milking such gigantic herds requires state-of-the-art equipment and is a constant, all-day affair.

More than one thousand cows are milked on this carousel twice a day.

(Three Sisters Farmstead Cheese Company)

It takes only six minutes to milk each cow on this carousel.

(Three Sisters Farmstead Cheese Company)

A Cut Above _____

Some dairy farms such as Three Sisters Farmstead Cheese in Lindsay, California, milk their cows on rotating stall carousels. After they're cleaned, cows walk directly into a milking stall, where they are hooked up to pumps. The stall slowly rotates around in a circle, with cows getting on and off every six minutes, making milking such larger herds easier.

Broken down by cheese type, California cheese is: 47.9 percent mozzarella, 22.5 percent cheddar, 14.6 percent Monterey Jack, 4.7 percent Hispanic cheeses, 2.9 percent parmesan, 2.3 percent provolone, and 4.8 percent other. California produces more Monterey Jack cheese than any other state, which is not so surprising because this cheese was created in California and is a descendent of mission cheeses. It's also the largest producer of Hispanic-style cheeses, and the largest producer of mozzarella in the country, making 1 out of every 4 pounds of mozzarella, which helps satiate the American appetite for pizza.

Some of the world's largest cheese factories can be found in California, but plenty of smaller, artisan producers also make their home in "the Golden State." Small, hand-crafted cheeses, such as Cowgirl Creamery's organic, triple crème Mt. Tam rounds or Andante Dairy's innovative mixed-milk varieties, not only tie in seamlessly with California's abundant organic agriculture, but they thrive in the gourmet markets of San Francisco and Los Angeles. They've also developed a following among turophiles across the country and around the world.

What's also interesting is that some of its farmstead operations are on large dairy ranches. But while the dairy operations push agricultural technology to its outer limits, with everything from waterbeds in cow stalls and carousel milking parlors, the cheesemaking operations remain decidedly old-fashioned. Often, the cheeses are made by only one or a handful of cheesemakers, and they're crafted in small batches in decidedly small vats.

California cheesemakers at both large and small operations are starting to get noticed, especially at national and international competitions. In 2006 alone, 16 creameries won more than 50 awards at both international and national competitions, many of them first or "best of" their class. In 2003, they won 26 awards at the American Cheese Society competition, and Cowgirl Creamery's washed rind Red Hawk took Best of Show honors.

Big Herds, Big History

California's long dairy history traces its roots way back to 1769, when Father Junipero Serra began setting up 21 missions along California's coast. Not only did this Spanish priest introduce the first grapes and set up the foundation for the state's rich wine-making legacy, becoming known as the Father of California Wine, he could just as easily be considered the Father of California Cheese, as he brought along dairy cattle and introduced the art of cheesemaking.

Cheesemaking didn't expand much beyond the missions until the 1850s when the Gold Rush hit the state. Many miners rushed in with dairy cows towed behind their covered wagons. By 1860, the state's cow population reached 100,000, and cheese production grew to 1.3 million pounds. Commercial dairies and cheesemaking weren't far behind.

Pioneer woman Clara Steele is often credited with establishing what could be considered the country's first commercial dairy in 1857. A New England native, Steele used recipes from her grandmother's cookbook and made cheese from the milk of wild cattle. She and her family began a 6,000-acre dairy farm on Point Reyes, and by 1861, they were making 45 tons of cheese a year.

Dairying and cheesemaking continued to grow, and a distinctly Californian cheese called Monterey Jack evolved. Though the cheese itself is believed to be a descendant of the original cheeses that the Franciscan friars made in the missions, its actual origin is sort of fuzzy. Some credit Senora Juana Cota de Bornoda, who went door to door selling cheese that she made using a housejack or press. Others credit a Carmel Valley man named Domingo Pedrazzi. But most likely this distinctive cheese was adapted from mission recipes by savvy Monterey businessman David Jacks, who sold the cheese as "Jacks' cheese" in 1882. The cheese later became known as Monterey Jack.

This later led to the creation of another American original, dry jack. But whereas the creation of Monterey Jack was intentional, dry jack was one of those delicious mistakes. San Francisco cheese wholesaler D.F. DeBarnardi simply left an order of fresh Monterey Jack in storage for a little too long in 1915. Upon tasting it, DeBarnardi discovered that the aged cheese had acquired a sweet, nutty flavor. It grew in popularity after World War I interrupted the shipments of aged Italian cheeses, and by the 1930s, about 60 California cheesemakers were crafting this aged cheese.

A cheesemaker loads a tray filled with wheels of brie in the aging room of the Marin French Cheese Company in the early 1900s.

(Marin French Cheese Company)

Cheesemaking continued to grow steadily, and in 1940, cheesemakers had reached an annual output of 16 million pounds. Bovine residents in the state numbered about 705,000. But from about 1940 until the early 1970s, cheesemaking and cattle numbers remained pretty stable.

The "me decade" of the 1970s could also be considered the decade of bovine growth in California. In 1970, cheese production hovered at about 17.5 million pounds; by 1978, it had grown to 137 million pounds, more than five times the levels it had maintained for more than 30 years. During the 1970s, dairy herds also began to grow in size, fueling unprecedented levels of milk production and cheesemaking.

Big wasn't the only cheesemaking word for the 1970s. Small was also big, as Laura Chenel got her first herd of goats. After purchasing goats to make a little milk, Chenel ended up with too much, so she decided to make cheese on her little farm. After an apprenticeship in France where she learned how to make chevre, she became the first person in the United States to make chevre in 1979. Chef Alice Waters was introduced to her cheese, and that was, in a sense, the beginnings of the artisan cheese movement in California.

From the 1980s to the 1990s, California's milk production grew. And it grew. And it grew. In 1984, the state set up a Real California Seal to certify that a cheese would be made in California using exclusively California milk. In 1993, it knocked out Wisconsin to become the largest milk producer in the country; three years later, its cheesemakers made a record 1 billion pounds of cheese.

Today, its 55-plus cheesemakers produce more than 250 different kinds of cheese, and the state's factories run the gamut from very large to very small, with both big commodity and small artisan coexisting peacefully and productively. Both its artisan and larger cheesemakers continue to press on with greater production levels, and they also work at perfecting their craft, striving to create better cheeses. Their ongoing efforts continue to garner attention and awards, and at 2007's World Cheese Awards in London, Fiscalini Cheese's 18-month-old, bandage-wrapped cheddar became the first non-English cheese in the competition's 20-year history to win top honors in the traditional, extra mature cheddar category. In 2005, Marin French Cheese Company became the first non-French company to win gold in the brie category; in 2007, Marin won again, once again beating the French. State cheesemakers are dubbing the wins "the 2007 Judgment of London."

A Cut Above

The "Judgment of London" is a historical riff on the 1976 "Judgment of Paris," which is when California wines beat out traditional French wines in a tasting, proving to the world that California and the United States could produce world-class wines. But where as the "Judgment of Paris" taste test was organized by one man, the World Cheese Awards is an international competition with judges and cheeses from across the globe.

Diversity in Terroir and People

Though the dairy industry can be found in many different regions across California, the Central Valley and the Chino Basin are the largest two regions. In fact, according to the 1997 Census of Agriculture, 8 of the top 11 dairy-producing counties in the nation are in these two California regions: Tulare (1), Merced (2), San Bernadino (3), Stanislaus (4), Riverside (5), Kings (6), San Joaquin (9), and Fresno (11).

This terroir can be described as warm or hot, and cows are typically fed special diets that include fruits and vegetables from the state, including citrus. On hot days, cows are kept cool by large fans.

The dairies in the Central Valley and Chino Basin are typically large in size of herd and scope of operations. Smaller but not tiny dairies can also be found in Marin and Sonoma counties. The cows in this terroir often graze on hillsides as the fog from the coast rolls in. This diversity in terroir is also mirrored in the state's cheesemakers themselves. As California boasts a multicultural heritage, so do its cheesemakers, and there are perhaps more Latino cheesemakers in California than anywhere else in the country.

Cheesemakers in California also make about 25 different Hispanic-style cheeses, of both fresh and "aged" or *anejo* varieties.

Say Cheese

Calling a Hispanic-style cheese "aged" or **anejo** is not the same as calling a cheddar aged. Anejo or aged Hispanic-style cheeses is a bit of a misnomer. Unlike European-style aged cheese, which are aged for a period of several months to several years, aged or anejo cheeses have a curing period of weeks, not months or years, and they are considered aged because they are drier, as more whey is pressed out during their making.

The most popular Hispanic-style fresh cheese that California makes is queso fresco, a moist, soft cheese that crumbles easily but does not melt. Other fresh favorites include panela, which is similar to mozzarella, and Oaxaca, which is similar to string cheese. Two popular anejo varieties made in California include asadero, which is similar to provolone, and cotija, which is similar to feta.

Great California Cheesemakers and Their Cheeses

A lot of great cheese is coming from those happy cows. That's a good thing for those of us whose tummies are happier when filled with such cheese. In fact, there's quite a bit of amazing cheese being crafted by cheesemakers with equally amazing stories. Here are more than a dozen golden examples of cheesemakers from the Golden State (in alphabetical order).

With a name like Andante Dairy, you might not be surprised to learn that its founder (or soloist, as she refers to herself and her one-woman operation) is an accomplished amateur pianist. And indeed, cheesemaker Soyung Scanlan is just that, and the cheeses she creates are musically delicious. Scanlan, who was born in Korea, had a background in food engineering, biochemistry, and dairy science before she began making cheese. A trip to Europe inspired her to leave behind the science of food making for the art of cheesemaking. The cheeses she creates are some of the most beautiful-looking cheeses around with such melodic names as Nocturne, Legato, and Minuet. All her cheeses are made from the fresh milk of neighboring Jersey cows or goats that live on her dairy. She makes cow's milk cheeses, goat's milk cheeses, and mixed-milk blends.

Nocturne is a soft-ripened cow's milk cheese that's been gently rubbed in vegetable ash—it has a delicate flavor, and the younger it is, the tarter it tastes. Legato is her personal version of camembert. Minuet is a triple crème goat's milk cheese that has added cow's milk crème fraîche to give it a velvety richness.

Just north of San Francisco, in Sonoma County, you'll find Bellwether Farms. This is a family-run operation started by Cindy Callahan, who left a career in nursing in 1986 to pursue sheep farming and, at a friend's suggestion, began making cheese. Her son Liam and later Liam's wife, Diana, joined the family business. Together, they make beautiful sheep's milk and cow's milk cheeses, and they've traveled several times to Europe to learn more about their craft.

Their cheeses are sublime and original. Crescenza is a square-shaped, rindless, oh-so-soft cheese that offers up a buttery, creamy taste and spreads easily on pizzas and breads. Carmody Reserve, made with the raw milk from an all-Jersey herd, is a firm cheese with caramel undertones. Pepato is a semi-soft sheep's milk cheese aged two to three months and flecked with whole peppercorns, which adds a nice bite. They also make a delicious fromage blanc and crème fraîche.

Jonathan Van Ryn is perhaps one of the youngest cheesemakers in the country, but he's not unseasoned. With partner and fourth-generation dairyman Bill Boersma, they formed Bravo Farms Handmade Cheese. They use milk from Van Ryn's uncle's farm to craft some big, brave cheeses, which visitors can watch being made at their little artisan factory, which has an attached restaurant and store, in Traver, California. The cheese is made in very small batches using recipes that Boersma developed when he first began making cheese in 1995 after decades in the more traditional dairy industry. They're known for their cheddars, both big-flavored, cloth-bound, aged versions and big-flavored varieties such as chipotle and sage.

Their Silver Mountain is a bandage-wrapped, raw-milk cheese that's rubbed in olive oil and aged for at least nine months. It has almost a cheddar/manchego blend of a taste. The Tulare Cannonball is a Dutch Edam-style cheese aged for up to seven months, and it comes in a big 4-pound ball. Using a 500-year-old recipe as a basis, the Tulare serves up a bold, spicy flavor with depth. The chipotle cheddar is spicy and hot,

A Cut Above

Though there aren't any milk-producing animals at the Bravo Farms store in Traver, California, do stop in its courtyard to visit a flock of birds, including chickens, a cockatiel, and some love birds. The birds aren't involved in the cheese-making, but some of their eggs (only the chickens) end up in the restaurant's omelettes.

but not overwhelmingly so—a perfect complement to burgers or grilled-cheese sandwiches.

Bubalus Bubalis is perhaps one of the funniest names around for a cheese company, but there isn't anything funny about their authentic mozzarella di bufala, or water buffalo mozzarella. As one of the few cheese factories making authentic mozzarella di bufala, this Butte County cheese is a prize. Owners Grazia Perrella and Hanns Heick bought the buffalo from an Italian man who had brought the herd from Florida to Chino, California. This husband-and-wife team relocated the herd to the Sacramento area, and because Perrella comes from a family of mozzarella makers in Italy, making mozzarella was the next step.

Their fresh, sweet mozzarella di bufala comes in soft, 8-ounce balls or the smaller bocconcini. They also make a smoky aged mozzarella called scamorza, the firmer mozzarella provoletta, and fresh, sweet ricotta. And nothing tastes better in a summer Capri salad than their fresh mozzarella.

With a name like Cowgirl Creamery, you know the cheese is going to be anything but boring. In fact, Cowgirl Creamery makes some of the most exciting cheeses in the country. Cheesemakers Peggy Smith and Sue Conley's little cheese factory in Point Reyes Station has been written up in numerous magazines, and it's no wonder—their background as chefs comes through in their creative, decadent cheeses.

Using only organic milk from the Marin Valley, they handcraft a variety of soft and delicious cheeses, named for some of the region's landmarks and bounties. They add wine, herbs, nettles, and other local organic ingredients to some of their cheeses, and in both their Pointe Reyes Station store and retail outlet in the Ferry Plaza Building in San Francisco they showcase not only their own cheeses but other handcrafted cheeses from California and around the globe. Their Pointe Reyes Station location also includes a small café where you can find some of their creations paired up with other local organic produce in delicious combinations.

Perhaps most well known is their washed rind, triple crème Red Hawk, a creamy American original that's bursting with flavor. The red-tinged Red Hawk took Best of Show at the American Cheese Society 2003 competition. They also make a buttery, bloomy rind cheese called Mt. Tam, a nettle-wrapped triple crème called St. Pat, and a Muscat wine-washed, seasonal cheese called Pierce PT. But although most of their press has been about their American originals, they also do some pretty stylish traditional cheeses, including one of the most divine cottage cheeses on the planet. Their clabbered-cream cottage cheese is rich, velvety, and it just oozes with flavor.

Cypress Grove Chevre's cheesemaker Mary Keehn might not have as much name recognition as Laura Chenel, but her cheeses are not only just as good, they come in an amazing array of original flavors and textures. Keehn began with a few goats on a small family farm, opening up her farmstead operations in 1983. Today, her company buys milk from several farms.

This California creamery, located near the Oregon border, makes fresh, bloomy rinds and flavored chevres. Purple Haze is a fresh, semi-soft chevre that's coated with lavender and fennel pollen with a light purple hue and a delicious tang. Humboldt Fog is an aged, ash-coated, soft-ripened cheese with a layer of ash added in the middle. Humboldt Fog is one of those addictive cheeses, and its complex flavors grow on anyone who tastes it.

Fiscalini Farmstead Cheese Company not only makes award-winning cheese, but it also crafts history-making cheese, as its 2007 aged cheddar became the first traditionally aged, bandage-wrapped cheddar to best the English in the World Cheese Awards in London. The cheese comes from a partnership between dairyman John Fiscalini and cheesemaker Mariano Gonzales. Fiscalini comes from a long history of dairymen, and his ancestors were farmers in the Swiss Alps. His grandfather first started dairy operations in Modesto way back in 1914, and he took over from his father. In the 1990s, after visiting Lionza, Switzerland, where his forefathers raised cattle and made cheese centuries ago, Fiscalini started thinking about cheese.

Around the same time he began experimenting with cheese, cheesemaker Mariano Gonzales had just closed up shop in his cheese factory in Paraguay. Trained in Vermont, the instability of his country led him back to the states where he met Fiscalini, who was so proud of the "fontina" that he had just made. "It was a good cheese, but it wasn't fontina," Gonzales explained to Fiscalini. Instead, that cheese became San Joaquin Gold, a sweet and buttery hard cheese. While Fiscalini Farms is a rather large dairy operation with a herd of more than 1,000 cattle, the cheesemaking operation remains very small and artisan. (It's so small that some cheeses have to be aged in an old Penguin Icee retail refrigerator.) Fiscalini is building a newer cheese plant and visitor's center on his farm, and that will give Gonzales more space to develop new cheeses.

Besides San Joaquin Gold, Gonzales makes several award-winning cheeses, including what was deemed the best cheddar in the world in 2007's World Cheese Awards.

That bandage-wrapped cheddar is aged between 18 and 30 months, and it offers a smooth, clean cheddar taste. Similar to Alpine cheeses created in the Ticino region of Switzerland, Leonza offers a sweet, almost caramel flavor and a semi-soft texture. Gonzales also crafts a variety of flavored cheddars including the more exotic saffron and a scotch ale that offers a taste of sweet hops blended with the cheddar.

In Armenian *Karoun* means "springtime," but in Los Angeles it means incredible cheese. This urban cheese factory was founded by Ohannese Bagdassarian, who learned how to make cheese and yogurt in Lebanon, where his family owns one of the largest dairies in the country. Bagdassarian not only studied cheesemaking in the Middle East, but he also traveled to Denmark to continue his education. In 1989 he moved to the United States, and he decided to make Middle Eastern styles of cheese using California milk.

Bagdassarian makes several varieties of cheese, including a cheese he calls California cheese, a brined, whole-milk cheese that is unripened and salty. He also makes what is perhaps the most unusual string cheese in the United States, called Mujaddal. This Middle Eastern string cheese is flavored with *majleb*, a spice made from cherry pits.

Say the name Laura Chenel, and you think goat cheese. Chenel's name is synonymous with chevre, as she became the first fresh goat cheesemaker in the United States back in the 1970s. Chenel's first inspiration came from her goats, and she experimented with making cheese. Not happy with the way her cheeses were turning out led her to France, where she learned traditional techniques.

Thus armed, she returned to the states, began making cheese, and Alice Waters, chef of Chez Panisse restaurant, tasted her cheese. Waters fell in love with her chevre, and the rest is history. In 2006, the French company Rians Group purchased her cheese factory, but Chenel still supplies milk from her herd of 500 goats.

Though Laura Chenel Chevre no longer has Chenel at the helm, the chevre logs, tangy chabis, crottins, and other goat lovelies remain as fresh and tangy as ever, beautiful chalk-white testaments to what one woman and a few goats can do.

Marin French Cheese Company is the oldest continually operating producer of cheese in the United States. This venerable company was founded in 1865, and it's still at the same location in Petaluma. Jefferson Thompson started the company making what he called "breakfast cheese," which was shipped to San Francisco taverns as a replacement for the unavailable pickled eggs. That original breakfast cheese is still made today by Marin French, and it's also evolved into a second cheese, the Schloss, which is an aged washed rind cheese.

Around the turn of the century the company took on its current name, and its owners changed its focus to hone in on soft-ripened cheeses like bries and camemberts. The cheese is made in 20-pound plastic buckets, the old, old-fashioned way. Both goat's milk and cow's milk versions of their cheeses are made, and in 2007 an accidental mixing of the milks led to a purposefully delightful mixed-milk line as well. Both the cow's milk and goat's milk versions have won several national and international awards, most notably beating the French in the 2005 and 2007 World Cheese Awards in London.

The cow's milk camembert offers up nutty and mushroomy aromas, as well as a rich mouth feel. The triple crème brie is sweet and very, very creamy. The Schloss serves up bold aromas and an incredibly delicious and complex array of flavors. The Yellow Buck Chevre is creamy and mild, aged just four weeks. All three lines of cheeses also include some blue, bloomy rinded cheeses, which are a delightfully different kind of blue. The blues have fewwer veins than traditional blues, and they taste almost like a combination of a triple crème and a blue cheese, which is what they basically are.

Marisa Simoes is the only one of three sisters who actually makes cheese at Three Sisters Farmstead Cheese in Lindsay, California, but someday her younger siblings might join the family business. Simoes's father, Rob Hilarides, is a third-generation dairy farmer, who supplies milk to the large Hilmar Cheese Company. After Simoes returned from college, she and her father took a cheesemaking course, and they experimented and came up with an Italian-style cheese that they made with their fresh Jersey milk.

What they came up with was Serena, a smooth, nutty, and complex cheese that boasts a yellow, creamy color from the richness of the milk. Their second cheese, Serenita, was created after a power outage forced them to use different techniques in making the cheese. The result is a milder, sweet, and herbal cheese that's equally delicious and easy to nosh on.

Though they farm a herd of 8,000 cattle, their cheesemaking operations are definitively farmstead in both the size and the nature of their creamery. All the cheese is made by hand, in small batches, and it is aged on the farm in special cellars.

Ignacio "Ig" Vella is an icon among California cheesemakers. His father Tom started the Vella Cheese Company in Sonoma, in an old stone building that was once a brewery. "I learned to make cheese among the vats," Vella will tell you, and he began learning when he was just 3 years old, back in 1931 when his father started Vella Cheese.

Ig Vella, one of the fathers of the American artisan cheese movement, shows off a wheel of his Dry Monterey Jack, an American original cheese.

(Jeanette Hurt)

The milk used to come in cans, but it still comes from a local dairy. In fact, for the last 20 years it has come from the same dairy, from George F. Mertens Sr.'s cows in Schellville.

Vella and his able staff, including cheesemaker Charles Malkassian, make cheese just the way his father did—by hand, in small quantities. Vella makes a Dry Monterey Jack that's coated with oil, cocoa powder, and pepper, and it's either aged from seven to nine months or from one to two years. The jacks are rolled by hand and shaped in muslin cloth—in fact, every cheese has an imprint of this cloth on the back, an attribute that no factory cheese will ever show. Besides the dry jacks, Vella also makes Mezzo Secco. This cheese was developed in the 1930s when consumers wanted a Monterey Jack that wasn't as dry as a dry jack, but wasn't as perishable as a regular jack during the summer months so it could keep more easily in

A Cut Above

Vella has been recognized internationally and nationally as a role model for cheesemakers. Slow Food International recognized him as a global gastronomic treasure in 2003, and the American Cheese Society gave him their first ever Lifetime Achievement Award.

iceboxes. It fell out of favor after refrigeration became widespread, but Vella revived this special cheese in 1999, winning awards for its singularly delicious flavor. Vella also makes several Italian cheeses, including the Romanello, which is a cow's milk version of Romano, and the Toma, a creamy semi-soft cheese that originally was made in the Piedmont area of Italy. (Vella is the only American company to make this special cheese.)

The Least You Need to Know

◆ California is poised to knock Wisconsin out of its place as the biggest cheese-producing state in the country.

◆ California has a long history of cheesemaking, tracing its cheesemaking roots as far back as its wine-making roots.

◆ California and its plethora of happy cows make not only large volumes of cheese, but some of the most exquisite varieties around. The Golden State is definitely a dairy-centric state, with diversity of cheese and cheesemakers.

16

Vermont Cheese

In This Chapter

- ◆ How Vermont became an artisan and farmhouse cheese mecca
- ◆ Exploring the history of this cheese-centric state
- ◆ Big cheeses and cheesemakers of this little state

Vermont doesn't call itself "America's Dairyland," nor does it have national television commercials showing off its happy cows. In fact, it's not even the third biggest dairy state (that title belongs to New York). As Jed Davis, spokesman for the Vermont Cheese Council, said in a newspaper interview, "In the cheese world, there's Wisconsin, and then there's California, and then everything else, and somewhere way, way down that scale, in terms of volume, is Vermont."

Even though dairy is its largest agricultural output, Vermont only ranks fifteenth in overall production. But what Vermont lacks in quantity, it makes up for in quality. In fact, many in the Vermont dairy industry describe their state as "the Napa Valley for cheese."

Though Wisconsinites and Californians might quibble with that self-promoting title, Vermont does have some bragging rights when it comes to cheese and dairy products. Almost all of this New England state's cheese-makers fall into the artisan, farmhouse, and specialty arenas, meaning that just about everyone making cheese is doing so on a small or at least very selective scale. Cheese in Vermont is made from the milks of cows, sheep, goats, and even water buffalos. And a lot of Vermont's cheesemakers place or clean up in different cheese and dairy contests. That's why Vermont deserves to be singled out and championed as the incredible cheese state that it is.

Putting the "Art" into Artisan: How Vermont Got Milk

When people used to think of Vermont and agriculture, the thick, viscous liquid they thought of wasn't milk, it was maple syrup. Real Vermont maple syrup has been a symbol of quality for years, but over the last two decades Vermont's always credible dairy industry has risen like cream to the top, and suddenly, when people think of the Green Mountain state, they not only think of maple syrup, they also think of cheese.

Say Cheese

Farmstead cheesemaking means that the cheeses are made right on the same farm where the animals are raised and milked.

Cheese and dairy have always been a part of Vermont's agricultural heritage, but not until recent years has its artisan dairy industry really flourished. Of Vermont's 40-plus cheese factories, the majority of them are on the small side and are *farmstead* operations, where the cheese is made right there on the farm. Those creameries produce dozens of different varieties of cheese, butter, ice cream, and other dairy products.

Some experts say that Vermont has more cheesemakers per capita than any other state. A lot of them have entered into cheese as a second career, and many of them were professionals in other fields—several of them have advanced degrees from prestigious universities—before they decided to pursue cheesemaking. Most of them support and cooperate with one another, and that cooperation helped foment the artisan and farmstead cheese movement in Vermont.

The dairy business in Vermont is valued at $26 million. Of the state's top five agricultural products, the top two are dairy products and then cattle and calves. (Greenhouse/nursery, hay, and maple products round out the top five.) While most of Vermont's dairy industry is of the handcrafted, specialty variety, Vermont also has a few dairy giants or larger factories, most of which tend toward the specialized varieties of cheese, too.

Both large and small factories in Vermont also often welcome visitors, and the state's tourism department has a Cheese Trail map of creameries that accept visitors, making the state not just at the forefront of artisan cheesemaking, but also at the head of the agritourism movement.

Vermont's fine cheeses can be found not only in New England, but also around the country, and in some cases around the world. Their cheeses can hold their own, and often they are the only cheeses of their kind on the planet.

Discovering the History of Cheesemaking in Vermont

When Vermont became a state in 1791 (the fourteenth state in the union, the first one added after the original 13 colonies), the main agricultural product was wheat, and Vermont was considered the breadbasket of New England. Besides wheat, some of the early settlers brought sheep with them for meat and wool.

The first cows came to Vermont by way of William Jarvis, who brought two Holstein cows and a bull from Holland in 1810. (Jarvis also brought Merino sheep over from Portugal, after seeing them while he was the U.S. consul in Lisbon.) In a few years, other prominent farmers and merchants imported Jersey and Guernsey cows from the Channel Islands and Ayshires from Scotland. Soon, people realized that it wasn't just sheep that could live well in Vermont: the grazing conditions in Vermont were ideal for cattle, and the state soon became known for its high quantity and quality of milk production.

Like so many other states, Vermont's first cheesemaking efforts were farm-based, and it was originally considered women's work. Cheese and butter were made on the farm to preserve the milk. As Vermont's notable herds began to improve and produce more milk, there was a larger and much more significant surplus, especially in the north of Vermont. Add to this growth the coming of the railroad in 1850, and suddenly Vermont's delicious dairy products were being transported to Boston and New York City. Things really exploded after 1854 when the first iced railroad car was invented, which allowed Vermont (and other producers of dairy and perishables) a greatly expanded market base.

Vermont's first cheese factory was built in 1864 by Consider Bardwell. Bardwell set up the first cooperative creamery in the Champlain Valley. Within the next five years, Vermont was considered a dairy powerhouse of sorts, and almost every farming community had a cheese factory or creamery. Milk production peaked in Vermont in 1869, at 9 million pounds, and factories grew from this output of milk. By 1895 there were 58 cheese factories in the state, some of which are still operating today.

A Cut Above

The Consider Bardwell factory didn't last, shipping out its last wheels of cheddar in 1932, but in recent years cheesemaking has resumed on the original Consider Bardwell farm. Angela Miller and Russell Glover purchased the farm in 2000, and cheesemakers Peter Dixon and Peggy Galloup make the cheese. They make a variety of goat's milk cheeses, as well as one cow's milk cheese.

Crowley Cheese, of Healdville, is the oldest, built in 1882 to expand the cheesemaking operations of Winfred and Nellie Crowley; the Crowleys originally started making cheese in 1824. Today, Crowley Cheese is considered the oldest continually operating cheese factory in North America, and still makes cheddar using its 1882 recipe. Other early factories include Plymouth Cheese Factory, of Plymouth Notch, which opened in 1890, and Grafton Village Cheese Company, of Grafton, which opened in 1892. What's interesting to note about Plymouth Cheese is that it was started with the milk of Col. John Coolidge, father of President Calvin Coolidge.

By the end of the nineteenth century and the beginning of the twentieth century, cheesemaking in Vermont was evenly split between factories and small farmstead operations. Of Vermont's cheesemaking prowess, Vermont Gov. Josiah Grout wrote in 1898, "Vermont is peculiarly a state of farms and farmers, which accounts for the noble character of her people."

By 1900, Vermont was the number-one cheese-producing state in New England, and about 80 percent of all the milk in Vermont was turned into cheese and butter. Vermont was also first in the nation in butter production, with production peaking in 1915. At that time, the Franklin County Cooperative Creamery in St. Albans was the single largest butter producer in the world. That number shifted dramatically by the 1920s. Though milk production remained relatively stable, butter and cheese production declined because fluid milk sales offered farmers a better income and lower production costs. Cow population in 1930 actually exceeded human population in Vermont 421,000 to 359,000, respectively. What happened in Vermont at that time also was happening around the country: smaller farmers were consolidating, and commercial dairies became the growing trend.

That led to the decline of smaller family farms. What's interesting, however, is that despite the decline, it never quite faded away. Then, in the late 1970s and early 1980s, a wonderful resurgence happened. Some dairy farmers turned to cheesemaking to increase and diversify their incomes. Others, led by the love of cheese, went to Europe to study artisan methods and came back to make cheese—good cheese.

Two of those cheesemakers were Allison Hooper and Bob Reese. Hooper had studied cheesemaking in France when she was a college student, and Reese was the marketing director for the Vermont Department of Agriculture. Their partnership started when Reese was stuck in a hard place: he was organizing an important state dinner, and his French chef needed chevre. Goat's milk cheese was not easy to come by in the early 1980s, but Reese knew that Hooper, his colleague in the state dairy lab, had worked at creameries in France. Could she make chevre? She could, and she did, and the rest is history, as her chevre was the talk of the dinner. In 1984, they formed the Vermont Butter and Cheese Company, which today uses the milk from 20 different dairy farmers, making goat's milk cheeses and some cow's milk cheeses and dairy products, including crème fraîche and cultured butter.

Vermont Butter and Cheese Company was just one of many smaller companies that got started, and by the 1990s, the artisan cheese movement in Vermont was more than well underway. Then, in 1996, the Vermont Dairy Producer's Council was formed to help cheesemakers increase their markets and get the word out about their great cheeses, and that eventually evolved into the Vermont Cheese Council. In 1999, the council published *The Vermont Code of Best Practices*, the first domestic publication on how to improve a region's cheeses, and in 2000, the council created the Vermont Cheese Trail, which promotes agritourism and visits to artisan cheesemakers.

The University of Vermont had always helped cheesemakers, and in 2004 it started helping smaller cheesemakers even more by establishing the Vermont Institute for Artisan Cheese, the only comprehensive center in the country devoted just to artisan cheese. The center not only offers classes and educational support, it also promotes research and technology development.

Today, Vermont boasts almost 40 artisan cheese producers (not including some of the larger factories), which is the most per capita in the country. Today, those cheesemakers make more than 150 different kinds of cheeses—cheeses that regularly win at national and international cheese competitions. The Vermont Cheese Institute was one of just two American delegations at the 2006 Cheese Art festival in Sicily, and in 2007 Vermont hosted the American Cheese Society's national convention and competition. Vermont's tremendous cheeses just keep growing—in reputation, quality, and quantity.

Identifying the Great Vermont Cheeses

With dozens of amazing cheesemakers constantly turning out a variety of high-quality cheeses, it's almost impossible to narrow down the list. But this is a book about the cheeses of the world, not just Vermont, so here is just a sampling of some of Vermont's finest, starting with two notable cheddar makers.

Like so many states, Vermont's reputation for fine cheese began with its cheddar. Vermont cheddar is considered to be among the best in the world, and it has a subtly different flavor from cheddars made in California and Wisconsin. It also has a different look from many cheddars, as Vermont cheddar typically is not colored with annatto.

Two of the best places for Vermont cheddar are Crowley and Grafton Village Cheese, which are two of the oldest cheese factories in the state. Both companies only make cheddar. Crowley makes mild, medium, sharp, extra sharp, and flavored varieties of cheddar. Crowley's distinct cheddars are often called a colby type of cheese, but they are not really colbies, and they're made from a herd of Holsteins.

Grafton makes cheddar of different flavors and degrees of sharpness, and offers cheddars that are aged for up to six years. All Grafton's cheddars are made from Jersey cows' milk, and much of the process is done by hand.

Another great maker of cheddar, Cabot Creamery, based in Montpelier, also has some history to it. Cabot, which bills its cheddar as "the world's best natural cheddar," first dates back to 1893. In 1919, however, it was formed into a cooperative, with 94 farmers joining together. Today, the cheese plant uses milk from about 330 Vermont family farms, and the cows are a mix of Guernsey, Jersey, and Holstein. Cabot is Vermont's largest dairy producer, and its cheddars have taken numerous national and international awards, including the American Cheese Society's Best of Show. The cheese is aged anywhere from a year or more, and it also comes in a cloth-bound variety.

A Cut Above

The Cabot cooperative cost each original farmer $5 per cow, plus a cord of wood to fuel the broiler. The creamery first produced only butter, under the Rosedale brand, but in 1930 the company hired its first cheesemaker to make cheddar.

Another well-known Vermont cheddar maker is Shelbourne Farms on the eastern shore of Lake Champlain. Shelburne Farms was originally established in 1886 by William Seward and Lila Vanderbilt Webb as a model agricultural estate, but in 1972, it was transformed into an educational, agricultural nonprofit. A herd of 125 pure Brown Swiss cows makes the milk that goes into the cloth-wrapped and aged cheddars, which are aged up to three years. The farm is noted for its educational offerings for cheese lovers, and it is also recognized for treating its cattle so well: in

While France is known for its goat cheeses, other countries, including South Africa, make delicious chevres, including this Foxenburg Crottin.

(*Agri-Expo South Africa*)

Gruyère is an integral ingredient in many Swiss fondues, prized for its meltability, and this Gruyère is made in Wisconsin by a Swiss company.

(*Wisconsin Milk Marketing Board*)

When pairing wine with cheese, sometimes fruit helps to bridge the flavors of the cheese with the wine, as with South African washed rind Porto Bello Choice with this South African red wine.

(Agri-Expo South Africa)

For many years, South Africa just produced cheddar and Gouda, but today this country's cheesemakers create many other versions of international cheeses, including Stellenbosch Cheese's feta and Zandam Cheese's Fior de Latte, a type of fresh mozzarella.

(Agri-Expo South Africa)

Bread and cheese are a classic food/cheese pairing, as these homemade bread sticks add a crisp bite to the soft, crumbly cheeses on this flight.

(Destination Kohler)

A horizontal tasting offers an array of different cheeses, whereas a vertical flight picks just one cheese or one producer in a single flight. This is a good example of a horizontal tasting, which is augmented by dried fruits and spiced nuts.

(Destination Kohler)

Pont L'Eveque was first produced by Trappist monks in the Normandy region of France, but Fairview Cheese's version of this aromatic washed rind cheese, La Beryl, is made in South Africa, and in 2003, it won first place in the Pont L'Eveque category at the World Cheese Championship.

(Agri-Expo South Africa)

Nut breads, along with nuts and fruits, pair up extremely well with blue cheese and cheddar, as they bring out the inherent sweetness in the cheeses themselves.

(Wisconsin Milk Marketing Board)

In arranging a cheese tasting or cheese plate, sometimes purchasing a large wheel or half-wheel adds panache to your display, as the big wheels of cheese add visual appeal to this assortment of Wisconsin cheeses.

(Wisconsin Milk Marketing Board)

The cheesemaking tradition in Mexico and most of Latin America began with the Spanish conquistadors; today, the wide variety of cheeses that originated in Latin America are made in the United States (and sometimes exported to Latin America) like these cheeses, which are made in Wisconsin.

(Wisconsin Milk Marketing Board)

Cheese curds, if they're freshly made, squeak in your mouth when you bite into them.

(Wisconsin Milk Marketing Board)

Van Gogh Gouda is one of the few cheeses that actually pairs well with chocolate.

(Roth Kase)

Brie was first made in a region just outside of Paris, France, but today it's made all over the world, including Wisconsin.

(Wisconsin Milk Marketing Board)

Like Brie and Camembert, Les Freres is a bloomy rind cheese, but it's an American original produced in Wisconsin.

(Wisconsin Milk Marketing Board)

Stilton is considered to be one of the best blue cheeses in the world.
(Roth Käse)

Wisconsin Gorgonzola has taken top honors at many cheese competitions, even when competing against versions made in Italy.
(Wisconsin Milk Marketing Board)

2006, it received a "Certified Humanely Raised and Handled" designation for its herd. There's also an inn on the property, where visitors can stay overnight and enjoy meals.

Consider Bardwell isn't making cheese any more on the Consider Bardwell Farm, but at the site of Vermont's very first cheese factory, cheesemaking continues. Unlike the farm's original cheddars, owners Angela Miller and Russell Glover wanted to do something different, so they hired some able cheesemakers to make some incredible goat's milk cheeses from their herd of Oberhasli goats. The goats are rotationally grazed, and they also purchase cow's milk from neighboring farmers who also believe in the organic lifestyles for their livestock. Their signature cheese is the fresh and bloomy rind versions of Mettowee, a delicious goat's milk cheese. Dorset is an aged, washed rind, cow's milk cheese similar to Italy's stinky Taleggio.

Vermont Butter and Cheese Company, despite the butter coming before cheese in its title, is all about the cheese. The company, which started from that first state dinner in need of chevre, has three basic lines of products: cow's milk cheese and dairy products, goat's milk cheese, and artisanal cheeses. The cow's milk category includes quark, mascarpone, crème fraîche, fromage blanc, and cultured butter. The goat's milk category includes chevre, feta, and creamy goat cheese, which is sort of like a goat's milk ricotta. The artisan cheeses include Bijou (a French crottin-style cheese), Bonne Bouche (an ash-covered, aged goat's milk cheese), and Coupole (which is sort of like a combination of Bijou and Bonne Bouche).

Vermont Shepherd is another one of the leaders in Vermont's artisan cheese community. It was started in 1990 by Cindy and David Major. Cindy is the daughter of a New York milk processor, and David grew up on the sheep farm, but they didn't automatically decide to make cheese. A suggestion by Cindy's father led them to try their hand at making cheese, but the first cheeses they made were pretty bad. So bad that a lot of their cheeses ended up in the garbage, and their first entry into the American Cheese Society's annual competition came in dead last.

Determined to make it work, Cindy read a French cheese book and then wrote the author for advice. He told them to go to the Pyrenees in France to study sheep's milk cheesemaking. They did just that, and their cheeses are now considered among the best in the world by sources ranging from *Gourmet* magazine to *The New York Times*. Their cheeses are seasonal and aged in a cave—the first natural cave for cheese in Vermont. The Vermont Shepherd cheese is their signature cheese, which has won the American Cheese Society's Best of Show award; but they also make two cow's milk cheeses: Putney Tomme, a rustic farmhouse cheese, and Timson, a creamy washed rind.

Whenever people talk about Vermont and cheese, one name often comes up, and that's Jasper Hill Farm in Greensboro. This small family farm was purchased by two brothers and their wives—Mateo and Angie Kehler and Andy and Victoria Kehler—in 1998. They wanted to come up with some sort of sustainable production, and they tried both farmstead beer and baked tofu, which didn't meet with success. Fortunately for caseophiles everywhere, the Kehler family turned their attention toward cheese. In 2002 they purchased 15 Ayrshire cows, and the next year they started making cheese. Right now, they make three types of raw milk cheese: Aspenhurst, a variation of the English Leicester; Bayley Hazen Blue, a blue cheese with a dense paste; and Constant Bliss, a soft, mold-ripened cheese. A writer for *The New Yorker* described Bayley Hazen Blue in a 2004 article: "It was tangy, sweet, creamy, velvet on the tongue, the most delicious blue cheese I'd ever tasted."

Another old farm was taken over and transformed into a great cheesemaking site by Kate and Jon Wright, who purchased their Londonderry farm in the early 1990s. They started just by running a traditional dairy on the 180-year-old Taylor Farm, but then, in 1999, they started making cheese. Today, they make several varieties of award-winning goudas, including a young version, aged two to five months, a one-year-old Gouda, as well as a smoked gouda and several flavored goudas.

A Cut Above

Plenty of cheesy cow jokes abound, but some of the best puns can be found on the kid's fun page of the Taylor Farm website (www.taylorfarmvermont.com). Two favorites are: "First cow: What do you think about this mad cow disease? Second cow: What do I care? I'm a helicopter!" and the perennially good, "Why do cows wear bells? Because their horns don't work."

The Three Shepherds of the Mad River Valley is one of the more creatively named farmstead cheese operations. The three shepherds are Francis, Heather, and Jackie, who are the children of Linda and Larry Faillace. After Linda and Larry completed graduate school, they took their whole family to Great Britain, where their family decided that they wanted to make cheese. Their first cheese was created in 2000 by their daughter Jackie, who at the time was only 12 years old. The family today makes a variety of raw cow's milk and raw sheep's milk cheeses. Their cow's milk varieties include Aurora, which is a Trappist-style washed rind cheese, and Vermont Brabander, a nutty, crumbly cheese. Their sheep's milk varieties include Cosmos, which is sort of like an extra-virgin olive oil–marinated feta, and Montagne, a three-month-old, hand-pressed cheese. The family also offers three-day cheesemaking lessons for serious amateurs and people who are interested in starting a career as an artisan cheesemaker. The classes are offered numerous times of the year and have received rave reviews.

One of the more unusual cheesemakers in Vermont has neither sheep, nor goats, nor cows. The Woodstock Water Buffalo Company makes authentic mozzarella di bufala from, well, water buffalos. Owner David Muller started his water buffalo farm in Woodstock in 2003. After selling his technology company, he decided that he wanted to make water buffalo cheese. After building a pristine dairy for his buffalo, he brought in Italian cheese experts to teach his employees the art of making mozzarella di bufala. Besides making a very authentic mozzarella, Woodstock Water Buffalo also makes a water buffalo yogurt.

The Least You Need to Know

- Vermont may only be ranked fifteenth in terms of overall cheese production, but it has more artisan cheesemakers per capita than any other state.

- Vermont's cheese history dates back to 1810, and it was a cheese and butter powerhouse in the 1800s and early 1900s.

- Like both California and Wisconsin, Vermont is home to some great cheddar makers, but Vermont cheddar tastes a bit different than California or Wisconsin cheddar.

- Vermont's artisan cheesemakers make cheese from goat's milk, sheep's milk, cow's milk, and even water buffalo's milk.

Chapter 17

Other Great American Cheeses

In This Chapter

- The different artisan cheese organizations across the United States
- Great cheeses from the East Coast
- Great cheeses from the South
- Great cheeses from the Midwest
- Great cheeses from the West Coast

Not every state has great cheese, not every state even produces cheese, but the fact is, most states—at least 38 at last count—make cheese, and a lot of those cheesemakers make some pretty darn good, if not downright fabulous, cheeses. The American artisan cheese movement continues to grow, and more and more cheesemakers are turning up in some of the more unlikely places (the Big Island of Hawaii, for example). The more cheesemakers who show up in a region, the more cheesemakers tend to flock to a region, and the more organized these cheesemakers become. What's interesting is that as people are eating more organic and locally grown foods, they're discovering the exotic realm of locally made cheeses.

While European countries have been constrained by traditions, American cheesemakers are open to experimenting, and you'll find, for example, great blue cheeses made on both the East and the West coasts. Yes, terroir plays into these cheeses, but they aren't restricted to any specific terroir. These new cheeses are only limited by the creativity and ingenuity of their makers, which means the sky's the limit.

Cheesemaking Around the United States

California and Wisconsin are the big cheeses, where both specialty and conglomerate cheeses coexist, and while Vermont has carved out a distinctively farmstead niche, plenty of other states, from Maine to Washington and Michigan to Texas, are starting to develop their own cheesemaking identities.

Now, some of these states—New York is a prime example—have always been cheesemaking states, with deep dairy heritages. And some of these states have been in the process of becoming more dairy-centric states, as big cheesemaking and dairy plants have moved west and southwest because of the larger space needed to operate large, large herds of cattle. But what's interesting about these types of states as well as those that don't have deep dairy heritages yet are producing incredible cheeses, is that in the 20 or so years since the pioneers of the American artisan cheese movement got started, the general American public now readily embraces new cheeses, especially new and locally made cheeses.

There are at least six individual state cheesemakers guilds or organizations, including the Maine Cheesemakers Guild, New York State Farmstead and Artisan Cheesemakers Guild, Ohio Farmstead-Artisan Cheese Guild, Oregon Cheese Guild, Washington State Cheesemakers Association, and the Slow Food Minnesota Cheese Forum—and this doesn't include any dairy or cheese organizations in Wisconsin, California, or Vermont. Not to mention the Southern Cheesemakers Guild and the Great Cheeses of New England, as well.

All of these individual organizations help cheesemakers, promote regional cheeses, and introduce the public to new cheeses. It also, indirectly, means that because of this organized support, the individual cheeses continue to improve and gain recognition. At national and international cheese competitions, there are plenty of cheesemakers who continue to win award upon award—they're that good and that consistent. But every year there are also surprises—new cheeses that either haven't been made for very long or haven't participated in competitions, suddenly recognized as the gems that they are.

A good example of this is Anne and John Hoyt, of Leelanau Cheese. This couple, with the help of just one part-time employee, had been making good Swiss-style cheese for 12 years in Michigan, operating their creamery out of a small winery in Suttons Bay, where they sell most of the cheese they make. Then, in 2007, they took top honors at the American Cheese Society (ACS), winning Best of Show and beating out more than 1,200 different cheeses.

America's "Other" Cheesemaking Regions

Long before Wisconsin farmers even discovered white gold, New York knew dairy. It wasn't the first state to have dairy production, but in the 1800s it was where dairy and cheese flourished. Jesse Williams created the world's first cheese assembly-line factory in 1851 in Rome, New York, and hundreds of cheesemakers and their small creameries eventually dotted the state.

By the early 1900s, though Wisconsin dairies had risen in prominence, the center of cheesemaking in the United States was New York. In fact, not only did New York export a lot of its cheese to Great Britain, but New York cheese was the standard that Wisconsin had to live up to and compete against. Cheese markets first came on the scene in 1871, bringing buyers and sellers together especially in the western region of the state. One such cheese market, which started in the early 1900s, was in the Kinney Hotel in Cuba, New York. That market eventually moved to Plymouth, Wisconsin, and then to Green Bay in 1958, where it became known as the National Cheese Exchange.

Around the same time as the cheese markets migrated, so, too, did much of the dairy industry. New York's thriving dairy industry took a downturn, slipping behind Wisconsin in production. But dairy never died in New York, and today New York is the third largest dairy-producing state in the country. New York not only has larger production numbers than most other states, but it also has a thriving artisan and farmstead dairy movement. In 2002, the New York State Farmstead and Artisan Cheesemakers Guild was organized. The guild has 25 members who make cheese from cow's milk, goat's milk, and sheep's milk, and it also supports and assists new cheesemakers who want to set up shop within New York State.

After New York, perhaps the largest cheesemaking state in New England is Maine. Though never as prominent as New York, dairy and cheesemaking has been a part of Maine's agricultural scene for generations, and in recent years, it has seen a tremendous growth. The Maine Cheesemakers Guild formed in 2003, and it now boasts at least 20 members. In the last few years, the guild has also sponsored a wine and cheese festival, and the guild's members can barely keep up with the demand for their cheese.

A Cut Above

Both Maine and New York have cheese-related museums. Maine has the Matthews Museum of Maine Heritage, which details Maine's agricultural history, including that of dairy and cheese. New York actually has two cheese museums, the New York State Museum of Cheese at the Erie Canal Village and the Cuba Cheese Museum.

A Cut Above

Every year Tillamook Cheese sponsors a mac n' cheese recipe contest, and the winner who creates the best new variation on this old favorite gets $5,000.

The New England Dairy Promotion Board, besides promoting cheesemakers in Maine and Vermont, also promotes cheesemakers in Connecticut, New Hampshire, and Massachusetts.

Outside of New England (and California and Wisconsin), perhaps the greatest concentration of cheesemakers lies in the Pacific Northwest. Oregon has at least 17 artisan cheesemakers, and Washingon boasts more than 20. Throw in a handful of cheesemakers in Montana, Idaho, and Utah, and there's a whole lot of great cheesemaking going on.

The cheesemaking history in both Oregon and Washington dates back to the 1800s, and some of the most prominent—and award-winning creameries—were founded in the early 1900s. Tillamook, of Tillamook, Oregon, actually started back in 1894 when T.S. Townsend set up the first commercial cheese plant in that area. But the region's dairy roots go back to the 1850s, when farmers would ship their butter to Portland. The first cheesemaking award Tillamook received was in 1904 at the St. Louis World's Fair, and to this day, Tillamook enjoys a great reputation.

Within the past decade or so, artisan dairies in both Washington and Oregon have grown tremendously. There are some pretty big industrial milk operations going on in the Pacific Northwest, too. For example, in eastern Oregon, there are several industrial-size farms, including one, Three Mile Canyon Farms, that has about 15,000 cows. Like California, big dairy seems to coexist with small farmstead operators, both producing some pretty memorable cheeses.

You might not think of Ohio as a huge dairy state, but it has more than a dozen artisan cheesemakers, as well as an active Ohio Farmstead-Artisan Cheese Guild, which promotes Ohio cheese and helps educate new cheesemakers.

Even the South, also not traditionally a dairy region, has the Southern Cheesemakers Guild, featuring about 20 different cheesemakers from everywhere from southern Indiana to Virginia. (North Carolina has the largest concentration of cheesemakers in the South with eight different cheesemakers.) Some of them, such as Capriole, in southern Indiana and close to Louisville, are internationally recognized. Then there are the cheesemakers scattered across the country in regions not necessarily known for cheesemaking. It might be surprising, but there are at least three farmstead goat's milk cheesemakers in Hawaii—on three different islands, Kauai, Maui, and the Big Island or Hawaii. And there's at least one cheesemaker in Alaska.

What this means is that cheesemaking, especially the artisan kind, is growing, and there are a lot of good—sometimes great—cheeses being made in places that have never been known for it before. And that's good news for cheese lovers.

Great American Cheeses

Even excluding the three big cheeses—Wisconsin, California, and Vermont—there are literally hundreds of fine artisan cheesemakers scattered across the United States, and every year more open up shop. Unfortunately, some cheesemakers also close shop every year, but the number of new factories tends to exceed the number of shuttered shops. Here is just a taste of what these innovative cheesemakers have to offer.

One of those innovative—and pioneering—cheesemakers is Caitlin Hunter, of Appleton Creamery. This Maine cheesemaker first developed an interest in dairy goats in 1979, and for the first 15 years, she just made cheese for family and friends. Then, in 1994, she was licensed, and she's been selling fresh and aged chevres ever since. Later on, she started making cheese from the milk of a neighbor's herd of sheep, and she even makes some cow's milk varieties, too. She's particularly known for her chevre buttons, which are marinated in olive oil, rosemary, juniper berries, and hot peppers.

Most cheesemakers don't open creameries right in the middle of a big metropolitan area, but that's exactly what Kurt Dammeier did when he started Beecher's Handmade Cheese in 2003 in Pike's Place Market, right in the middle of Seattle. Dammeier and his cheesemaker, Brad Sinko, turn out some delicious cheddars—especially the Flagship Reserve, which took second runner-up and best aged cheddar in the 2007 ACS Competition.

Dixie and Jake Schneiderer's families have been involved in dairy farming for more than a century. Dixie's ancestors started farming in the 1820s, and Jake's ancestors started raising Jersey cows in the 1860s. In fact, the herd they milk today for their

Buckeye Grove Farm Cheese is descended from that same herd. They make a variety of delectable washed rind cheeses including French Munster, Penn Brick, and Gouda Boeren Kaase.

Judy Schad and her husband, Larry, are also no strangers to awards. Schad has been making goat's milk cheese since 1988, winning the ACS's Best of Show in 1995 for her Wabash Cannonball. The Wabash Cannonball, which is aged for two to four weeks, is an ash-coated, bloomy rind goat's milk cheese that has been internationally acclaimed, setting cheese lovers' hearts all aflutter for its distinctive taste. Equally beloved is her O'Banon, which is wrapped in chestnut leaves and soaked in Kentucky bourbon.

Four Amish goat farms supply all the milk for Firefly Farms creamery in Bittinger, Maryland. Fresh chevres, ash-coated bloomy rinds, and even blue cheeses are made at this family farm. The cheeses boast an array of colors, flavors, and awards.

Leelanau Creamery, located in Blackstar Farm in Suttons Bay, Michigan, has been making Swiss-style cheeses for more than a decade. Cheesemakers John and Anne Hoyt actually met in the Valais region of Switzerland, where they were studying Alpine cheesemaking. Besides their 2007 ACS Best of Show Raclette, they also make a variety of flavored fromage blancs, including one made with Michigan cherries. Not only can you taste the cheese at the farm, but you can also stay there, as it is a working farm, bed and breakfast, stables, winery, and creamery combination.

Maytag isn't just the name of a respected appliance company in Iowa, it's also the name of a distinctively American blue cheese. Fred Maytag, who was president of such appliance company, started Maytag Dairy in 1941. For more than 60 years, Maytag cheesemakers have crafted the blue cheese by hand, aging it in local caves.

Born in France, Pierre-Louis Monteillet met his wife in Mexico, and today they make goat's milk, sheep's milk, and blended-milk cheeses in the Walla Walla Valley in Washington. At Monteillet Fromagerie, they make fresh, bloomy rind and aged varieties, some wrapped in ash, others mixed with herbs, but all quite delicious.

Birgit Halbreiter and her husband, Robert Poland, met at a beer conference and both worked in a brewery, but cheese was in their destiny. The daughter of a master German cheesemaker, Halbreiter had worked for a German cheese company, and she and her husband had experimented with making different cheeses at home for several years. Then, in 2001, armed with three tried-and-tested recipes, they opened MouCo Cheese Company in Fort Collins, Colorado. Today

A Cut Above

Brigit Halbreiter's father, Franz Halbreiter, developed the German bloomy rind blue cheese, Cambazola.

they make two washed rinds, ColoRouge and Affinity, as well as MouCo Blu, a bloomy rind blue.

A trip to Italy led Paula Lambert to fall in love with fresh mozzarella, an affair so passionate that she started the Mozzarella Company in Dallas in 1982. Lambert's interest in other cuisines and her travels abroad led her to expand not only into other cow's milk cheeses such as Crescenza and Oaxaca, but also to start making goat's milk chevres. Lambert is one of the country's leading artisan cheesemakers, reflecting not only her travels but also her native Texas cuisine and culture in her creations.

One of the first sheep dairies in the United States, the Old Chatham Sheepherding Company has quite a following. Not only is it the largest sheep dairy in the country, with more than 1,000 sheep, it also has received several national and international cheese awards. It's most well-known cheese is the Hudson Valley Camembert, made from the milk of both cows and sheep. They also make a Roquefort-style Ewe's blue, fresh ricotta, feta, and darling "Mutton Buttons," or little bloomy rounds of cheese.

Plenty of religious orders preserved cheesemaking in Europe during the Middle Ages, but you don't often hear of modern religious orders making cheese. However, that's exactly what an order of Cistercian nuns do in Crozet, Virginia. Our Lady of Angels Monastery handcrafts 2- and 4-pound wheels of Golden Gouda. By making this sweet, heavenly cheese, these nuns support their little monastery.

The name might suggest otherwise, but it wasn't just fortune smiling that led to the success of Pure Luck Dairy in Texas. Since 1995, this family-run company has been making amazing varieties of goat's milk cheeses. One of its signature cheeses is Del Cielo, a soft-ripened, bloomy rind that has an unctuous and deliciously sweet taste.

Considered by many to make some of the best blue cheese in the country, the Rogue Creamery has historical connections to Kraft, though its cheese is nothing like processed cheese. Rogue Creamery started in 1935 when an immigrant cheesemaker, Thomas Vella, learned from his brother back in Italy that World War II was imminent. Vella predicted that milk used in his Sonoma, California, creamery would be diverted for military uses, and that there might be a need for large quantities of cheese for troops. With the backing of Kraft, Vella purchased a defunct cheese factory in Oregon in 1935, and that was the start. Then, in 1956, Vella spent three months studying cheesemaking in Roquefort, France. The company passed down to Vella's son, Ignacio, and in 2002, Ig selected Cary Bryant and David Gremmels to continue in the tradition. The following year, this duo won the London World Cheese Award for best blue cheese. Ig Vella still makes cheese in Sonoma, California.

Sally Jackson is another Pacific Northwest cheese pioneer. She and her husband, Roger, started making farmstead cheese back in 1979. Sally makes cheese on a wood-burning stove in large stainless-steel pots, and she makes cheese from goat's, sheep's, and cow's milks. Her sheep's milk cheese is wrapped in chestnut and grape leaves that her family and friends gather in the fall. Old-fashioned, flavor-filled, and just exquisite, her cheeses have quite a reputation.

You have to love a creamery that goes by the name of Surfing Goat Dairy. Such a name also might indicate that the cheese is not made in Kansas, and indeed, it's crafted by hand on the island of Maui. The Aloha chevre, made by Eva Maria and Thomas Kafsack, comes in 13 different flavors, including the exotic Mandalay, which is a blend of apple, banana, curry, and chevre. They also make Oyster chevre, which is made with smoked oysters.

The Hawaii Island Goat Dairy doesn't have such a fun name, but cheesemakers Heather and Dick Threlfall have been making goat's milk cheese on the Big Island since 2001. Their cheeses can be found at the Hilo farmer's market on Wednesdays and Saturdays, as well as several local restaurants. Perhaps their most unusual cheese is a guava wood smoked pyramid.

Tillamook, a regional Oregon cheesemaker with deep roots, is known not for blue cheese, but for its fantastic cheddars. It makes a wide array of Monterey Jacks, too. Though one of the larger factories, it nonetheless is quite notable.

The Willamette Valley has become internationally known for its outstanding pinot noirs, but this wine-making region in Oregon is also home to a splendid cheesemaker, the Willamette Valley Cheese Company, run by husband-and-wife team Rod and Melissa Volbeda. Rod spent a year studying cheesemaking in Holland, and after working at Tillamook, he and his wife set up their own dairy in 1992. Today, they make a variety of all-Jersey cow's milk and sheep's milk cheeses, including Gouda, Brindisi Fontina, and even the pinot noir pomace–coated Pinot Crush.

The Least You Need to Know

- Besides the big cheese-producing states, there are also numerous cheesemakers in New York, the Pacific Northwest, and even the South.

- Small but fine cheesemakers operate small factories everywhere from Alaska to Hawaii, from North Carolina to Texas, and just about everyplace in between.

◆ Some creameries such as Rogue Creamery and Tillamook have long histories; others such as Beecher's Handmade Cheese have been operating less than a decade, but all make amazing cheese.

◆ Cheese is made in at least 38 different states, and it wouldn't be surprising to see more artisan cheesemakers set up shop in other states.

Chapter 18

Canadian, Mexican, and Latin American Cheeses

In This Chapter

- Canada's cheesemaking heritage
- The great cheeses of Canada
- A historical account of cheesemaking in Mexico and Latin America
- Popular Mexican and Latin American cheeses

Sandwiching the world's largest cheesemaking country, Canada and Mexico both make some really good, distinctive cheeses, but neither country makes nor consumes huge amounts of cheese. Still, both have interesting cheese-making histories, and the cheeses they do make are quite noteworthy.

Canada, in particular, has some great cheeses and an interesting blend of French and Scandinavian cheesemaking traditions. Not only that, Canada is one of the biggest exporters of cheddar, especially to Great Britain.

Mexico's cheesemaking heritage hails from Spain, but it makes very different cheeses from Spain. Its cheeses are also quite entwined with its rich culinary traditions, and you really can't think about Mexican food and not include cheese in your thoughts. Although many Mexican and Latin American cheeses are similar, there are some very distinct cheeses coming out of Brazil and Argentina. Argentina makes very good Italian-style cheeses, for example.

The History of Cheesemaking in Canada

While the origins of cheesemaking in many countries is a little fuzzy—even the United States doesn't have an exact starting date for cheesemaking—Canada's cheese-making history is rather, though not exactly, specific. It dates back to Samuel de Champlain's introduction of cattle into Quebec in either 1608 or 1610. An explorer and the founder of Quebec City, Samuel de Champlain is also known as "the father of Canada."

As Champlain and others encouraged more French settlers to move to Quebec, they brought with them more cattle, and cheesemaking became an established activity. Cattle from Normandy and Brittany came over in about 1660 and were eventually bred to become the Canadian or Black Jersey breed of bovines. The French settlers made soft-ripened cheeses, and several of the monasteries also made cheese.

Because Quebec and later the rest of Canada shifted hands between the British and the French, Canadian cheese has somewhat of a dual heritage. Tories loyal to the crown during the American Revolution moved up north and brought their cheddaring traditions. These two distinct traditions continued and became established Canadian methods of making cheese.

For much of Canadian history, the cheeses were made in small batches on farms. Despite their small size, Canada first began exporting cheeses in the early 1800s. Things changed and expanded rapidly in 1864, when an enterprising American, Harvey Farrington, opened Canada's very first cheese factory in Norwich, Ontario. That region had already been one of the country's leading producers of butter and cheese by the 1850s, so he took it a step further. Farrington's factory was called the Pioneer Cheese Factory, and he later built four more in the same area. Many business-men followed his lead. In nearby Ingersoll, the Canadian Dairymen's Association was established in 1867. In fact, by 1867, the same year that Canada became a dominion of the British Empire, there were 200 cheese factories in Ontario alone.

That specific region where Farrington set up that factory is known as Oxford County. Oxford County's dairy prowess continued to grow in the late 1800s, and in 1866, a group of cheesemakers led by James Harris created a mammoth cheese, weighing about 7,300 pounds, which was an attraction at the New York State Fair. Today, Oxford County is known as the "dairy capital of Canada."

A Cut Above

The dairy capital of Canada was also home to James McIntyre, known as the "best of Canada's worst poets." Circa 1866, this poet for the common man penned a great little ditty titled "Ode on the Mammoth Cheese." Perhaps the most memorable lines of the poem are "We have seen the Queen of cheese, Laying quietly at your ease, Gently fanned by evening breeze, Thy fair form no flies dare seize." There's an annual James McIntyre poetry contest for Oxford residents, and for a short time contest organizers also held a dairy ode contest.

Cheesemaking not only grew in Ontario, but it also expanded where it all started, in Quebec. In 1865, the first cheese factory was built in Quebec, in Dunham. But more importantly, in 1881, Edouard-Andre Barnard cleaned out his barn, whitewashed its walls, and installed a cheese vat, thus setting up not only the first cheesemaking school in Canada but the first in North America, in Saint-Denis-de-Kamouraska, Quebec.

Another dairy and cheese school opened in 1892 in Saint-Hyacinthe, Quebec, and is still around today. In fact, the Saint-Hyacinthe Food Research and Development Centre is considered the chief center for dairy research and innovation in Canada.

Also in 1892, a group of monks who settled in Quebec created a new, washed rind cheese similar to the very French Port du Salut. This Canadian original was called Oka cheese, and it was aged on cypress wood planks from South Carolina. The wood addressed a special need in the curing of the cheese, as it would absorb excess humidity while restoring moisture to the cheese when needed. The cheese, which was made by Marie-Alphonse Juin, was named for the monastery where it was created: the Oka Cistercian Trappist Monastery in Oka, Quebec. The year the monastery's cheese made its debut it won first prize at the Montreal Exhibition, and it again won first prize the next year at the Quebec Exhibition.

Canada became one of the first countries to implement pasteurization, and it also was one of the first to set up strict sanitation laws in milk processing and cheesemaking. Canada also continued in its "mammoth" tradition, and in 1893, for the World's Fair in Chicago, 12 cheese factories in Ontario banded together to meet a challenge thrown down by the government's department of agriculture: create the world's largest cheese.

That super-mammoth cheddar weighed 22,000 pounds, stood 6 feet high and was 28 feet in circumference. Ten thousand cows had to be milked for three days to create enough milk to make that cheese, which became known as "Le Fromage Elephant."

It was so large it had to be created in a Canadian Pacific freight shed, and it drew crowds at every train stop on its journey to Chicago. As soon as it arrived at the fair, it crashed through the floor.

In the early 1900s, a certain Canadian immigrated to Chicago and not only started what is perhaps the most well-known cheese dynasty on the planet, but changed cheese history as we know it. J.L. Kraft, a savvy cheese marketer, started his wholesale business of buying cheese and reselling it in 1903. In 1915, however, he revolutionized the cheese world with his method of processing cheese. Kraft didn't forget his native land, as he also brought his processed wonders to Canada. To this day in Canada, folks refer to boxed macaroni and cheese as "Kraft dinner," even if they're using a generic brand.

> **A Cut Above**
>
> While specialty cheese did not become widespread until after World War II, the dairy school in Saint-Hyacinthe experimented with Canadian Camembert and feta in 1901. Those experiments tanked with the general Canadian population, who weren't ready for such foreign tastes.

By the early 1900s, there were more than 2,000 cheese factories in Ontario and Quebec, and cheesemaking operations continued to grow, reaching a high of 2,300 cheese factories and 570 combined cheese and butter factories. Much of this cheese, especially cheddar, was exported, and a lot of it headed to Great Britain.

After World War II, Canada saw an influx of European immigrants who brought with them cravings for more exotic cheeses like feta, Edam, and Parmigiano-Reggiano. So Canada imported master cheesemakers to satisfy their hungers. The twentieth century not only saw the launch of processed cheese in Canada, but it also saw greater variations in kinds of cheese, as well as methods of making cheese. Factories were consolidated, and today most cheese is made in larger factories. In 1973, factory at Notre-Dame-du-Bon-Conseil in Quebec was the largest cheese factory in the world when it opened, as it made about 100 tons of cheese every day.

Although factory methods of making cheese are quite widespread, some of the cheeses yielded are of extremely high quality, and recently several Canadian cheeses are winning awards on the international stage. There are also some artisan or farmstead cheesemakers popping up.

Canadian Cheeses

Cheese is made throughout Canada, but the biggest cheese-producing provinces remain Ontario and Quebec. Cheddar remains the number-one cheese produced in

Canada, accounting for at least 55 percent of the total production of cheese in the country. Canadian cheddar, especially those varieties made in Quebec, are rather similar to cheddars made in Vermont or New York State. Almost all are white cheddars, and they have a bit drier curd than a Wisconsin or Californian cheddar. They are delicious, and quite a few Canadian cheese companies export their cheddar to the United States.

Black Diamond is Canada's biggest cheddar manufacturer, with a wide variety of cheddars from light and mild cheeses to the extra aged cheddars. They also make processed cheese. Black Diamond is owned by Parmalat, which is headquartered in Toronto, Ontario. Parmalat also owns Balderson, another cheddar maker, and Lactantia, which makes cheddars, cream cheeses, and several other milk products.

Besides cheddar, Quebec cheesemakers make a lot of French-style cheeses, from bries to washed rinds, as well as both fresh and bloomy rind goat's cheeses. One of the big European-style cheese companies is Damafro, which manufactures that whole spectrum. In recent years, Damafro purchased Tournevent, an artisan cheesemaker known for its superb fresh and aged chevres.

Another great French-style manufacturer, but smaller, is La Vache a Maillotte in La Sarre, Quebec. This small factory makes a mix of sheep's milk and cow's milk cheeses, including Allegretto, a firm sheep's milk cheese with a subtle yet not too soft flavor, as well as the washed rind cow's milk cheeses La Sonatine and La Farondole. All of La Vache's cheeses are made from the milk of very specific herds of cows or sheep in order to produce the flavors they are seeking.

A Cut Above

The Quebecois have a unique cheese dish called *poutine*. Poutine is made with french fries, fresh cheese curds, and brown gravy. In some rather upscale places, poutine is elevated with the addition of fois gras.

Besides French-style cheeses, one of the big cheeses made in Quebec is Oka, which was produced by those Trappist monks for 75 years. Today, the washed rind cheese is made by a company that the monks license, but the wheels of cheese are still aged in the monastery's cellars. Oka can be made from both pasteurized and unpasteurized milk, and it has two different varieties: regular, which is aged for 30 days, and classic, which is aged for 60 days. It has a fresh, mellow, nutty flavor with hints of fruits and butter, and it has a smooth, creamy texture.

Other monks in Quebec produce cheese, including the Benedictine monks at the Saint-Benoit-du-Lac Monastery. These Benedictines have been making cheese since

1943, and perhaps their most famous cheese is Bleu L'Ermite. Today, these monks produce more than a dozen different cheeses including their original blue, which today is one of Canada's most famous blues.

Moonstruck Organic Cheese Company, based in Salt Spring Island, British Columbia, makes several different organic cheeses from its all-Jersey herd of cattle, including a line of blues. Its blue cheeses include: Blossom's Blue, Baby Blue, Blue Moon, and Beddis Blue—all original, artisan cheeses.

British Columbia is actually home to more than a dozen different artisan cheesemakers who craft everything from cow's milk cheeses to goat's and sheep's milk varieties to even water buffalo. Besides Moonstruck, another great one to check out is Carmelis Goat Cheese, in Kelawna, British Columbia. Carmelis is an artisan goat's milk cheesemaker who makes some incredible bloomy rind varieties, goat's milk fetas, fresh chevres, as well as even some goat's milk yogurt and gelato.

One of the newest kids on the Canadian artisan block is Fifth Town Artisan Cheese Company in Picton, Ontario. This sustainable, green company in Prince Edward County combines modern technology—green architecture, sustainable energy—with age-old artisan cheesemaking techniques. It just opened its doors in the fall of 2007, and makes a handful of handcrafted goat's milk and sheep's milk cheeses of both the fresh and bloomy-rinded varieties. Besides cheese, they also acquired the publishing rights of Ontario's cheesy poet, James McIntyre, and they have republished his laudatory dairy book, *Oh! Queen of Cheese* (1979).

The History of Cheesemaking in Mexico and Latin America

Though civilizations in Mexico and Latin America date back thousands of years, cheese production only started after the Spanish conquistadors went a' conquering. In 1521, Hernan Cortes and his armies began their final assault on conquering Mexico. Not only did they conquer the native peoples, they brought their culinary traditions. Spanish monks followed, bringing their cheesemaking skills as well as cattle, goats, and sheep. They also—along with the Portuguese—spread cheesemaking to the rest of Central and South America. Justo Sierra, a Mexican educator, summed up their impact this way: "The grocer, not the conquistador, is the real Spanish father of Mexican society."

The first cheeses may have been made by monks, but the monks taught farmers, and for several centuries, cheesemaking remained completely regional and farmstead operations, and distinct cheeses from Spain evolved. Up until the twentieth century, cheesemaking was basically farmstead, but gradually more and more factories have opened, and the diversity of cheeses being made in Mexico and Latin America has grown tremendously. Argentina, for example, makes and exports a variety of Italian-style grana cheeses. But in many rural regions, cheesemaking occurs in sometimes primitive and not always hygienic conditions. That means that there's a real distinct mix of high-quality and low-quality cheeses.

Stinky Cheese

In recent years, some people have smuggled Mexican cheeses across the border in both the United States and Canada, and sometimes these cheeses have caused salmonella and listeria outbreaks. There also have been illegal cheesemaking or "bathtub cheese" operations of Mexican cheese that have been shut down in several places, including California and Illinois. As a rule, it's not a good idea to buy cheese that isn't made by a USDA–certified cheesemaker or to purchase cheese off the street.

The Cheeses of Mexico and Latin America

There's a rather diverse array of Latin American and Mexican cheeses, and sometimes confusion arises because there is no uniform naming system and some cheesemakers call the same cheese by different names.

The most popular cheese in Mexico and Latin America is *queso blanco*, which means "white cheese." Made from skimmed cow's milk, it used to be coagulated with citrus juice, but today is usually made with rennet. It's sort of a cross between cottage cheese and mozzarella. Though it becomes soft when it is cooked, it doesn't melt. It's often crumbled over regional dishes.

Another popular cheese is *queso fresco* or "fresh cheese." It sometimes has been made with a combination of cow's and goat's milks, and it's similar to a farmer's cheese. Crumbly and slightly acidic and salty, it's used as a topping or filling. When it's sold in larger pieces, it's called *adobera*. An aged version of queso fresco is called *queso anejo* or "old cheese." But calling it aged is a misnomer, as it's aged for a period of extra weeks, not months.

Another popular cheese is *queso panela*, also known as *queso de canasta* or "basket cheese" because it has an imprint of the basket in which it is molded. It tastes similar to a fresh mozzarella, but it doesn't melt like mozzarella.

Queso Oaxaca, also known as *quesillo*, is the cheese most commonly used to fill quesadillas. Oaxaca cheese is a stretched-curd cheese that originated in Oaxaca, Mexico, and it's a Mexican version of string cheese.

Queso asadero, which means "well done" or "aged," is a melting cheese similar to provolone in taste. It's an incredible melting cheese often used in making Mexican fondue or *fundido*.

Queso chihuahua or *queso menonita* was first made by the Mennonite communities who lived in northern Mexico. It is not white like most Mexican cheeses, but instead it boasts a pale yellow color. It is similar to Gouda, and it can be mild or very sharp.

A Cut Above

Many traditional Mexican cheeses are made in California and Wisconsin, and the United States is the biggest exporter of cheese to Mexico, exporting a record 35,084 metric tons of cheese to Mexico in 2006.

Queso cotija is named after the town of Cotija where it was first made. It is a firm and very salty cheese that could be described as feta-like. It can be crumbled or grated, and it's often used as a condiment with soups, salads, and beans. *Cotija anejo* is an aged version of the cheese.

Queso Requeson, which means "curd" or "cream cheese," is a ricotta-like cheese used as a filling in tamales, enchiladas, and other dishes. A fresh cheese, it has a soft, grainy texture and very milky taste.

The Least You Need to Know

◆ Most Canadian cheese is made in large factories, and most cheese in Canada is made in Ontario and Quebec.

◆ Canada has a mixed French and English cheesemaking heritage, but today, the most popular cheese made and exported from Canada is Canadian cheddar.

◆ Oka is a Canadian original washed rind cheese, similar to Port du Salut, made first by monks in Quebec.

◆ Spanish conquistadors introduced Mexico and Latin America to cheesemaking.

◆ The most popular Mexican cheese is queso blanco.

Chapter 19

Australian, New Zealand, and Other Unexpected Cheeses

In This Chapter

- ◆ The history of cheesemaking in Australia
- ◆ The cheesemaking heritage of New Zealand
- ◆ Popular Australian and New Zealand cheeses
- ◆ The history and cheeses of India, South Africa, and Japan

Australia and New Zealand came to the dairy table a bit later than a lot of other big dairy nations, but both the Kiwis and the Aussies have made up for lost time. Today, they rank among the world's top 10 dairy producers, much of it cheese, and much of it exported everywhere from Great Britain and the United States to all over Asia and South America.

Cheesemaking started as a farmstead endeavor by the first European settlers in the eighteenth century in both Australia and New Zealand, but by the middle of the nineteenth century, dairy cooperatives were formed, thus beginning the modern dairy industry. The most popular cheese produced in both countries is, not surprisingly, cheddar.

While the dairy scene in both countries is heavily dominated by large conglomerate companies, including some of the world's largest dairy plants, farmhouse traditions are being revived, and today both countries not only produce bulk cheese, but some absolutely amazing world-class originals and extremely well-done European varieties.

Though you may not associate cheese with South Africa, Japan, or India, all three of these unlikely dairy countries do have a thriving dairy industry. Cheese is an important part of Indian cuisine; Japan is perhaps the most dairy-interested country in Asia; and South Africa makes a wide variety of good European-style cheeses and is now developing newer cheese varieties. Each of these countries is producing if not world-renowned cheeses, some very, very good cheeses, and they all are countries to watch in regards to new dairy developments.

Australia's Cheesemaking Origins

The original Aborigines in Australia didn't make cheese. Cheesemaking as an endeavor didn't begin in Australia until European settlers came in the late 1700s. Those settlers brought sheep, goats, and cows, and they made cheeses on their farms. Most likely these first cheeses were of the English cheddar or Cheshire varieties, made in crude, handmade presses which were crafted from tree branches, tree stumps, and large rocks.

As the different herds of animals grew during the 1800s, farmers gradually formed dairy cooperatives. The first cooperatives were set up on the north coast of New South Wales, southern Queensland, the Gippland area, and the western part of Victoria. The dairy industry spread to other areas of Australia, including South Australia's extremely fertile Adelaide Hills region.

A Cut Above

Bega, Australia's biggest dairy today, makes Australia's most popular cheese, Tasty Cheese. Tasty Cheese is a variety of Australian cheddar. Bega makes not only the famous Tasty, but also Mild, Extra Tasty, and Strong 'n Bitey Vintage cheeses. A mountain climber even took Tasty Cheese with him to the top of Mount Everest in the late 1980s.

By the 1840s, dairy had really grown, and some farming entrepreneurs had even begun to export cheese and butter to areas of India and southeast Asia. The 1880s led to the introduction of more scientific know-how into the dairy industry, and machine technology had begun to be implemented in the milking of animals and the production of cheese and butter. Those changes, coupled with the growth and expansion of dairy cooperatives, caused the dairy industry to grow at a rather rapid pace. Australia's biggest cheese producer, Bega, started in 1860 with some smaller farmers who were making cheddar. In 1899, the Bega Cooperative Creamery Company was officially formed.

The Australian government got more involved in the dairy industry during World War II, setting pricing and hygiene standards. Australia—and New Zealand—have perhaps some of the toughest standards on hygiene, and no local cheese factories can make any raw milk cheeses; in fact, very few nonpasteurized milk cheeses can even be imported into Australia or New Zealand. Government involvement in the dairy industry solidified dairy cooperatives, and larger and larger dairy cooperatives were formed, setting the precedent of factory-produced cheeses and other dairy products.

Along the way, Australians also began making non-English vintages of cheese. This began in the early 1930s when the first Greek, Italian, and Slavic immigrants began flocking to Australia. As cheese was part of their native cuisines, it didn't take long for cheese manufacturers to realize there was a market for more unusual varieties of cheese. Also, European cheesemakers made their way to Australia, as more and more immigrants continued to move to Australia through the 1950s, '60s, and '70s.

A Cut Above

A signature Australian food—Vegemite, a yeast extract protein spread—was created in Australia by a scientist at a cheese company. The cheese was created by Dr. Cyril P. Callister at the Fred Walker Cheese Company. But Vegemite didn't really take hold in Australian households until 1935, when Walker used the success of his joint venture making processed cheese (with Kraft in the Kraft Walker Cheese Co.) to promote Vegemite.

One of the most renowned specialty cheese factories is Lactos. Milan Vhnalek, a Czech immigrant, set up the Lactos cheese factory in Tasmania in 1955. The first cheese he made was called Romadur, a soft-ripened cheese. More than half a century later, Lactos has grown and expanded, and several other competitors have also set up shop, feeding the Australian and international markets' hunger for specialty cheeses. This growth can be seen in the sheer number of cheeses produced in Australia. In the 1960s, there were really only about 20 different kinds of cheeses. By 1970, that had more than doubled to over 40, then 50 by the mid-1980s. Today, there are more than 100 different kinds of cheese made in Australia.

Growth and change in the dairy industry continues to this day. Despite the removal of government subsidies and deregulation of milk prices in recent years, production continues to increase, and it's up 75 percent higher than it was 15 years ago. In fact, more than 17,000 tons of Australian cheese were exported in 2006.

Even though the focus is on big factory cheeses, there are more than a few fine farmstead cheesemakers. Coinciding with the explosive growth in Australia's fine wine industry is the rise of the farmstead cheese producers. Still very small, the farmstead producers make a variety of interesting cheeses from a variety of milks, including buffalo's milk.

Farmstead and specialty cheese has taken hold so much in Australia that author and cheese guru Will Studd started *Cheese Slices*, a cheese-focused television show on Australian cable television that features notable Australian cheesemakers, and the host travels the globe in search of great cheese. That show, which began in 2005, is now in its fourth season, and it is shown all over the globe and on some international flights. (Unfortunately, it is not yet available in the United States except through some DVDs.)

The History of Cheesemaking in New Zealand

New Zealand's first tribal settlers, the Maoris, didn't raise any mammals for meat or milk. In fact, they didn't find any indigenous mammals on the islands so they really only ate birds, fish, and plants. The islands' first British settlers, who arrived in the late eighteenth century, brought cattle with them. The actual official start of the dairy industry occurred in 1814, when the English Christian missionary Samuel Marsden brought in a bull and two heifers as a gift.

That tiny herd started what would become one of New Zealand's biggest economies. To accommodate cattle, forests had to be hacked and burned, and that's just what the earlier European settlers did. Sheep and goats were also imported, but the sheep were (and still are) primarily used for wool and meat. Today, New Zealand has more sheep than people.

Dairy cooperatives were set up to better manage production, and the 1840s saw the very first exports of cheese. The initial export, of cheddar, happened in 1846, and it was sent to Australia. Other exports to England soon followed, and cheese production branched out into the realm of blue cheeses, too. The growth of the dairy industry in New Zealand followed the British occupation and eventual conquest of the islands. In 1840, Britain began setting up settlements in earnest, and battles for land ensued until 1872 when the British declared victory over the native Maoris. Despite the conflicts of that time period, dairy farmers continued to cultivate cattle and produce cheese.

The first refrigerated shipment of meat and butter from New Zealand to England followed, and because perishables could be better shipped, cheese production also increased. By the early 1900s, most of New Zealand's dairy production centered around cooperative factories, and a lot of it was exported. New Zealand's exported dairy goods boosted the local economy, and in 1907, the value of cheese exported just to London was 662,000 pounds.

In 1923, New Zealand's first dairy board was established, and the government took over export marketing in 1935. New Zealand cheddar was especially important to Great Britain during World War II when rationing cut into local supplies. But in 1947, a Dairy Products Marketing Commission was set up so that the government and farmers could both have a say in marketing dairy products abroad. In the 1960s, New Zealand dairy cooperatives began to diversify their cheese offerings for both local and especially international markets. Cheese factories continued to grow in size and output from the 1960s to the 1980s, and today, some of the world's largest and most efficient dairy factories are established in New Zealand.

A Cut Above

Just as most Americans can probably recite a Kraft jingle or two, many folks in New Zealand can recite the Chesdale song. Two dancing cartoon farmers, Ches and Dale, espouse the virtues of cheese. "Chesdale, slices thinly, never crumbles. There's no waste. And, boy, it's got a mighty taste. It's finest cheddar, made better!"

As a general rule, bigger was considered better, but in the 1980s, smaller and farmstead producers made a comeback—in a big way. Ross McCallum was perhaps the first. McCallum started his company, Kapiti Cheese, in 1985, with the goal of producing original New Zealand cheeses, not imitations of European cheeses. McCallum honored New Zealand history by christening his cheeses with traditional Maori names, and he was instrumental in encouraging New Zealanders to take pride in locally produced cheeses. Today, Kapiti produces more than 50 different cheeses. McCallum's once little company was also instrumental in introducing New Zealand (remember: more sheep than people) to the wonders of sheep's milk cheeses. In 1990, his Hipi Iti sheep's milk, feta-inspired cheese was perhaps the first New Zealand cheese made out of sheep's milk.

In the 1980s, New Zealand also saw an influx of Dutch cheesemakers who recreated traditional Goudas and Edams, adding to the diversity of New Zealand's cheeses. Some large factories actually began mass production of Camembert and Brie-like cheeses, and a few of them even introduced fresh chevres to the New Zealand market.

Another interesting occurrence happened in the New Zealand dairy industry in the 1980s: in 1984, the New Zealand government eliminated farming subsidies.

As a result, farm profits actually increased. In 2003, the New Zealand Specialist Cheesemakers formed their own organization, the result of 20 years of working together informally. Today, this organization has more than 20 different cheesemakers as members.

> **A Cut Above**
>
> New Zealand is at the forefront of cloning cows. In fact, New Zealand scientists have cloned enough cows to make the first genetically modified milk. Could genetically modified cheese be that far behind?

The dairy industry in New Zealand remains the country's largest single industry, with both large factories and small farmstead producers making a variety of delicious cheeses. New Zealand continues to be a very agricultural country, with virtually the same percentage of its population employed in agriculture today as there was three decades ago, and the exact same rural population as it did in 1920.

Cheeses from Down Under and New Zealand

Australia and New Zealand are such big dairy and cheese producers, it's hard to narrow down all of the choices, but here is a selection of some of the best. Some of the cheeses are made by rather large or industrial factories and others are crafted by hand in small production facilities.

As cheddar is their most popular cheese, here are a couple of varieties worth trying. The first would be King Island Dairy Black Label Cloth-Wrapped cheddar, which is made, not surprisingly, on King Island. (South of Melbourne, it is one of the few remains of a land bridge that once linked Tasmania to Australia's mainland.) All the cows who live on King Island benefit from the bucolic pollution- and chemical-free environs, and the cheddar, which is aged for a minimum of six months, has a sweet, nutty flavor.

> **A Cut Above**
>
> There are plenty of cheese contests around the globe, and New Zealand and Australia boast a few notable ones. In New Zealand, the New Zealand Cheese Awards were started in 1993 to raise the profiles of New Zealand's fine cheeses. In Australia, one of the biggest competitions is the Australian Grand Dairy Awards.

Another notable Australian cheddar is Pyengana cheddar, which is made in Tasmania. The cheddar is made using intensive handcrafting methods, and the resulting year-old cheese is nutty, rich, and boasts a depth of flavor.

One of the best New Zealand cheddars is Barry's Bay cheddar, made in the Banks Peninsula on the South Island. Cheddar has been made in this region since 1844, and by the 1890s there were nine dairy and cheese factories in the region. Barry's Bay is the only one around today, and they still make amazing traditional cloth-bound cheddars, the only ones in the country. This cheddar is aged from six months to three years, and as it ages, the flavor intensifies and develops a delicious rich taste.

One of the best Swiss-style cheeses made in Australia is the Heidi Gruyère, made by Lactos in Tasmania. This delicious Gruyère has a sweet, fruity, yet nutty taste that just improves over time. It's made by a cheesemaker who was born in Switzerland, and the cows are naturally grazed.

Some terrific blue cheeses come out of both Australia and New Zealand. One of them, made by King Island, is called Roaring 40's Blue. This blue has a creamy texture and a sharp yet buttery taste, and it pairs beautifully with Australian shiraz vintages.

Some other notable blues are made by the small Milawa Cheese Company in Victoria. They make the Milawa blue, more of a mild blue, as well as an aged version of Milawa blue, which is aged for a minimum of six months. Both Milawa blues are made from cow's milk, but they also make a goat's milk blue called Mt. Buffalo, which is a rather creamy blue.

Ferndale Dairies, which is part of the large conglomerate Mainland Group, makes a delightful Blue de Montagne. This smooth and creamy blue has a pronounced and spicy tang.

One of the very first New Zealand blue cheeses was Blue Vein, launched in 1951 by the NZ Rennet Company. To celebrate Blue Vein's fortieth anniversary, the company launched Jubilee Blue, which has an almost Brie-like texture, a delicate aroma, and a buttery taste.

Besides blues, both Australia and New Zealand make a variety of soft-ripened cheeses. Timboon Brie is made by Timboon Farmhouse Cheeses, and is crafted by hand in Victoria. It has a greater depth of flavor than many Australian Bries as it's made with organic milk, and the cheese doesn't have any stabilizers added so it's quite luscious.

Two good New Zealand Bries are made by Te Mata Cheese in Havelock North. Kidnappers is a traditional Brie, while Pania is a vine ash–rubbed Brie. Both are delicious, and they're made by cheesemakers who also happen to be winemakers.

Another good New Zealand Brie is made by Kapiti, and Kapiti's Brie is called *Aorangi*, which means "white cloud" in Maori. Kapiti also makes French International Choice French Brie, a double-cream version.

Kapiti, which is based in Wellington, also makes a wide array of Brie-like cheeses and Dutch and Swiss styles, and also works with a variety of milks. In 1990, it introduced New Zealand to sheep's milk cheeses with *Hipi Iti*, which means "little sheep" in Maori. Hipi Iti is fresh, feta-style cheese that is slightly salty and definitely citrusy. Hipi Iti is packed with herbs in jars of oil.

Both Australia and New Zealand also make some notable goat's milk cheeses. The Yarra Valley Pyramid, made in Victoria, is a farmhouse goat's milk cheese that comes covered in ash or plain. This cheese is melt-in-your-mouth smooth and slightly acidic.

Kapiti Cheese, not surprisingly, makes a great soft-rinded goat's log called Sainte-Maure. Velvety smooth, Sainte-Maure is both nutty and sweet, with loads of flavor.

One of the most unusual cheeses in Australia is a fresh mozzarella made with the milk of water buffalos. Purrumbete mozzarella began in 1996, after Roger Haldane's successful campaign to import water buffalos from southern Italy to Australia. Haldane hired a cheesemaker who studied in Italy to learn the correct process of making fresh Mozzarella di bufala, and the result is a delicious and authentic cheese.

The Cheesemaking Origins and Cheeses of South Africa

Most of the cheeses in Africa are made by nomads, though international cheese consultants have been working with several nations to develop better and more distinct cheeses. Perhaps the most cheese-centric country on the continent would be South Africa, due to the European immigrants who brought their hunger for Gouda and cheddar cheeses. Though South Africans hanker for hunks of cheddar more than ever before, as consumption of cheese has nearly doubled since 1995, South Africans only eat about 6 pounds of cheese per person per year (way below what Americans, French, and Greeks eat).

Much of the cheese in South Africa is made in 12 large factories. However, there are a growing number of farmstead producers. Cheese is made throughout South Africa, but the big cheese region is Western Cape, which makes more than 50 percent of all cheese in South Africa.

To increase quality and awareness, the South African Dairy Championships and the South African Cheese Festival promote local cheeses. Several producers also compete on an international level, and some South African cheeses are exported to other African countries and to Asia.

One cheesemaker who has won international awards is Chrissie Brisco, of Chrissie's Country Cheese, in Natal. This farmstead cheesemaker makes English-style cheeses, including cheddar, Sage Derby, and Leicester.

Another award-winning South African cheesemaker is Fairview Estate in Paarl, which makes a variety of soft-ripened cheeses, including a soft, Brie-like blue cheese.

A larger but also quite notable and award-winning producer is Lancewood Cheese in George. This dairy factory, started in 1996, makes a variety of soft, hard, and creamy cheeses, including cheddar, Gouda, cottage cheese, and mascarpone.

As several South African cheesemakers have their sights set on improving quality and exporting more cheese, it probably won't be long before some of this country's fine cheeses make their way to the United States.

India and Paneer

Milk consumption in India is growing, and as a result, desire for cheese is also growing. But currently, though there are some European-style cheeses being made in India, the most popular is India's native paneer.

Paneer (sometimes spelled panir), is a fresh, nonrennet cheese similar to unsalted, pressed ricotta. It's one of the only native Indian cheeses and is basically made from buttermilk or yogurt; then vinegar or citrus juice (usually lime or lemon) is added to curdle it. It's a very fresh cheese, and it's used quite often in Indian cuisine. One American cheesemaker, Cowgirl Creamery in California, makes a delicious farmhouse version.

Indians might not eat as much cheese as other peoples across the globe, but they do eat quite a bit of yogurt, one of the staples in their diet.

A Cut Above

Though similar to cheese, yogurt is not quite the same. This fermented dairy product is made from two bacteria cultures, *lactobacillus bulgaricus* and *streptococcus thermophilus*, which are either added to milk or introduced after pasteurization. Unlike cheese, the whey isn't separated out of yogurt, and that's one of the main differences between yogurt and fresh cheese; also, rennet or curdling agents aren't added to yogurt.

A Few Words About Japan and Cheese

Whether it's coffee, wine, or cheese, the Japanese have a hunger for new and exotic tastes. So much that Japan actually has a very active dairy industry. Most of Japan's cheese and dairy products are made on the northern island of Hokkaido. The country's first cheese factory was Seiraku Hanbai Kumiai (forerunner of Snow Brand Milk Products), which opened in 1933.

One native Japanese cheese is Sakura cheese. *Sakura*, which means "cherry blossom" in Japanese, is a soft cream cheese that is flavored with cherry leaves.

Most cheeses are manufactured at big factories, but there's at least one group of farmstead cheesemakers in Hokkaido, a group of female cheesemakers who call themselves the Milky Ladies Group.

Most Japanese cheeses are created for domestic consumption, but Japan remains a great market for other countries that export or are seeking to export their cheeses. Also, as Japan is known for such advancements in technology, it's not hard to speculate they might also soon make an imprint on the international dairy industry.

The Least You Need to Know

- Most cheese producers in Australia and New Zealand are large companies, but both countries have experienced a renewed farmstead cheese industry that continues to grow.

- Cheese is mostly made from cow's milk in Australia and New Zealand, but goat's milk, sheep's milk, and even water buffalo's milk are also used, creating a variety of European-style cheeses and original creations.

- The South African cheese industry continues to grow, and it's only a matter of time before its best cheeses reach the United States.

- The number-one cheese consumed and produced in India is paneer, a fresh, non-rennet cheese.

- Most cheese made in Japan is crafted on the northern island of Hokkaido.

Part 4
Shopping and Enjoying Cheese

Wow. We've covered a lot of ground, and by now, we know what cheeses are out there, and if we haven't tried them yet, we're more than ready to taste them.

This is the most practical part of the book, where the pedal meets the metal, so to speak. Now that we have the knowledge about cheese, this is where we can put it into practice. It's where we will learn how to shop for cheese, store cheese once we've got it home, pair cheese with food and beverages, cook with cheese, and even make some simple cheeses in our own kitchens.

This part will teach you how to get the most out of your cheese, so grab a cheese knife—or plane—and get tasting. Happy munchings.

Chapter 20

Shopping for Cheese

In This Chapter

- How to discern a good cheesemonger
- How to pick out cheese at a store
- Finding good cheese at bad stores
- Reading labels
- Shopping for cheese outside grocery stores

Finding good cheese is worth the trouble, and finding a good, knowledgeable cheesemonger is essential if you love cheese. It's like finding a knowledgeable wine seller or liquor store owner if you love wine—you can pick out some decent bottles by yourself, but if your purveyor loves what he or she is selling, he or she will be able to introduce you to new loves you didn't know you were missing.

Right now, it seems that just about every big box grocery store and commodity store sells gourmet cheese. But just because they're selling it doesn't mean that they know what they're doing. Plenty of mediocre stores mangle amazing cheeses—it happens enough to make me cry. And even good gourmet stores may still not know how to care for their cheeses properly. Jeanette can think of a certain local grocery store where she regularly shops, but where she won't purchase cheese. Although she loves this store, they treated a half-wheel of Humboldt Fog so badly that it brought tears to her eyes.

So rather than crying about spilled milk or mishandled cheese, a little know-how not only helps you navigate stores, it helps you traverse the cheese shelves within stores as well. An educated consumer is a happier consumer, and who doesn't want to be happy?

What to Look for in a Cheese Store

Practically every store—even the little 24-hour groceries—carries cheese. And plenty of stores carry "gourmet" or "artisan" cheeses. But not every store is created equal. Not every deli or cheese counter orders cheese direct from producers, and not every store has an educated staff who can help you decide between a Brie and a Brillat-Savarin. There are, however, plenty of great stores and cheese purveyors if you know where and how to spot them.

When selecting a cheese store, pretend you're a detective, coming in to check out the circumstantial evidence or how the shop is caring for its cheeses. First, look at how the shop displays its cheese. Does it have a cheese counter, or are most of its cheeses—even gourmet cheeses—plastic-wrapped in pieces, already priced for sale?

A good cheesemonger will have a cheese counter—a gorgeous, refrigerated case where you will see wheels and half-wheels and quarter-wheels of cheese. The cheeses will look good. The cheeses will look organized. Different cheese counters might organize cheeses differently—by region, by milk, and so on—but they will have an organization system that is either easily discernable or easily explained.

Free Samples

Most importantly, though, if you point to a blue and ask what it is and where it came from, the person behind the counter will not only be able to answer your questions, he or she will offer you a sample.

Samples—and not the kind just stuck under a cheese dome and left to sit there all day—are a sure sign of a good store. A good cheesemonger will want customers to try his or her cheese. He or she will have nothing to hide and will actively encourage people to try the cheese. It's a pretty basic concept, but it's a good sign if someone encourages sampling.

When you sample a cheese or two or more, watch to see how the cheesemonger handles your samples. Do they use a fresh knife or plane when offering samples? What do they say to you when you ask for samples? What is their attitude? You can tell a lot about a store and its staff by how they handle sampling. A good cheesemonger will also not serve you a cheese if it has gone beyond its optimum freshness. A good cheesemonger not only has a good cheese counter, but also carries all the accoutrements you'd want for a cheese plate. This is the kind of store that knows a chutney from a jam, and probably has a selection of olives, too. The store also probably sells some great cutting boards, fondue sets, and knives. In short, a great cheesemonger will have not only cheese, but everything else you'd want to go with your cheese, too.

In the Know

Sampling not only will let you see if the cheese passes muster, but it's also a good way to interact with the store owner or employees. Good stores have owners and employees who are knowledgeable and enthusiastic about their products. They may not know everything about them, but they like answering questions, and when they don't know answers, they will share your curiosity and get them for you. Jeanette's personal favorite stores are the ones where a manager or employee not only bends over backward to assist her, but they actually take the time to call her when they find the answers she's looking for.

The store's manager, owner, and employees will all take the time to get to know you and your personal cheese preferences. This kind of store will also alert you when your favorite chevre comes in season, and it will also probably host tasting events or other cheese-related festivities from time to time.

In talking with a store's staff, find out how many cheeses they typically carry at one time and how often they receive cheese shipments. If you are really into cheese, you will want to go to a store that carries a lot of cheeses. For Jeanette, 50 is a good number of cheeses. But quantity is not the same as quality, and some very fine little shops carry only 20 or so cheeses, but they carry them well.

Unless the store just specializes in imports or American artisans, a good store will likely carry a mix of both. A good cheesemonger will also be able to speak intelligently about cheese trends, and he or she will not only be able to talk about his or her distributors, but will also be able to talk directly about the cheesemakers themselves.

A Cut Above _____

And while it's not a guarantee, membership in the American Cheese Society or participation in different cheese events is a sign that the store's owner, manager, or employees are into cheese. A sure sign that the store's manager, owner, or employees *don't* know cheese is if they look dumbstruck at the very mention of the American Cheese Society.

A good cheese store's employees will also, more importantly, be able to speak intelligently about the cheeses that store sells. They will know when they got that Brie in, and they will know when it's getting to the end of its delicious life cycle. They will be able to tell you, "Yes, we still have X brand of cheese, but it's getting to be a bit strong."

Lastly, a good cheesemonger knows what he or she doesn't know, and if you happened to discover a new favorite while traveling, he or she will try to find out more about that cheese for you. A good cheesemonger is always thirsting for more knowledge about cheese because there's always more to know. And learning about cheese can almost be as addicting as the cheeses themselves.

What to Avoid in a Cheese Store

The little things count in life, and as a consumer you deserve to have a store that understands this basic principle. Just about every gourmet store on the planet sells artisan cheese, but just because they have a deli case with wheels in it doesn't mean they know what those wheels are or how to care for them.

When you ask for a sample, if they hem and haw and don't want to give you a sample, then you probably don't want to buy their cheese. This is definitely a case where if you buy, you want to try. If it's not store policy, then you really don't want to be their cheese customer.

Also, when you are given samples, if they use the same plane to give you blue that they just used for cheddar, without even cleaning it off, then that's more than a bit gross. It might not technically be unsanitary, but it does show that they cross-contaminate their cheeses. Also, if they exhibit any sniffing, coughing, sneezing, and don't wash their hands … well, that's just disgusting, too.

Many great cheese stores do put samples up on their counters, perhaps under a cheese dome or on a little tray. But they don't just leave them there. While cheeses do taste best at room temperature, they aren't that appealing if they've just been left on a shelf to languish until a hungry customer comes by.

Jeanette has also seen gourmet stores—which do a great job of selling everything from fresh cuts of meat to top of the line produce—flunk her cheese tests. And one of those tests is, do they have cheese that is cut to order or not? If their cheese is only sold precut, precryovacked, and prepriced, then chances are their cheese isn't as fresh as it should be. Jeanette has been to quite a few reputable, upscale grocery stores that just don't handle their cheeses with the same care that they handle their grapefruits. If snooping around the aisles leaves you without the cheeses you want or the accoutrements to cheese you desire, then it's probably not a good store for cheese.

A Cut Above

Some stores will cut your cheese to order and then also have a barrel or shelf of precut, precryovacked cheese that's "on sale." It's likely on sale and prepackaged for one simple reason: it's past its prime. Jeanette remembers distinctly buying one of her favorite Irish cheeses that was prepackaged ... and as soon as she got it home and opened it, she discovered an unpleasant ammonia smell and an excessive amount of mold.

And just because a store has a reputation as a good store doesn't mean it'll live up to it. Check the store out, see how you are treated, and see how the cheese is cared for. Some gourmet grocery stores do a great job with other foods, but they just don't know their cheese. Though Jeanette still shops at some of those stores, she never buys cheese from them.

Learning the Signs of Freshness

Even at the best stores, sometimes good cheeses go bad. The shipment they received ended up at a sweaty customs dock for too long a period of time; someone forgot to watch the Crescenza, or the cheese case refrigerator went on the fritz. There are, fortunately, tell-tale signs for good and bad cheese so if someone else makes a mistake, you won't end up paying for it.

Here are the basic rules for fresh, semi-soft, bloomy rinds, firm, hard, and blue cheeses. Fresh cheeses should be fresh. That means they need to get from the cheese-maker to your store to you within a finite period of time. They have a short shelf life. Good fresh cheeses smell fresh and they look fresh. Sour smells and discolorations are signs that they've gone bad.

Semi-soft cheeses have a range of different shelf lives. The softer ones have a shorter shelf life. Harder semi-softs like Gouda have a fairly long shelf life, and it's pretty easy to see if they've gone over to the dark side. They should smell nice, have smooth rinds, and look good. If their rind looks dried or cracked and if there is any mold, it's a bad cheese.

Just by sight, soft-ripened cheeses should be white, not pink. They should be firm, but have a little give to them if you press your finger into them. And if they smell like ammonia, they're bad.

Washed rind cheeses, by their nature, have a variety of colors and smells. But their overall rinds should have a uniform appearance and color. Cracking is a bad thing. And though a good washed rind will likely have a strong smell, it shouldn't have a strong bad smell—again, no ammonia scents. Some washed rinds will be a bit runny— that just means they're ready to eat and at their prime.

> **A Cut Above**
>
> The exception to the rule of firm cheeses with mold is that some of the finest English cheddars will sometimes be "infected" with blue molds (from blue cheeses), and in Great Britain, these cheeses are prized because only the very finest cheeses attract molds.

Firm or semi-hard cheeses have good long shelf lives, and they generally don't spoil as easily as other cheeses. They should look dry, but not dried out. Dry spots and cracks on the rind are bad. In general, their aromas should be mild. Mold on them is a bad thing.

As with firm cheeses, hard cheeses should be dry, but not dried out. They should appear to be solid, and there shouldn't be too many cracks in them. Because hard cheeses already are pretty dry, air exposure should be kept at a minimum, and good retailers know to keep them well wrapped, or they cut them by the wheel.

Blue cheeses have a variety of shelf lives. The younger ones like Gorgonzola last from two to four weeks, Roqueforts last a week or two longer, and Stiltons last the longest of the bunch. The softer blues shouldn't be mushy or smell like ammonia. The firmer ones should have clean-looking pastes with distinctive blue veins, and again, no ammonia aromas. Stiltons might have a little bit of cracking, but they shouldn't be too hard to the touch, as that's a sign they're past their prime. They should have nice veins, too.

Label Reading 101

A little bit of label reading can tell you a lot about a cheese. The ingredients of most cheeses will all be pretty similar—milk, enzymes, salt. The label will also tell you its type of milk and the fat content. Sometimes, but not always, it will tell you the sodium content, as well as the calories.

The other parts of the label can tell you interesting and important things. Label reading can, at times, save you heartache or heartburn—or at least prevent you from wasting good money on bad cheese. Some gourmet and artisan cheesemakers will print a sell-by or made-on date on their cheese. That is the first and most important thing to look for. Don't ever buy any cheese that is too old. It might be okay, but chances are, it probably isn't that good.

A typical label will include the name of the cheese, its origin, and its producer. It might also tell you whether it's farmhouse-made or produced by a dairy cooperative. On imported cheese, it'll tell you its status—if it's protected by laws or regulations that guarantee it's a certain type of cheese from a certain region.

Finding Cheese at a Mediocre Store

Jeanette's favorite cheese store in the entire world is about 40 minutes from her house. Sometimes, she just can't get to them when she needs a fix of cheese. And if she suddenly gets a craving for cheese on a Sunday or in the late evenings when they're closed, she has to go somewhere else.

Though she hates it when that happens, she is a savvy enough cheese shopper that she can make do in practically any grocery store. Some cheeses are harder to ruin than others, and when she needs a cheese fix on a Sunday—or in a strange city where she hasn't yet discovered the best cheese counters—she seeks out those cheeses.

In general, harder cheeses are harder to ruin than soft, bloomy-rinded cheeses and fresh cheeses. An aged cheddar will probably be okay. A packaged cheese spread (by a good, reputable cheesemaker) will also probably incur minimal damage by mishandling. A packaged log of chevre, after you check its label, is probably going to be just fine for a tossed salad.

Again, basic cheese shopping advice still holds true: if Jeanette wants something, she tries to get a sample of it first. If she can't get a sample and she still wants the cheese, she uses her eyes, and then, after she gets the cheese home or to her hotel room, if it doesn't taste right, she returns it.

Even at the biggest of big box stores, chances are you can find some decent cheeses. It's important to use your eyes. That means you need to really look at the cheeses. Are they the color they're supposed to be? Are there any cracks or discolorations on the rinds? Is there any obvious mold that shouldn't be there? If a cheese doesn't look fresh, it probably isn't.

Next, use your nose. What does the cheese smell like? Strong smells are okay for stronger-smelling cheeses; ammonia is not. Sour smells are also bad. If something smells—or looks—off, then don't buy it. What does it feel like? If it's a firm cheese, is it firm or is it rock hard? If something feels off, don't buy it.

A Cut Above

> The English author Osbert Burdett wrote a charming little book in 1935 titled *The Little Book of Cheese*, describing a cheese-shopping adventure: "In spite of the grocer's assurance that the Stilton was perfectly mature, we waited a month, tried yet again, and in the end declined to accept the Stilton, which had been chosen in November, until the following February. The perfection of flavour then reached is unforgettable."

Also use common sense when you're shopping. If you're at an Italian grocery store and you're not familiar with the store's cheese, don't buy the Camembert or Port du Salut; buy the aged Parmesan or the fresh mozzarella.

And don't be afraid to ask questions. The staff might not be as knowledgeable, but if it's a decent store, they'll be as helpful as they can be, and armed with your own knowledge of cheese, you will be able to satisfy your craving for Gruyère.

Buying Cheese from Other Sources

One of the best places to buy cheese is direct—from the cheesemakers themselves. You can buy them after visiting them, or you can buy them via phone or e-mail. Sometimes it's a little harder to buy obscure, international cheeses or purchase them directly from the cheesemakers themselves, but it's quite easy to buy cheese directly from American cheesemakers. Most American artisan cheesemakers are connected to the World Wide Web these days. Not only do many of them have websites, but they also have websites that allow you to directly order cheese from them.

Also, plenty of great cheese stores, including Larry's Market in Milwaukee, Wisconsin, Zingerman's Creamery in Ann Arbor, Michigan, and Murray's Cheese Shop in New York City, have websites where you can order cheese directly from them.

Cheese, unlike wine, doesn't have any regulations that would prohibit it from being shipped within the United States, but some cheeses—such as fresh or bloomy rinds—can be a little bit trickier to ship. They will either require refrigeration, or they might be packed with cold freezer packs within the packaging. One thing to keep in mind when ordering direct from a cheesemaker or a great cheese store is that depending on where you live and what time of year it is, they might not ship to you. Some cheese-makers don't ship their cheeses at certain times of the year—e.g., summer.

Also, here's a little secret. If you're at a great restaurant where you just enjoyed one of the best cheese plates of your life, chances are, that restaurant will sell you your favorite cheese to go. At the American Club in Kohler, Wisconsin, which has a fantastic cheese bar, people can even buy the cheeses at checkout. Most restaurants and bars, especially those that specialize in cheese, will be more than happy to sell you cheese directly. Consider it a form of take-out. Even if the restaurant doesn't advertise this service, most will accommodate your wishes.

Buying the Right Amount of Cheese

When confronted with a gorgeous selection of creamy triple crèmes, delicate blues, and aromatic washed rinds, it can be quite easy to go overboard. Most people, Jeanette very much included, have eyes that are bigger than their stomachs.

Unless you are hosting a great big party or making a super large dish of mac n' cheese, be careful how much cheese you buy. Great cheese doesn't last forever in your refrigerator (see Chapter 21). A good general rule to keep in mind is to buy only the amount of cheese you are planning to eat within the week. Buy less, not more, and remember, if you have a favorite cheese store, you can always return to it to get more cheese.

A little bit of great cheese goes a long way. If you're just starting on your cheese journey, just purchase one or two, *maybe* three, to take home and enjoy. If you're a cheese nut, try to reign yourself in. Jeanette generally sets her limit at seven, and she also sets a spending limit because it's easy to get caught up in the moment.

For parties, try purchasing between 1 and 2 ounces per cheese per person, and don't buy too many different kinds of cheese. For a small cheese tasting, 3 to 5 should suffice; for a larger tasting, don't do more than 10. And the more cheeses you're offering, the less of each cheese you will need to provide. (See Chapter 22 for more on tastings.)

The Least You Need to Know

- A good cheesemonger will introduce you to new cheeses and help you enjoy old favorites.

- Good cheesemongers encourage questions and sampling of their fine cheeses.

- Most stores carry cheese, but not every store knows how to care for cheese properly.

- Examine your cheeses before you buy them—and that includes reading the labels.

- One of the best ways to buy cheese is to buy it direct—from the cheesemakers themselves.

- Don't buy too much cheese at one time.

Chapter 21

Storing Cheese

In This Chapter

◆ Storing good cheese

◆ Wrapping cheese properly after serving

◆ Refrigerating versus freezing cheese

◆ Extending the life of good cheese

Once you've taken the trouble to find a good cheesemonger and you've purchased good cheese, you want to take good care of it after you get it home. If you're spending upwards of $20 a pound on good cheese, you're not just going to want to throw it in your cold-cuts bin and call it a day. Remember that cheese is a living organism, and as such, it has certain needs.

Storing and caring for good cheese not only extends the life and usefulness of your cheese, but it also ensures that the cheese tastes just as good as it did when you were trying it at the cheese counter. A little know-how goes a long way, and you won't ever cry over spoiled milk (as Jeanette once did, when she had to throw away a great hunk of Brillat-Savarin that got ugly).

Caring for your good cheese isn't too terribly difficult, but it's a lot different than the way you handle a bag of shredded, industrial-style cheese.

That stuff is meant to last for long periods of time, in both warehouses and in grocery stores. But fine cheeses don't have indefinite life spans. Knowing the different characteristics of fine cheeses and how to keep them fresh makes you a happier customer.

Getting Your Cheese Home

If you've just purchased your cheese at a local grocery store or specialty gourmet store, then take it home in the bag they put it in. There's no issue. But if you've taken the time, say, to visit some cheesemakers out in the countryside, and you're traveling in a car for several hours, you should make sure that the cheeses are refrigerated. Either carry the cheeses home in one of those plug-in car refrigerators or just put them in a cooler with a few frozen ice packs. Many cheesemakers or cheesemongers carry little frozen packs you can place in your cooler.

If you've traveled to another state by plane, your best bet is to put your cheese into an insulated bag or Styrofoam cooler, add a few ice packs and either put that in your suitcase or in a box, and then check your box or your suitcase. Even with travel delays, your cheese should be okay.

Things get a little trickier if you've traveled to another country and you want to bring home some of their great cheese. If the cheeses are either pasteurized or raw milk cheeses that are aged 60 days or longer, then legally you should be able to bring them back into the United States. Just put them in an insulated bag with a few frozen packs and then put that in your luggage.

Some French cheesemongers who are used to selling to American customers will cryovac your cheeses, which then are easy to check into your suitcase. It used to be pretty easy to just take these as carry-ons, but with new regulations regarding liquids, it's not a good idea to take them with you on the plane—especially cheeses like triple crèmes that get gooey; they're considered liquids, so you wouldn't be able to carry on more than 3 ounces.

Now, plenty of caseophiles have gone to great lengths to bring back some of these "illegal" or raw milk cheeses that haven't been aged 60 days. If you plan on doing that, be prepared to lose it. You might get lucky 9 out of 10 times, but that tenth time, you could end up losing your cheese.

Keeping Your Cheese at the Right Degree

After you bring your cheese home, the normal thing is to put it in the refrigerator. Cheeses keep best at an optimal temperature from 34°F to 38°F. Your home refrigerator typically will be set from 36°F to 40°F so you probably won't have to change your set temperature unless you happen to keep it more at freezing. Cheeses don't like to get too cold; they typically prefer it to be moderately cool instead of chilly. If it gets too cold, their natural textures might change, and that could also adversely affect their taste.

A general rule of thumb is to put your hard and fresh cheeses in one of the coldest parts of your refrigerator. That usually means placing it at the back and toward the bottom, as cold air sinks. Your vegetable crisper—not your cold-cuts drawer—is actually pretty ideal for keeping cheese.

Although it's okay to store your cheeses next to each other, it's not okay to place your cheeses next to other aromatic food items. Do not, for example, put your cheese next to some cut onions or garlic, as your cheese will take on the flavors of those onions or garlic, and unless you want, for example, onion-seasoned chevre or garlic-enhanced Roquefort, keep them separated.

Put your bloomy and washed rind cheeses in a warmer part of your refrigerator, and again, do not put them next to any other aromatic foods. Also, if you happen to have a penchant for stinky or blue cheeses, consider placing those cheeses in a sealed container so they won't lend their aromas to other foods. They also will lend their aromas to other, milder cheeses, so you might want to keep them separate from other cheeses, as well.

A Cut Above

If you buy good cheese and store it in your refrigerator, then you don't want to clean your refrigerator with straight ammonia or an ammonia-based cleaner such as Windex. As cheese ages, it naturally releases ammonia, and the presence of ammonia in a cooler will speed up the aging process. In effect, your cheeses will get moldy a lot sooner than if you cleaned with soap and water.

Cheeses are living organisms so they require some humidity to keep them fresh. Most cheeses do well at the normal levels of humidity within your refrigerator, but if you keep your cheese in the vegetable crisper, don't set it at the highest level of humidity, as that will provide a better environment for molds that are attracted to cheese.

A Cut Above

Fresh cheese curds will not only squeak in your mouth, but they will also squeak in your dog's mouth. This was discovered, through difficult scientific study, when Jeanette made her dog dance for a cheese curd.

Another cheese storage rule to follow is to keep it refrigerated, not frozen. If you freeze cheese, it'll change the texture, taste, and aroma of the cheese. But, as with any rule, there are exceptions, and the three exceptions are cheese curds and fresh goat's milk and fresh sheep's milk cheeses. Cheese curds contain a bit of whey so it's okay to freeze them. But if you freeze fresh curds, they won't squeak when you thaw them out. To get them back to their squeaky selves, nuke them in the microwave for about 20 seconds or so; then they will regain their squeakiness.

Fresh goat's milk cheeses and fresh sheep's milk cheeses have a different chemical composition than fresh cow's milk cheeses and aged cheeses. In fact, some cheesemakers freeze their curds before making cheese. Freezing those cheeses won't alter their composition, and their taste and texture won't be changed by the freezing process.

Wrapping and Keeping Your Cheese

Some cheese experts insist on wrapping the cheese first in parchment paper and then putting it in a plastic baggie or sealing it in plastic wrap; others say it doesn't make much difference. Other experts insist on wrapping cheese in slightly moistened cheesecloth, which is then wrapped in wax or parchment paper. And some experts say that going to such lengths is nice, but not necessary, especially if you are planning on eating the cheese within a short period of time.

A Cut Above

Most cheeses shouldn't be wrapped in aluminum foil, the exception being blue cheeses, many of which come wrapped in foil.

A good cheese store will cut and wrap your cheese correctly, and that goes a long way to keeping your cheese. The main thing, however, that all experts agree on is the need for rewrapping. Whether it was wrapped in parchment paper, plastic, or foil, whenever you take that cheese out of the refrigerator to nibble on, you should wrap it in fresh or new wrap before returning it to your refrigerator. If you only follow one rule to extend the life of your cheese, this is the one.

Rewrapping cheese keeps bacteria and molds from infecting the cheese, and although some molds and bacteria are good for cheese, the kind cheese gets from being rewrapped in the same piece of plastic is the kind that your five-year-old child would describe as "icky." It's a little bit of an extra step to rewrap your cheese, but if you're going to spend the extra money to buy good cheese, taking care of it will let you enjoy it more in the long run.

One word about cryovacking your cheese. Although you can now get home cryovacking or vacuum-packing systems, it's generally not a good idea to buy good cheese that was carefully wrapped in parchment or plastic by your cheesemonger and then cryovac it at home.

Cryovacking cheese isn't a good idea because of the simple reason that cheese is a living organism. It needs to breathe a little, so sucking the air out of its container is a bad idea. The one exception to the rule is if you want to shred your own cheese instead of buying bags of shredded cheese, which contain food starch and other ingredients to prevent the cheese from clumping. Some cheese experts are fine with the idea of cryovacking your own shredded cheddar, mozzarella, or Monterey Jack.

Cheesy Lifetimes

Just as different cheeses have different aging requirements, different cheeses will last for varying amounts of time in your refrigerator. A general rule of thumb is the softer the cheese, the less time it takes to go bad or ripen past its prime; the harder or the more aged the cheese, the longer it will last.

Fresh cheeses usually are sold right at their prime. That means they will only keep for three to four days, at most, in your refrigerator, and sometimes they'll go bad even more quickly. The more air they're exposed to, the more quickly they'll sour. Fresh ricotta, fresh cottage cheese, and fresh chevre should all be eaten within days of purchasing. To keep them fresh, keep them in the containers you purchased them in or spoon them into an air-tight container, which will extend their life a little bit.

Fresh mozzarella, for example, typically doesn't last much longer than three days. But to keep it fresher for a little bit longer, change its water (and be sure to add a little salt to the water) when you get it home and then change it every day. You can also replace the water with skim milk. If the brine starts to stink, rinse the cheese off and then smell the cheese to see if it's the cheese or the brine that's gone bad. Fresh mozzarella should be springy or bouncy, so if it's lost its bounce, it's started to break down and turn to the dark side.

Bloomy rind cheeses like Brie or Camembert typically last for only a week or maybe a week and a half, and if they're double or triple crèmes, they will go bad even more quickly. A Brillat-Savarin, for example, typically will last no longer than four days. Sometimes when you buy these cheeses they are pretty runny, so if you cut off a bit, you might want to just put the remainder on a plate and then cover the plate with plastic.

Semi-soft cheeses typically have a lot of moisture in them, and they will go bad quickly, too. Monterey Jacks and Port du Saluts will last for only a few days or a week. The reason for this is that their high levels of moisture tend to attract molds, and they'll mold faster than most other cheeses.

Washed rind cheeses can last for a week or two, depending on how old they were when you purchased them. A young Limburger, for example, will last longer than a more aged Limburger. The other thing to keep in mind is that even if these cheeses haven't technically gone bad, you might not find their taste or aroma pleasing to you, the longer they age. A washed rind will get stronger the longer you have it around, and that can be a good or a bad thing, depending on your personal taste.

For blue cheeses, it depends on the texture. The softer blue cheeses will last only a few days. The harder blue cheeses will lose their moisture, but they can last for a week or longer.

Firm cheeses and hard cheeses tend to last longer than any other cheeses, and they can last from a few weeks to a few months. Some cheddars can keep for a few months; some Parmigiano-Reggianos or Dry Jacks can last for even longer. Think of it this way—it was aged for a couple of years, so it ought to last in your refrigerator for a few months.

A Cut Above

In France, goat cheese crottins are not only enjoyed fresh, they also are enjoyed when they get dried out. The French simply let the crottins dry out, and then they grate them over soups, salads, sauces, and so on.

The longer you keep a harder cheese in your refrigerator, the more moisture it will tend to lose. Some people rub a little extra virgin olive oil on it to prevent moisture loss, but mostly, this is an unnecessary step.

When cheeses lose their moisture, it doesn't mean they've gone bad, but it will mean that you might not want to cut a hunk of it for a snack. Instead, you should grate those cheeses onto your pizzas, toss them into your soups, or add a bit to your pasta dinner. You can also throw them into sauces, make fondues with them, or even create a homemade cheese spread with them.

If you have some particularly old Parmesan, you might want to throw that rind into some soup for flavoring; that's something that good Italian cooks do to flavor their minestrone. But you don't want to do that with a washed rind cheese, which could adversely affect the taste of your soup.

With harder cheeses, if they have attracted a bit of mold, you can always cut it off. Remove the mold by slicing it one quarter of an inch to one half of an inch away from the good part. You can do this with harder blue cheeses, too.

But just because you can keep a harder cheese for a longer period of time doesn't mean you can forget it in the back of your refrigerator. Just because your cheesemaker aged your cheddar for six years doesn't mean that it's going to taste good if you've kept it around for another year. It doesn't mean that you now have a seven-year-old cheddar, it just means you've got old cheese.

How to Tell If Cheese Goes Bad

Some people say that once a cheesemonger cuts the cheese out of its original wheel, it stops aging. That's not really true—cheese will continue to age, but not necessarily the way it is supposed to age.

It's pretty easy to tell when milk sours—the smell and the taste just makes you wince. But because cheese is, essentially, properly soured milk, it sometimes can be a little difficult to tell if it's just aged a bit or if it's gone bad.

If a fresh cheese such as ricotta or mozzarella develops a color, it's gone bad, so just toss it. If a cheese is supposed to be chalky white and suddenly is more ivory, then you should not eat it. If it smells sour or of ammonia, then it's gone bad as well.

Bloomy rind cheeses, as they age, tend to develop more ammonia aromas, and if they have a really overpowering smell, then you don't want to eat them. A lot of them will tend to develop a rusty orange color, and that means you should toss them, too.

Blue cheeses tend to attract the wrong kinds of mold as they age in your refrigerator. If it's a firmer blue, you can just trim it off, but if the cheese starts becoming runnier and runnier, or if it starts turning yellowish and then brown, it's gone past its prime.

With firm or hard cheeses, if they've really changed color, begin smelling like ammonia, or have any green fuzz around them, just get rid of them. If they've just dried out a bit, then you can grate them or use them in cooking.

Keep It Cool ... in a Special Refrigerator

Though companies have realized that wine connoisseurs prefer to keep their precious vintages in an exact temperature environment, they haven't yet realized that turophiles have similar needs. If you've seriously gone off the deep end in terms of wanting to keep your delicious wheels in a perfect, temperature-controlled environment, then you'll have to get a little inventive to have your refrigerating needs met.

Fortunately, it's relatively easy to convert a wine refrigerator into a cheese refrigerator. Basically, you will want to remove the wine racks inside the refrigerator and replace them with wood or glass shelves, and voilà! You have a cheese refrigerator, which you can keep at a perfect temperature for cheese.

Mailing Cheese

If you've fallen in love with a certain cheese and you want to introduce your loved ones to that cheese, you can have your cheesemonger or cheesemaker send the cheese, or you can mail it yourself.

It's not that hard to mail cheese, and most cheeses won't even require refrigerated packs. If you mail a firm or hard cheese across the country via overnight or two-days shipping, you don't even need to enclose a freeze pack within your box. But if you have a fresh, soft, or semi-soft cheese, you will definitely want to enclose a freeze pack within the box. You will also want to enclose a freeze pack if you are mailing the cheese to warmer climates.

In any case, however, do make sure that you ship the cheese to the correct address; if it gets returned to you, it's probably gone bad.

The Least You Need to Know

♦ If you are traveling long distances with your cheese, make sure you have some freeze packs to keep it cool.

♦ Cheeses do best when refrigerated from 34°F to 38°F.

♦ The most important thing you can do to extend the life of your cheese is to rewrap it every time you take it out of your refrigerator.

♦ The softer the cheese, the less time it'll last in your refrigerator.

Chapter

Chapter

22

How to Taste

In This Chapter

- ◆ Cheese serving basics
- ◆ Cheese flights, tastings, and plates
- ◆ Cheese parties
- ◆ How to order a cheese plate at a restaurant

Tasting and eating cheese is the best part about cheese. And although it's easy to just pop a few pieces of cheese into your mouth, you can really savor and enjoy cheese even more when you know how to set up the tastings and when you know the basics of cutting and serving cheese.

With the right flavor components, accessories, and accoutrements, you can take a good cheese and make it taste even more divine. You'll also know how to make the cheese look as appetizing as possible, and because we eat with our eyes, not just our mouths, the whole experience is enhanced. It is also fun to set up different kinds of tastings for your family and friends when you know how.

When you go to a restaurant or bar that boasts a cheese specialty, it's also quite enjoyable to order cheese when you know a little bit about ordering cheese and setting up a cheese plate. Basically, this is where the real fun starts.

Ready to Serve

Cheese tasting can be as easy as grabbing some string cheese from the refrigerator on the go or as elaborate as plating and pairing 20 different cheeses for a party. But whereas grabbing some cheese to go requires no thought or planning, true enjoyment of cheese requires a bit of knowledge and forethought.

The first, most basic cheese tasting rule is that cheese should be served at room temperature. The colder a cheese is, the less flavor you will enjoy. A great cheese is filled with nuances of flavor, delicacies of aroma, and a most definitive texture—all characteristics that will be muted by refrigeration. Serving cheese at room temperature is not only safe, it's recommended. If there is one tasting rule you follow, this is the one to adhere to. The one exception to this rule is very fresh goat's milk and sheep's milk cheeses, which can be served lightly chilled.

Cheese experts recommend removing the cheeses you are planning on eating at least 30 minutes before serving. Some will even suggest that they be set outside the refrigerator an hour before serving.

A Cut Above

If you have to grab and go, cheese maven and author Laura Werlin recommends you use your thumb and forefinger to warm up the cheese. Just role the cheese around between your fingers before popping it in your mouth. That's actually kind of similar to the what cheese judges do when they taste cheese—except the cheese is already served to them at room temperature.

Cut the amount of cheese you are planning to eat or serve, and then return the rest of the cheese to the refrigerator, following the instructions explained in Chapter 21. The process of warming and then cooling the cheese repeatedly could adversely affect its flavor.

Cutting the Cheese

Almost any good knife can adequately cut the cheese, but certain tools do a better job and make the task easier. Though there seems to be a different knife for every type of cheese, you don't have to buy 10 different knives to cut 10 different cheeses. In most cases, just two essential tools will suffice for any cheese lover: a cheese knife and a cheese plane.

A cheese knife looks like a utility knife with a fork attached to the end of it. A cheese knife has a serrated blade that curves up at the tip into two distinct points. A skeleton cheese knife differs from a regular cheese knife in that it also has the addition of holes in the middle of the blade. The holes allow the knife to cut smoothly into semi-soft cheeses without crushing or smashing them, and they also allow the knife to glide more smoothly through aged cheeses without too much crumbling. The forked tip allows you to pick up individual pieces of cheese and serve them to guests or pluck them up and pop them in your mouth. A basic cheese knife will cost $5 to $10, while some of the fancier models will run $20 and upward.

A cheese plane, sometimes known as a cheese shaver, looks a little like a pie cutter, except it has a little horizontal blade in the middle of it for shaving cheese. Cheese planes are used for slicing firm cheeses such as Gruyère into wafer-thin slices. Cheese planes are usually rather inexpensive, costing only $10 or less. An even less expensive substitute is to use a vegetable peeler to shave cheese.

Another useful tool, especially for cutting very soft cheeses, is a French tool called a wire butter knife, which is a U-shaped contraption involving a wire strung between two points. This is traditionally used to cut fragile cheeses such as logs of chevre.

Wire slicers, which are different from wire butter knives, are used for semi-soft or firm cheeses. The simplest version is a hand slicer, which typically costs about $10 and looks similar to a vegetable peeler. The fancier ones can slice larger blocks or wheels of cheese, running $17 and up. The fancier versions also might be attached to wood or marble—they look a little bit like a wire cleaver.

A Cut Above

A cheaper and more practical solution, which is advocated by Ryan Andersen, executive sous chef at the American Club in Kohler, Wisconsin, is to use a clean guitar string or wire to cut soft cheeses and chevres. It works just as well, and you don't have to import it.

Hard Italian cheeses traditionally aren't "cut" at all. Instead, they are broken out in natural pieces using a cheese wedge or a short, stubby knife. There also are special cheese cleavers, which are also used for this purpose. But a basic chef or utility knife can do the same job nicely, and you don't have to add any more utensils to your kitchen.

If you plan on buying cheeses by the wheel, then you probably need a big knife, preferably a two-handed cheese knife. This knife is not really practical for most people, but it is an interesting tool. It is basically a chef's knife, but with two handles, one on each end, and the blade runs between the two handles. The two handles allow for cleanly slicing through a wheel.

If you plan to cut the cheeses before serving, cut them before they are warmed up to room temperature. It is easier to cut most cheeses if they're still chilled. The exception is extremely hard cheeses, which are easier to cut when they are warmed up to room temperature. Sometimes, scoring the rind makes it easier to cut into a wedge of cheese.

The best way to cut cheese is the logical way—you cut cheese according to its shape. Small round cheeses should be cut into halves or thirds, depending on how tiny they are. Diamond-shaped small cheeses should be cut into two separate halves along the diagonal, then cut each half into two triangles.

Round, drum-shaped cheeses, pyramids, or cones should be sliced into wedges as you might slice into a bundt or angel food cake. Wedges of Brie should be simply sliced into thinner wedges. A wedge of Roquefort or other blue should be cut into additional wedges, radiating out from a center point along the thin edge of the wedge. Logs of chevre and other cylindrical cheeses should just be sliced into little rounds. Soft cheeses that come in plastic or wooden tubs should just be spooned out.

When you are cutting two or more cheeses, clean your knife between cuttings. If you are serving and cutting them all at once, provide individual knives for each cheese. Also, cut them on separate plates or cutting boards, especially if one or more of the cheeses are strong or blue. Not adhering to these suggestions will result in commingling of the cheeses, and that might not offer an optimal taste of each cheese.

Presenting and Plating Cheese

Just as there are different knives for cutting cheese, there also are a plethora of options for plating cheese. Because cheese is such a natural, wholesome product, many cheese snobs advocate using plates and platters of natural materials.

Wooden boards are usually the traditionalists' first choice for presenting cheese. There are tons of great boards, some meant for presenting cheese, others meant for general use, but the nicer the board, the nicer your cheese will look on it. Cowgirl Creamery in California sells some absolutely gorgeous cheese boards, crafted from logs with bark still rustically attached to the underside of the smooth boards. They simply are the most stunning boards I've ever seen.

Marble platters can also be quite stunning. In fact, they've been used since the Middle Ages to keep cheeses cool, and their distinctive colors and veins provide a gorgeous contrast and background for the cheeses.

Wicker trays and straw mats are also appealing, natural choices, but, while they allow the cheese to breathe, which some experts advocate, crumbles of the cheese can also get caught or mashed into their woven textures. Glass platters are also quite a beautiful and natural option, and most people already have such items stored in their cupboards. Ceramic and china can also be used. Metal plates and platters can be used, too, but they are not recommended, as they could impart a metallic tinge to the taste of your cheeses.

A Cut Above

Instead of buying an expensive marble platter, head to your nearest home improvement store and purchase a couple of samples of large slate, stone, or marble tiles. It's a creative—and less expensive—way to present your cheese.

Some cheese platters or plates come with a nice glass dome. Cheese domes are great for warming up cheeses to room temperature—they allow the cheeses to warm up without drying out. They also can be used to keep a blue or other strong cheese's aromas from wafting into the other cheeses. But they aren't as necessary as a good cheese knife and a nice platter or board.

Whatever you choose to use to present your cheese, don't crowd your plate or your platter with too many cheeses. Leave room for accessing and cutting the different cheeses, as well as for adding a few decorative, presentation touches.

Greens can add color and visual punch to your plate. Traditionally, grape and chestnut leaves have been used, but they're not as easily found in your typical grocery store, not even a gourmet grocery. Instead, use Swiss chard, lemon leaves or even collard greens. Collard greens are particularly pretty, and they hold up nicely, too. Greens add a decorative color touch, but they won't affect the taste of the cheese. A few artfully strewn berries and nuts amidst the cheese can also add visual interest, but in general, any foods that are accompanying the cheese should be served separately from the cheese.

Stronger cheeses—blues, washed rinds, and smoked cheeses—should be presented on separate boards or platters, as their robust aromas and flavors have a tendency to overwhelm milder cheeses when they're immediately adjacent to them. At the very least, place them farther away on the tray or platter. Really creamy cheeses can be served in nice bowls or pottery. They can also be served in artful mounds on a board.

If you are serving cheese as a course within a meal, plan on serving just 1 to 2 ounces of cheese per person. If you are throwing a cheese-tasting party, allow for 4 to 6 ounces of cheese per person.

Cheese Tastings: A Guide

Whether serving individual cheese plates or throwing a cheese-tasting party, always start with the mildest cheese in the bunch and then work—or, rather, eat—your way up to the strongest cheese, ending with the blues. For a cheese course or tasting, you can most easily just present a single great cheese with a few accompaniments. Most tastings should average between three to six different cheeses.

You probably won't want to serve more than eight cheeses, because after that point, palates can get confused. Though experts recommend a maximum of tasting six cheeses, I've had and enjoyed many more on occasion; that said, you probably should stop at ten even if you're planning to go gonzo with your cheese.

Say Cheese

A **cheese course** is just that—a separate course within a meal that is made up of just cheese, with perhaps some bread and fruit on the side. It's served sixth out of seven courses or third out of four courses.

Cheese and cheese plates can be served at the beginning of a meal or at the end of the meal in place of dessert. In France, the *cheese course* is traditionally served just before dessert. It can also be served as an entire meal for lunch or dinner, and lighter cheeses can also be incorporated into breakfast.

For a basic cheese plate or course, serve from one to three cheeses, about a total of 1 to 2 ounces total of each cheese, and artfully arrange the cheese on a plate with a few greens and some fruit, and serve with bread and crackers on the side. It's simple, elegant, and easy. Make sure and some if you are serving three cheeses, that each cheese is distinct, and there is variety. Don't, for example, serve three triple crèmes.

This same rule also applies to more elaborate cheese tastings. The key is variety—in textures, ages, milks, and perhaps countries of origin. Serve one goat's milk or sheep's milk cheese, serve a semi-soft, add a bloomy or washed rind, and an aged, smoked, or blue cheese. For example, try Wisconsin's Driftless lavender and honey, Belgian Chimay, and Irish Blue Cashel. This offering would be a good variety in types, textures, countries of origin, ages, and milks. Some experts recommend getting an old favorite, trying something new or outrageous, and then tasting something in between.

One thing to note is that many people say they don't like goat's milk or sheep's milk cheeses. That's probably because they've experienced some bad versions of these lovely cheeses. If you happen to be one of those people, don't completely write off chevres. At a good cheese store, do try them, and ask to try some versions that are as "non-goaty" or "non-sheepish" as possible. Sometimes, too, an unfamiliar taste might require 8 to 10 tries and then, suddenly, you will find yourself enjoying the food or cheese. Also, do try different styles—such as a goat's milk cheddar.

Most traditional tastings are horizontal. That is, they include a wide variety of cheeses from many different places, served from mildest to strongest, with the blues always served last. Variations of horizontal tastings might be doing a tasting of all Spanish cheeses, all American artisanals, or all farmstead cheeses. Those are themed tastings, but they're still horizontal tastings.

For an interesting twist, try vertical tastings. Instead of choosing different cheeses, select one genre of cheese and pick a variety of makers. For example, choose different chevres or blues. Another type of vertical tasting could be even more specific—pick one cheesemaker, and then taste different aged versions of his or her same cheese. The American Club in Kohler, Wisconsin, for example, has a very popular vertical tasting of Hook's cheddar, starting with fresh cheese curds and going all the way up to a 12-year-old cheddar.

At a tasting, you might also want to serve a couple of different cheese flights. Cheese flights are like mini vertical tastings in which two to three different cheeses from the same family or maker are served—such as three different blues or two different chevres. You can set up two or three different flights and pair each cheese or each flight with a different wine or beverage for even more variety.

A Cut Above

A traditional English plowman's lunch consisted of cheese, bread, fruit, ale, and perhaps a little mustard or chutney served on the side. It is fun and easy to make up your own English plowman's meal, too.

Whether you plan on serving just one cheese in a cheese course or setting up an elaborate tasting, do learn a little bit about each cheese you serve. That will make it more interesting, entertaining, and educational for your guests. You can even type up a list of the cheeses, perhaps with a few facts on each cheese, to give to your guests before they leave. Or you can just print the names of each cheese on nice cards or on nifty ceramic, write-on/wipe-off display picks, placing them with each cheese.

You can also set up blind tastings and not tell your guests what cheeses they're trying until after they've tasted them. This form of tasting, which is common with wines, beers, and spirits, isn't as blind as it is for beverages, as different cheeses have different appearances, which your guests might easily be able to identify. Most people might not be able to identify a particular blue cheese on sight, but they'll know it's blue cheese.

Ordering Cheese at a Restaurant

Going to a restaurant or bar that specializes in cheese is a great way to try new cheeses and expand your palate. It's an enjoyable culinary experience, and if you like cheese, you'll want to seek out these places.

Most restaurants that specialize in cheese have a *maître fromager*, a cheese expert who will guide you through the cheeses in your tasting, and he or she will help you navigate your dairy selections just as a sommelier would help you understand a wine list. Much like sommeliers, maître fromagers require extensive training on cheese, and some maître fromagers are trying to develop a test and criteria for professional standards just like the sommeliers' education and testing.

A good maître fromager will look at what you are eating and drinking and then come up with a cheese plate or tasting that fits your meal. Sometimes he or she will present the cheeses on a cheese cart; other times the restaurant will have a display area for the cheeses. In most cases, the restaurant will also have a detailed menu list of what's available.

Maître fromagers will listen to you, discern your likes and dislikes, and be able to introduce you to new cheeses you might enjoy. Jeanette personally loves having a maître fromager surprise her with a couple of well-selected flights and pairings.

Even if a restaurant doesn't have a maître fromager, many still serve cheese courses. And some fine restaurants that don't list cheese plates on the menu will arrange one for customers on request. Jeanette's mother often asks for cheese plates, as she prefers not to eat desserts, and she has never had a restaurant refuse her request yet.

Say Cheese

A **maître fromager** is a cheese expert who has studied cheese and will help you navigate a restaurant's cheese selection. A maître fromager is, in effect, a sommelier for cheese.

The Least You Need to Know

◆ Always serve cheese at room temperature, except for fresh goat's milk and sheep's milk cheeses, which can be slightly chilled.

◆ The two most important pieces of equipment are a good cheese knife and a cheese plane. Natural materials such as wood and marble are optimal surfaces for presenting cheese.

◆ Never cut different cheeses on the same board or use the same knife for several cheeses.

◆ Arrange cheese tastings horizontally or vertically, from mildest to strongest, and serve only between three to six cheeses at a time.

◆ Have a maître fromager help you select cheese at a fine restaurant.

Chapter 23

Pairing Cheese and Food

In This Chapter

◆ Pairing breads and crackers with cheese

◆ Matching fruits with cheese

◆ Nutty pairings with cheese

◆ Pairing vegetables with cheese

◆ Determining how to pair meat and sauces with cheese

You could argue that cheese tastes good with anything. You could also argue that good cheese makes anything taste better. But while you could munch on an aged, bandaged English cheddar with fresh chocolate chip cookies, hot out of the oven, this is not an optimal pairing. Nor would your taste buds relish a California roll with a tart, ash-covered goat cheese. In both situations, you wouldn't get the most out of your cheese, nor the most out of your food.

The basic truth is that some foods just make a good cheese taste even better. The reverse is also true: great cheese, when paired perfectly, brings out different nuances and flavors in your food that you wouldn't otherwise notice or enjoy. Classical accompaniments to cheese include bread, crackers, fruits, and nuts, but other great sides include salads, meats, and even chocolate. That's right, chocolate. Provided, of course, that these foods are paired with the right cheeses.

Get Ready, Set, Pair!

Cheese, like wine, is a natural taste bud enhancer, and it's the sort of food that lends itself to improve and bring out the flavor of other foods. Likewise, other foods will bring out the nuances of a cheese, making its various layers of flavors and tastes sing. Cheese accompaniments not only round out a cheese course and make it more visually attractive (a plain old slab of cheddar, anyone?), but they can also turn a cheese snack into an entire meal.

> ### A Cut Above
>
> While many Americans serve a cheese course as an appetizer or hors d'oeuvre, cheese is served at the opposite end of a meal in France. In France, cheese is traditionally served as a course between salad and dessert, and the salad is served after the entrée. Cheese is also often served as the dessert.

Complementary Carb Overloads

Cheese goes with bread and crackers just the way peanut butter goes with jelly. They don't have to be served together, but they so often are, and they just taste good together. Crackers, breads, and other carb-laden foods have been served with cheese for centuries. It's a pretty fail-safe combination.

That said, not all breads are created equal. If you're going to go to the trouble of serving good cheese, you might as well put out some quality breads or crackers with it. Unless you're dishing out the kind of cheese that comes single-sliced and wrapped in cellophane, stay away from the squishy white breads—and the squishy whole grains, too. Trust me, it's not a wondrous combination.

Instead, go for the crusty French baguettes, the sensory multi-grained goodness, or the hearty Italian focaccias. As a general rule, though, you don't want your breads to overpower, clash, or detract from your cheese. That's why you should probably steer clear of the onion-garlic-jalapeño-blueberry combinations.

The same rule applies to cracker flavors as well. Simple, plain table crackers and bread sticks suffice and serve as great building blocks for cheese. Whole-grained crackers and crackers with texture are also nice, but forgo the fake cheddar cheese and ranch-flavored crackers.

> ### A Cut Above
>
> Two of Jeanette's favorite standbys for crackers are Carr's Table Crackers and Stonewall Kitchen's Olive Oil Crackers. Both are simple, crispy, and go well with all types of cheese.

Though simple reigns supreme, as with any culinary rule, it's made to be broken—with discretion, of course. Nut and fruit breads can be wonderful when they're paired with fresh chevre, blue cheeses, and fromage blanc. Try apricot, cranberry, walnut, and pecan breads and rolls, but make sure they don't have any artificial additives or too much sugar, which would definitely clash with the cheese.

Dark pumpernickel and ryes not only go well with blue cheese, but they taste divine with the stinky, washed rind cheeses as well.

Olive and herb breads can also be served with feta cheese, while sun-dried tomato–enhanced artisan breads match up nicely with Italian cheeses. As with the fruitier versions, just make sure the breads aren't overly olivey or herby.

Pretzels, especially the soft, homemade ones, are a salty delight, and they match up nicely with German and Swiss cheeses. Again, just make sure they're not dipped in cinnamon or sugar; added raisins could also raise a clash in tastes.

A Cut Above

Limburger on rye with red onions and mustard, and perhaps liver sausage, used to be the ubiquitous workingman's lunch in Wisconsin. If you're traveling in Monroe, Wisconsin, stop by Baumgartner's Cheese Store and Tavern to try this signature sandwich.

A Fruity Cocktail of Accompaniments

Nothing adds color to a cheese plate or brings out the inherent sweetness and tang of some cheeses like fruit. Almost as common an accompaniment as bread, fruit can really add another delicious layer to your spread of cheeses.

Obvious fruits to serve with cheese include apples, pears, and berries. Make sure the fruits are fresh and ripe but not overripe, and it's equally important that the fruits be of a good quality. Organic or locally grown produce is ideal. When you're serving fruits, slice and cut them up neatly.

Poaching, stewing, or turning your fruit into compotes, chutneys, and jams also creates interesting pairing combinations. Serve

A Cut Above

Apples and pears brown almost immediately after being sliced. To prevent browning, just squeeze a little lemon juice over them. The citric acid preserves freshness, and it shouldn't interfere with the cheese.

A Cut Above

While many people tend to use pears and apples interchangeably in a cheese course, they each pair slightly better with different cheeses. Pears tend to taste better with triple crèmes, blues, and bries; apples lend themselves to improving aged, sharp cheddars and harder cheeses.

A Cut Above

Membrillo or quince paste is a traditional accompaniment to Spanish cheeses, especially Manchego. Most fine cheese stores sell this delicious fruit concoction.

them separately in little bowls or even place spoonfuls on top of individual cheese portions. The spiciness and sweetness of cooked fruits adds layers of flavor and nuance to the cheeses. Poached pears, especially when cooked in port, taste absolutely divine with blue cheeses. Pears lend themselves to Parmigiano-Reggiano, too.

Berries of any kind lend beauty to a plate of cheese. Try strawberries and raspberries, but don't forget blueberries, blackberries, and even gooseberries. If you are using berries, serve at least two kinds for variety in shape, texture, and color.

Fresh figs, dates, apricots, and peaches are also great to add to the plate. Quince is also an interesting addition.

Dried fruits are also traditional cheese enhancers, and they are especially good to serve when fresher fruits are out of season. Try cranberries, cherries, figs, and apricots for starters. Dried exotic fruits such as mangoes, papayas, and pineapples can also be interesting. If you're serving larger dried fruits—apricots or papayas—you can serve them whole, or you can serve them diced nicely.

Citrus and exotic fruits also can be served with cheese, but they're not as common or traditional on a cheese plate or in a cheese course. A good guideline to follow when experimenting with exotic, sweet fruits is to first taste them with simpler, lighter cheeses. Fromage blanc and fresh chevre are two good bets to start.

But let your taste buds be your guide. Many famed and not so famed chefs come up with unusual combinations—watermelon with salty hard cheeses, or mangoes with stinky, washed rinds, for example. You might come up with a surprising taste sensation.

Stinky Cheese

The one common fruit we haven't mentioned is grapes. Grapes are an almost ubiquitous accompaniment to cheese and wine plates, but the truth of the matter is, grapes can clash with wines. Grapes can mellow out sharp edges and flavors of cheese, and by themselves, they taste just fine with cheese. But forgo the grapes if you're serving an especially rare or vintage wine.

Nutty About Cheese

It's nutty but true: nuts taste great with cheese. In fact, some nutty nuanced cheeses—think Emmantaler or gouda—taste even nuttier when they're served with, well, nuts.

You can serve nuts raw, toasted, salted, or even sweetened. Lightly toasted nuts are a good basic, but sugared and spiced nuts can also mix up a delicious combination. They can, in fact, provide a sweet or spicy contrast to the cheese. To add visual interest, serve the nuts on the half shell or just add a couple of whole nuts (and a nutcracker) to liven up the plate.

Try walnuts, almonds, and pecans for starters, and hazelnuts, pistachios, and macadamia nuts for a more exotic taste. You can serve just about any nut—even peanuts—with cheese.

While seeds aren't exactly in the same food grouping as nuts, I'm including them here because of their texture. Toasted pumpkin and sunflower seeds can add a salty texture to a cheese plate. Pumpkin seeds, in particular, pair up nicely with Mexican cheeses.

A Cut Above

Marcona almonds are a special type of almond cultivated in Spain. They're a bit larger than the typical almond, and they taste wonderful when added to a Spanish cheese plate. Manchego, here we come.

Green Goodness

Most people, myself included, need to eat more veggies, and fortunately, vegetables actually do go well with cheese. Broccoli and cheese, anyone? Simple mixed greens, baby spinach leaves, and even chopped romaine can form the basis of a delightful accompaniment. Serve alone, dressed simply with a vinaigrette, or toss with dried fruits and toasted nuts. A drizzle of walnut, hazelnut, or macadamia nut oil with a splash of balsamic vinegar is all the dressing you'll really need; nut oil–based dressings are wonderful when also serving with nuts.

A Cut Above

This might be one of the oddest cheese and veggie combinations, but salsa and Juustoleipa pair nicely. Cube the Finnish bread cheese and either bake, grill, sauté, or nuke it in the microwave. Then serve it with salsa on the side. Weird, yes, but also quite delicious.

Tomatoes can make a tart and sweet veggie add-on to a plate. The classic combo is to serve fresh mozzarella, chopped basil, and extra virgin olive oil with tomatoes. But you can also cube a mild cheese like Monterrey Jack and skewer it between chewy sun-dried or fresh cherry tomatoes, then drizzle a little extra virgin olive oil and balsamic vinegar over the top.

> **A Cut Above**
>
> Gorgonzola cheese–stuffed olives can be served alone, or they make a marvelous addition to a martini.

Olives, though technically a fruit, taste particularly yummy with cheese. Forget the pimento-stuffed green and basic black varieties that your Aunt Dolores serves. Instead, try kalamatas, niçoise, or Spanish greens. Olives tend to taste best when paired up with harder cheeses, and a good rule of thumb is to serve olives and cheeses from the same country of origin together.

Experimenting with other vegetable and cheese combinations can also be fun, but the typical crudités platters served at cocktail parties everywhere just don't cut it. In fact, raw veggies just come across, well, raw. Lightly parboil your veggies, roast them, gently steam them, or even bake them with olive oil and balsamic vinegar. Try baked asparagus with chevre, marinated artichokes with Parmigiano-Reggiano, or sautéed eggplant with fresh mozzarella. Sautéed morel mushrooms taste heavenly when served with truffled cheese.

Meet a Meat Plate

Who hasn't eaten or prepared a platter of sliced deli meats and cheeses? It isn't much of a jump, then, to step up your salami and provolone slices to Pecorino-Romano and proscuitto, mozzarella and mortadella, or Gruyère and Black Forest ham.

Meats and cheeses, while definitely not kosher and not vegetarian, nonetheless can taste delightful together. When serving meats with cheeses, the high-quality rule applies.

> **Say Cheese**
>
> In France, cured and prepared meat is an art. **Charcuterie** is the realm of cuisine devoted to prepared meat products such as sausage and confit, and the word is derived from *cuiseur de chair* or "cooker of meats."

Forget cheap sausage and pepperoni, and don't buy any meat that's been pre-packaged. Instead, go to a real deli counter where they slice the meats or seek out a bona fide butcher. In France, cheese lovers head to the *charcuterie* shop to seek out such delicacies.

Quality ham—imported or domestic—is a good basic meat to marry with cheese. As with other food items, imported meats go best with cheeses imported from the same country of origin. Manchego, for instance, is traditionally served with Serrano ham.

But don't stop with the hams or salami. Pates, mousses, and rillettes can make delicious and decadent combinations as well. The richer and creamier the meat, the richer and heartier the cheese to go with it. Triple crèmes match up nicely with a great pate, for example. And though not pleasing to everyone's palate or political convictions, foie gras also can be a great addition to a cheese plate. (Just pretend it comes from a happy place.)

Duck breast, smoked or otherwise, can also make an unusual but tasty accompaniment. So can beef tenderloin, cooked but served cold; cooked medium rare, it goes marvelously with blue cheeses.

Dress your meats lightly—don't cover them up with sauces or too many spices. Less is always more.

Sassy Sauces

Cheese loves to get dressed up. Simple sauces, as well as honey, oils, and vinegars, can go well with cheese. Top the cheeses with the dressings or serve them up on the side—it's your choice.

Honey, for example, can be drizzled over a fresh chevre, an aged Parmigiano-Reggiano, or even an assertive blue. Honey brings out the natural sweetness of cheese, and it mellows strong flavors.

Like honey, real maple syrup can be used as a dip or drizzle over light cheese. But maple syrup has a more assertive flavor than honey, so don't serve it with strong cheeses.

Olive oil—extra virgin and cold-pressed—marries nicely with cheeses and cheese accompaniments such as leaf lettuces. Good olive oil goes best with harder cheeses such as Manchego.

Stinky Cheese

While good basic honey goes with cheese, fake honey does not. Like the ubiquitous "pancake syrups" that have replaced real maple syrup in some circles, honey-flavored syrups have begun to show up on grocery shelves. Just because the unctuous liquid comes in a bear-shaped squeeze bottle doesn't mean it's real, so check the label.

Stinky Cheese _____

When shopping for olive oil for a cheese platter, go for the extra virgin kind. Extra virgin means it was oil that was pressed out using mechanical, not chemical or thermal, means, which could alter the flavor of the oil. Avoid light or pomace oils; they're inferior grades, and light refers to the flavor, not the calories.

Balsamic and sherry wine vinegars are also cheese enhancers, served on the side or sprinkled on top. They both taste even better if they're reduced to a thicker syrup. Some cheese stores serve balsamic vinegar syrups that are already reduced; just check the label to make sure that extra sugar was not added.

Port wine can also be served, not as a drink, but right over the cheese.

A Cut Above _____

Put a dollop of blue cheese into an Asian ceramic soup spoon, then pour a teaspoon of port wine over it. And voilà! You have an elegant appetizer.

Sauces can also be served alongside cheeses. Fried cheese curds, for example, taste great with salsa or ranch dressing. Fruit-based syrups and concoctions can also be drizzled on top or served on the side of cheeses. In general, though, don't serve cheese with sauces that are too spicy, too sweet, or too hearty. Do also try to avoid cream sauces, though; as too much dairy is not always a good thing.

Unusually Sweet Pairings

Except for fruits, cheese seldom is paired up with anything sweet. However, though it might sound weird, some cheeses can be paired with chocolate, and some can also be matched with coffee.

While cheese might be considered more savory than sweet, there's no denying that cheesecake is one of the sweetest treats on the planet. But it's not just processed cream cheese that can serve the basis of a cheese and sweet pairing. It follows that some regular cheeses are also sweet enough to stand up to the flavors of chocolate and coffee. Mascarpone is an obvious example, as it naturally balances out coffee and chocolate in tiramisu, but other cheeses can also stand up to the sweetness.

A good rule when tasting cheese with chocolate, coffee, or another strongly flavored food, is to go with gentle, milder cheeses. Some goudas and even Monterrey Jacks can be paired up with coffee or chocolate, and that wonderful, Scandinavian bread cheese, Juustoleipa, is traditionally dunked in coffee or sprinkled with powdered sugar.

A Cut Above

Strong cheeses can also be paired with chocolate. At Vosges Chocolate in Chicago, chocolatier Katrina Markoff plays with exotic combinations, and she designed the Rooster truffle, a dark chocolate truffle shaped like a triangle that boasts a filling of Tallegio cheese.

The Least You Need to Know

◆ Like wine, cheese is a flavor enhancer that brings out the different flavors and nuances of food. Certain foods will also bring out the different layers of taste within cheeses.

◆ Breads, crackers, and carb-based foods go great with cheese.

◆ Fruits and vegetables also add color and texture to a cheese plate.

◆ Nuts and meats can also be added to a cheese course for flavor and variety.

◆ A basic rule in serving other foods with cheese is that the plainer the food, the better it'll go with the cheese. You want the foods to enhance and bring out the flavors of the cheese, not clash with them.

24

Pairing Cheese with Wine, Beer, and Spirits

In This Chapter

◆ Pairing wine with cheese

◆ Matching beer with cheese

◆ Determining how to pair spirits with cheese

◆ Nonalcoholic beverage pairings with cheese

◆ Bad matches and good matches

Wine and cheese go together. This classic pairing has been around for centuries, as "the wine of food" just goes wonderfully with, well, wine. But wine isn't the only beverage that brings out the best in cheese. Beer, spirits such as vodka and scotch, and even coffee can tango beautifully with cheese.

The right beverage, served with the right cheese, will bring out nuances and flavors of cheese, enhancing flavors and making the whole experience even more enjoyable. Pierre Androuet, French author and cheese expert, explains it this way: "Cheese stimulates the taste buds and readies them for wine. Wine permits cheese to attain unimaginable heights of flavor. These twin fruits of the earth were made for one another." (*The Complete Encyclopedia to French Cheese*, 1973)

But although wine has been classically paired with cheese for centuries, sipping the wrong kind of wine with your cheese can produce an unpleasant taste experience in your mouth. The same unpleasantness can be experienced with beer and other beverages, too.

This chapter outlines the basic principles of pairing wine with beverages, and it discusses some traditional match-ups. It also explores some new and unusual flavor marriages, as well as discusses some great options for those who prefer not to drink alcohol.

Of Wine and Roses: Pairing Wine with Cheese

Cheese and wine go together, almost no matter what. People have been sipping wine and noshing on cheese together for centuries, and it's no wonder. Good cheese and good wine both offer layers of flavor and depth, with enough similarities that make tasting them together a natural, almost foregone conclusion.

Sometimes, drinking wine with cheese is a neutral sort of experience—they both taste good, and they don't clash, but they really don't take the flavors of the wine or the nuances of the cheese to another level. Though most wines and cheeses tango nicely in step with one another on your tongue, when they're really dancing harmoniously, a good tasting becomes almost a sublime experience. When the wine and the cheese complement each other perfectly, there's just nothing better. A perfect pairing will bring out nuances in both the cheese and the wine that you never knew existed when you tasted them separately.

The inverse is also true. While some wines bring out the best in some cheeses, some wines clash so audibly that it's the tasting equivalent of scratching your nails across a blackboard. Some wines with certain cheeses will make you want to spit both out of your mouth. Jeanette remembers distinctly the very first time she encountered this experience. One of her dearest friends came to visit, and she had just purchased one of her favorite wines and one of her favorite cheeses: Cloudy Bay sauvignon blanc and Cypress Grove's Humboldt Fog. If you like sauvignon blancs, this New Zealand import is sublime, and if you like goat cheeses with bloomy rinds and a layer of ash in the middle, there's nothing like Humboldt Fog. But when she and her friend tried them together, it tasted like they were chewing on iron forks. It just didn't work at all.

Since that experience, Jeanette has been experimenting, searching, and questing to learn how to correctly pair wines and cheeses. The first rule she's learned is that for every "perfect pairing" or "traditional match-up," there are exceptions to the rule. Even though we will detail some common and often fabulous pairings, we will caution you that sometimes the individual cheese or the individual wine you choose won't work. Sometimes, they don't work because the vagaries of the individual wine and the individual cheese are just "off" enough, and instead of bringing out the best in each other, they bring out the worst. Also, keep in mind that your individual palate may not like what experts deem as perfect, and that doesn't mean that there's anything wrong with your preferences—it just means that yours are different.

A Cut Above

At the American Club in Kohler, Wisconsin, sommelier Jaclyn Stuart always includes a wine that she doesn't think of as a perfect pairing for her wine and cheese tastings. "Eighty percent of the people usually don't think it's the best match, but in every tasting, there is that 20 percent who just raves about that match," she says. "And usually, after they say that, I go back and taste the two together and discover some flavor combination I hadn't noticed was there. I can see their point of view, even if I don't enjoy it as much as they do."

Sauvignon blanc, for example, often is paired with goat cheese; it's considered a failsafe pairing. But Jeanette learned the hard way—how Cloudy Bay fouls the foggy flavors of Humboldt Fog—that this can sometimes not be the case. It can get tricky in that wines and cheeses have nuances that can vary from year to year. Most restaurants and bars that do a good job of pairing up wines with cheeses do so by trial and error—they taste, and they taste, and eventually, they find the togetherness qualities they were looking for.

Although taste and error come with the territory, there are some basic principles of pairing that can help you in your own personal quest for the perfect pairs. There also are some pretty good, cheese-friendly wines that will, at the very least, not disturb your tasting of the cheese.

The first, most basic wine and cheese pairing rule is to consider the characteristics of the cheese and the characteristics of the wine. Pairing cheese with wine starts with the basic ideas one uses when pairing any kind of food with wine—seek balance and harmony or look for good contrasts. To achieve this, one must start with the cheese or with the wine, and because this is a cheese book, we'll start with the cheese.

A creamy cheese, for example, goes well with a wine that is creamy, such as a luscious Brie with a buttery chardonnay. A light cheese goes well with a light wine—a delicate, tangy chevre with a tangy sauvignon blanc or Sancerre (a Loire Valley sauvignon blanc). A smoked cheese could emphasize the smoky characteristics of a wine, like a smoked cheddar with a cabernet sauvignon. Really taste the cheese you want to pair with wine, and really think about its characteristics, not only the flavors of the cheese, but also its textures. Then, either by yourself or with the help of a good cheesemonger or wine store owner, look for wines that have those characteristics, too.

A Cut Above

Wine expert Josh Wesson advises, "Don't have the wine step all over the food nor the food step all over the wine. Two different flavors can be synergistic, producing a third flavor experience."

For contrast pairings, you're going with the principle that opposites attract. Salty blue cheeses, for example, go really well with sweet dessert wines like Roquefort with a sauternes. Stilton also traditionally has been paired with port, and for good reason—they bring out the best in each other.

When many people think of wine and cheese, the wine that comes to mind is red. But in terms of actual pairings, red wines can sometimes be more prone to clashes than whites. The reason for this is twofold. White wines tend to have higher acidity levels that can match the acidity in different cheeses. The wine's acid can lift the cheese and cleanse the palate of the cheese's cloying nature.

Red wines, while sometimes absolutely incredible with cheese, are often denser, darker, and more complex. The bigger, bolder reds often are matched with big, bold tannins, and tannins do not always tango nicely with cheese. Heavily oaked chardonnays will also clash with many cheeses for the same reason—that bitterness won't meld with cheese.

White wines tend to go well with cheese because they often are fruity. Fruity red wines also will go well with cheese. Our favorite cheese-friendly wines are sauvignon blanc, riesling, viognier, pinot noir, zinfandel, and syrah.

But perhaps one of the most cheese-friendly wines of all is a brut champagne or dry sparkling wine. The bubbles of such wines naturally cleanse the palate, and that effervescence will not only cleanse the mouth of any lingering cheese flavors, it'll also match a variety of cheeses. In particular, champagne tends to go extremely well with double and triple crèmes.

We also enjoy pairing sweet wines such as gewürztraminer or port with cheeses, especially blue cheeses or cheeses with pronounced, strong flavors. The residual sugars in sweet wines pair nicely with many types of cheeses, and the cheeses tone down the sweetness of these wines, making them a really enjoyable combination.

It's also quite enjoyable to pair cheeses and wines that hail from the same geographic region—fresh chevres with Loire Valley Sancerres, for example. While regional wines don't always go with their respective cheeses, they do more often than not, and if you know where a cheese and a wine come from, then it's pretty easy to match them up. You can take that knowledge and apply it to American cheeses, too. For example, take Anne Topham's Wisconsin fresh chevre and pair it with a California sauvignon blanc.

A Cut Above

Here is a treat that Marin Co. French Cheese Owner Jim Boyce recommends. Take a small round of triple crème cheese and put it in the freezer for about a half hour or so. Then, use a cheese shaver to shave off just a small medallion of it. Place that in your mouth and then take a sip of champagne. It's a little bit of heaven.

Here is a list of pairings that you might enjoy trying. It's not a foolproof list, but it's a good place to start:

- Fresh cheeses such as ricotta and chevre often pair up nicely with sauvignon blanc or sangiovese.

- Semi-soft cheeses like colby and Gouda often match up nicely with rieslings, chardonnays, and zinfandels.

- Bloomy rinds such as Brie and Camembert go with sparkling wines and pinot noirs.

- Washed rinds tend to match up nicely with sweeter wines like gewürztraminer and muscat.

- Firm cheeses such as cheddar and Emmentaler tend to go with riesling and zinfandel.

- Hard cheeses such as Parmesan and Asiago tend to go with sangiovese and sparkling wines.

- Blue cheeses go with port and sweet wines like late-harvest riesling.

Lastly, remember that your tastes are your own personal guide, and if you like the cheese and the wine together, who cares what the experts or anyone else thinks?

Cheesy Beers

Some cheese experts, especially a number of them from Wisconsin, contend that beer makes a better partner for cheese than wine does. Beers tend to have less complex flavors than wines—or a lesser number of different flavors—so they have fewer flavors to clash with cheese. Beer is also effervescent and, like sparkling wine, cleanses the palate after eating cheese, lifting up your taste buds and readying your mouth for another bite.

Beer connoisseurs contend that beer has more in common with cheese than cheese does with wine. Both were traditionally made on the farm, and both come from grain (though cheese comes indirectly, through the milk of the animal). Cheeses often have nutty, caramel, and earthy qualities, which beers also boast of having.

One general rule for pairing that many advocate is that lighter beers go with lighter cheeses and darker beers go with stronger cheeses. This works well, especially when pairing lighter beers like pilsners with lighter cheeses such as mascarpone or chevre. And although some strong beers marry well with some strong cheeses—try a Guinness with Mary Falk's Trade Lake Cedar, a washed rind cheese that is sort of like cheddar and blue combined (though it's neither, and it's made from sheep's milk)—some strong beers have unhappy marriages with strong cheeses. Their complex flavors compete with (instead of complementing) each other.

Like wine and cheese combinations, think about the flavors of the cheese first and then seek out beers that will enhance that flavor by either matching (finding harmony and balance) or contrasting. Beer expert Lucy Saunders recommends keeping four points in mind when trying to pair beer with cheese: hops' bitterness, malt's sweetness, carbonation levels, and the extra flavors in beer. They all can play a role in pairing beer with cheese. Also, like regional wine pairings with cheese, consider regional beer pairings. Try the Belgian Trappist monk pair-up of Chimay Grand Reserve Trappist Ale and Chimay cheese.

Like sparkling wine's effervescent versatility, try a hefeweizen for a similar, almost perfect match-up every time. Another very cheese-friendly beer is Hacker Schorr, which is light and friendly and tends to bring out the best in cheese.

The best way to find out what cheeses and beers taste well together is to experiment. Buy a few cheeses and a few beers and taste them together. Here are a few pairings that experts recommend:

◆ Fresh cheeses like mozzarella go well with cream stouts as well as Belgian fruit lambic beers.

◆ Semi-soft cheeses such as Gouda go well with dark and amber lagers, as well as draft ciders.

◆ Bloomy rinds like Brie tend to go well with draft ciders and Belgian fruit lambic beers.

◆ Firm cheeses such as cheddar go well with nut brown ales, pilsners, and stouts.

◆ Blue cheeses go well with nut brown ales and amber lagers.

Spirited Pairings

Though many foodies swear that hard alcohol deadens the palate, there are some spirited pairings that work with cheese. Chef and hotelier Leah Caplan, of the Washington Hotel, makes her own artisan vodka, and she swears that cheeses can go really well with vodkas, gins, and whiskeys (or whiskies). "The thing with pairing spirits is that you are doing one-note pairings," Caplan says.

This means that, whereas beers and wines offer complex notes and layers of flavors and aromas, spirit pairings tend to be one-note symphonies. When you pair a spirit with cheese, you're looking to match one aspect of the spirit with one aspect of the cheese.

Vodka, for example, accentuates the tang of foods. That's why it goes into a Bloody Mary—it brings out the zip of tomato juice. That means it'll also bring out the tanginess of cheese. Fresh chevre goes really well with vodka. Vodka also brings out the tang or the punch in an aged cheddar or a Parmesan. And who hasn't had a straight-up martini with a blue cheese–filled olive?

Bourbons and scotches also go well with cheese—mainly because, as spirits, they

Stinky Cheese _____

Though cheese is best served at room temperature, that rule might make it clash more with vodka. Vodka tastes best chilled, and when it is combined with something at room temperature, it falls flat. That's one reason why fresh chevre, which can be served chilled, goes well with vodka.

often are complex with aromas such as vanilla, caramel, toast, and even nuts. They tend to pair up very well with cheeses that are smoky, nutty, and even fruity. Gouda, especially an aged version, pairs up sublimely with a nutty bourbon. Parmesans and Mimolettes also bring out those caramel and nutty aromas of the whisky or whiskey.

Gin, with its juniper nature, can be a little bit trickier to pair, but again, its tangy nature makes it a good bet with fresh and tangy cheeses like chevre. Tequila pairs almost instinctively with Latin American cheeses like queso fresco, especially when dressed with a bit of lime.

Even some liqueurs—especially those with inherent nuttiness—can match with cheese. Try Frangelico, for example, with a nutty Gouda or a sweet mascarpone. The key in pairing up liqueurs and spirits with cheese is to keep it simple. Because they are more simplistic in nature, it is also important to understand that a well-matched spirit and cheese won't necessarily sing the way cheese and wine or cheese and beer does.

Nonalcoholic Beverages and Cheese

The most natural nonalcoholic beverage that pairs with cheese is a sparkling juice drink. Sparkling juices offer the similar palate-cleansing prowess that champagne offers, but without the buzz. They taste amazing with bloomy rinds, and they also tend to go well with just about any cheese.

Straight apple cider also works well, as does cranberry juice. When you consider that fruits and cheese go together beautifully, so do the juices of the fruits. About the only fruit juice that doesn't always work well with cheese is orange juice.

Coffee and tea can also go well with cheese—but there's conflicting advice on whether they work with cheese, or how well. Some cheese experts say coffee goes with cheese but tea doesn't, and others say tea works but coffee doesn't. Our opinion is that they both can work—with some cheeses and to some degree. Think about tiramisu—a classic Italian dessert made with mascarpone cheese and espresso. Creamy, sweet cheeses tend to bring out the nuttiness of coffee. Sweet, young Goudas such as Vintage Van Gogh also tend not to clash with coffees. Juustoleipa, a Finnish cheese with caramel notes, is also traditionally dunked in coffee. A nice espresso can also go with a sweet, young cheese, and even hot chocolate can go with some sweet or chocolate-enhanced cheeses like Carr Valley's Cocoa Cardona.

Fruity tisanes also tend to go well with cheese, much like juices do. Dark, smoky oolong teas provide a smoky balance to smoked cheeses. And iced teas, especially when touched with lemon, can cleanse your palate.

Coffee connoisseurs and authors Kristine Hansen and Travis Arndorfer advise to have lighter-bodied coffees or teas pair up with lighter cheeses while heavier-bodied coffees or teas pair up with stronger cheeses. Look for certain attributes (acidity, tanginess, fruit notes, crispness) when pairing.

Water—including sparkling water—is also good to serve with cheese. It doesn't pair or match up with cheese, but it cleanses the palate, and it doesn't clash with cheese. For any cheese tasting you're planning, do provide lots of water. It never goes out of style.

Going to a restaurant or bar that specializes in cheese is a great way to try new cheeses and expand your palate. It's an enjoyable culinary experience, and if you like cheese, you'll want to seek out these places.

The Least You Need to Know

◆ When pairing wine or beer with cheese, look for harmony or contrast.

◆ White wines tend to pair up nicely with many cheeses, and sparkling wine goes with almost any cheese, especially bloomy rinds. Blue cheeses go well with sweet wines.

◆ The bubbly nature of beer makes it a great palate cleanser for cheese.

◆ Pair spirits with cheeses according to a single flavor in the spirit with a single flavor in the cheese—like the tartness of vodka with the tartness of chevre.

◆ Fruit juices, coffee, and tea can also pair up nicely with cheese.

Chapter 25

Cooking with Cheese

In This Chapter

- Cheese cooking principles
- Classic cheese recipes
- International cheese dishes
- Leftover cheese and what to do with it

Chances are, you've probably cooked with cheese, even if it's just to make a prepared box of mac n' cheese or a good old cheeseburger. But if you're like most people, most of your cheese cooking revolves around processed cheese or processed cheese products, with the occasional cheddar or maybe Italian variety thrown in for variety.

There's a big difference between cooking with real cheese and processed cheese, and if you want to be a better cheese cook, there are some dairy principles that can kick your cooking up a notch or two. It also bears mentioning that different cheeses not only have different flavors, but they also sometimes require different cooking techniques.

This chapter not only introduces you to techniques that help you better prepare your cheese dishes, but it also details both classic and international recipes. It also explains to you how a little ingenuity can transform leftover cheese into delectable treats.

What You Need to Know Before You Cook

Perhaps the most important thing to know when you cook with cheese is cooking with real cheese is nothing like cooking with processed cheese. Processed cheese is … well, *processed*, in such a way that when heat is applied, it doesn't break down—it melts and has a creamy texture. It doesn't matter how high you heat it, the basic components won't break down, and it's harder to burn.

Real cheese, on the other hand, will break down when you apply heat to it. That doesn't mean that you should only use processed cheese, but it does mean that you do need to know what you are doing when you cook with real cheese. If you heat cheese too high, the protein—*casein*—will separate from the fat and water and turn into a tough, rubbery, icky mass in a puddle.

Say Cheese

Casein is the milk protein in cheese.

A good general rule, then, is when you heat up cheese, be gentle with it, and never use extremely high heat. Instead, use medium or medium-low heat, or move it on and off of the stove. When broiling cheese, you will want to watch it and be careful not to burn it. Another tip to prevent cheese from curdling into rubber is to use starch, wine, or lemon juice, which can all prevent the cheese from becoming stringy when you cook it.

Also, the harder and more aged the cheese, the grainier it'll be when melted. The younger the cheese, the creamier it will be when melted. A good experiment to tell the difference in melting is to take a young cheddar of only a couple of months and an aged cheddar and then just broil a sprinkle of each on two separate pieces of toast—that will show you the difference.

Because real cheese separates into fats and other components, when you make a cheese sauce or a fondue, you will want to use some sort of binder—flour or corn starch, for example—to keep the cheese from breaking down and getting messy.

Another good rule of thumb is that cheese melts more quickly and evenly when you grate it or shred it. If you just slice it, it has more of a tendency to become rubbery. Unless you like your cheese rubbery, don't slice it.

It is also easier to grate your cheese if it is cold rather than warm, so don't warm it up to room temperature before you grate. Just take it out of the refrigerator cold, then use a grater.

Though you do not technically have to have a different grater for different types of cheese, be aware that the coarser the grater, the easier it is to grate softer cheeses; firmer cheeses are easier to grate with finer graters. And just about any cheese can be pulsed in a food processor with a grating attachment.

While you want your cheese cold to grate it, if you want to mash or spread it, you want it warmed up to room temperature. If you just want to crumble it, it depends. If you want the crumbles less mushy, crumble the cheese cold; if you want the crumbles more mushy, then room temperature.

Because all real cheeses have salt in them, don't ever just sprinkle salt into your dish. Do taste it first because it can easily become oversalted if you're not careful. We've found that with many cheese-based dishes—such as macaroni and cheese or quiche, for example—we never add extra salt. That is a personal choice, but you should be aware that the more cheese you add to something, the more salty it could potentially become.

> **A Cut Above**
>
> If you don't have a grater handy when you are cooking, a serrated knife, scraped against a hard or firm cheese will do the same trick. Jeanette found this tip to be particularly handy while remodeling her kitchen (when her favorite grater was packed away).

When you are adding extra cheese—let's say to the top of a broccoli and cheese casserole—add it just for the last few minutes of cooking so that it can melt and warm up without overcooking.

Also, know the cheeses you are using when you are cooking. Fresh cheeses can break down when cooking because of their high moisture content. The two exceptions to this rule are whey-based cheeses such as ricotta and stretched-curd cheeses like mozzarella. Also, many chefs tend to use fresh cheeses in summer and hard cheeses in winter; we personally use all cheeses all year-round (though it is less common to make fondue in summer!).

Soft, mold-ripened cheeses such as Camembert or Brie bake well, but they're harder to add into sauces. If you're adding them to a dish—like mixing your Brie with spinach and folding it into puff pastries—do remove the rind. But if you're just baking it, don't remove the rind—when you cut into it, it'll be gooey, unctuous, and just delicious, especially when topped with fresh berries, nuts, and honey.

Semi-soft cheeses are pretty good to cook with. The more elastic their texture, the better it'll melt when grilled on a burger or sandwich. Washed rind cheeses tend to melt and cook well, but because they tend to have very strong aromas, their pronounced flavors will season whatever dish you're using them in.

Blue cheeses will also strongly flavor whatever dish you are making, so, for example, if you add blue to mac n' cheese, use less of it than you would the other cheeses in your dish, and know that the dish will take on a blue cheese taste. Flavored cheeses—such as a garlic chive cheddar—will also add stronger aromas to dishes, so keep that in mind when cooking with them.

Firm and hard cheeses tend to be the best for cooking overall, whether it is using an Emmentaler for a fondue or grating some Parmigiano-Reggiano over pasta sauce. They tend to melt well and add flavor while at the same time not overpower other flavors of a dish.

In our mind, you can never have too much cheese in a dish. Other finer chefs might quibble with this rule, but we almost always add extra cheese to whatever dish we're cooking—if we have first tried the dish before. We tend to toss our salads with cheese (everything from blue and chevre to Gouda and Dry Jack), sprinkle it in soups, and toss it with pasta. In fact, we've never met a pasta that doesn't taste better with more cheese added to it. We've also added it to breads, mixed it in mashed potatoes, and served it baked with fruits as appetizers and desserts.

Lastly, we have at least three to five cheeses in the kitchen at all times (and usually a lot more): a hard cheese like Dry Jack or Parmigiano-Reggiano to grate over pasta, a chevre to toss in salads and pasta, cream cheese for mixing into things, cheddar for whatever, and at least some new cheese we're just dying to try out.

The harder cheeses—Jack, cheddar, Parmigiano-Reggiano—tend to last a few months in the refrigerator, and we always keep a spare chevre in the refrigerator. We also almost always have a box of cream cheese on hand—it's a fail-safe for throwing together dips, appetizers, and desserts for impromptu gatherings and for when you've got to bring a dish to the office potluck.

Although pure turophiles might wince at incorporating a fine Gouda into mashed potatoes, we never hesitate to use fine cheeses in our cooking. Though we absolutely adore them by themselves, when we cook, we always try to use the freshest and best ingredients possible, and that also goes for cheeses. But because the better cheeses tend to have stronger flavors, a little goes a long way. A sprinkle of real Parmigiano-Reggiano or BelGioioso's American Grana adds a real kick to pasta rather than dumping heap after heaping tablespoon of pregrated generic stuff from the grocery store.

Lastly, about $1/2$ pound of cheese equals 2 cups of grated cheese.

Classic Cheese Dishes, Revisited

This is cheesy cuisine you're probably very familiar with. Who hasn't had au gratin potatoes? This chapter will detail some common cheese dishes, explaining how to make them. It focuses on the cheese aspect of each dish. While you can make pizza dough, puff pastry dough, or pasta by hand, we are going to assume you either have your own favorite recipe to make those things, or you will purchase those items ready-made from the grocery store. So let's get cooking.

The first, basic building block of cheese cooking is to make a good au gratin or cheese sauce. This is the recipe we use for au gratin potatoes, broccoli and cheese casserole, and also for macaroni and cheese. This recipe is a derivative of one taught in a French cooking class by Jill Prescott. A good cheese sauce is a derivative of a good white sauce or béchamel sauce.

Cheese or Au Gratin Sauce

The infused milk serves as the foundation for the sauce; it lends just a hint of sweetness, and the resulting sauce is richer for it.

Yield: 2 cups
Prep time: 45 minutes

2 cups whole or at least 2 percent milk

1 slice (¼-in. thick) white or yellow onion

1 Turkish bay leaf

6 black or white peppercorns

3 to 4 whole cloves

1½ TB. unsalted butter

1 TB. plus 1½ tsp. unbleached, all-purpose white flour

1 tsp. Dijon mustard

½ cup grated cheese

Salt

Freshly ground pepper

Freshly grated nutmeg

1. In a medium saucepan over high heat, bring milk to just a boil, watching carefully so that it doesn't boil over. Add onion, bay leaf, peppercorns, and cloves, and stir to combine. Remove the pan from heat, cover, and let stand for 30 minutes.

2. In another saucepan over medium-low heat, melt butter. Whisk in flour and cook, stirring occasionally, for about 1 to 2 minutes or until mixture foams. Continue to cook roux for another 30 seconds, making sure it doesn't brown. Remove from heat.

3. Return infused milk mixture to high heat. As soon as it reaches a boil, pour milk through a fine mesh strainer into the pan with roux (which is off the heat), whisking milk into roux as you pour. Discard onion, bay leaf, and peppercorns.

4. Bring sauce to just a boil over high heat, whisking constantly. Decrease the heat to achieve a simmer.

5. Whisk Dijon mustard and cheese into hot béchamel sauce. Season with salt, pepper, and ground nutmeg.

For Au Gratin Potatoes: pour mixture over 4 thinly sliced and boiled russet potatoes. Broil, with an additional ½ cup cheese sprinkled on top.

For Au Gratin Vegetables like Broccoli with Cheese: steam 3 cups chopped vegetables like broccoli or cauliflower (or broiled or parboiled asparagus) and serve with cheese on top.

Macaroni and Cheese

This is a creamy, cheesy mac n' cheese, and it is my nephew's favorite dish.

1 recipe au gratin sauce plus

1 lb. pasta (penne, macaroni, wheels, etc.)

1 to 2 TB. olive oil

1 medium onion, chopped finely

1 cup shredded cheese, plus ½ cup reserved shredded cheese

½ cup breadcrumbs

1 to 2 TB. unsalted butter

Yield: 2 cups
Prep time: 30 minutes
Cook time: 15 minutes

1. Preheat the oven to 350°F.

2. Cook pasta according to package directions. Set aside.

3. Heat a medium saucepan over medium-high heat. Add olive oil. After 30 seconds, add onion. Cook for about 5 to 8 minutes, stirring constantly, until onions are caramelized.

4. In a large bowl, combine cooked pasta, au gratin sauce, onions, and cheese. Pour into a 4-quart casserole dish, and sprinkle breadcrumbs and dollops of butter over top.

5. Bake for 30 minutes, remove, add extra cheese. Return to oven for an additional 5 to 10 minutes until cheese is just melted.

A Cut Above

For just vegetables or potatoes, we tend to use a cheddar, Gouda, Jack, or an Emmentaler. But for macaroni and cheese, we often use two to three cheeses: start with a cheddar, add Parmigiano-Reggiano and add a fontina, for example.

The Perfect Grilled Cheese Sandwich

Entire books and websites have been devoted to this topic. There are four basic rules, however, that make sense to follow. The first is the type of pan you use. Experts debate whether you should use a nonstick pan, a cast iron skillet, or a griddle. Our personal preference is to use a griddle; but if not a griddle, use a large enough nonstick or cast iron pan that allows you to fit your spatula into the pan to flip the sandwich over.

The second rule is that you should grate the cheese rather than use slices. Unless you are using processed American cheese, grated cheese melts quicker and more easily.

You should also use a high-quality bread, typically either a thick white or whole wheat. Lastly, you need to butter the bread (and warm the butter to room temperature before you butter your slices).

As with macaroni and cheese recommendations, we suggest using more than one cheese, and also adding other ingredients to spice it up. Some of our favorite add-on ingredients include caramelized onions; fresh or sun-dried tomatoes; fresh herbs such as basil or thyme; fig spread or jam; olive tapenade; and fresh, sliced avocados. We love, for example, combining cheddar and fontina, and that goes beautifully with sun-dried tomatoes. Gouda, by itself, naturally pairs with caramelized onions. And nothing tastes better with fig spread or jam than Brie, by itself or combined with cheddar and Parmigiano-Reggiano.

A Cut Above

Laura Werlin, general cheese goddess and prolific cheese author, recommends using bread that is ¼ inch in thickness.

Perfect Grilled Cheese

On a cold winter day, there's nothing better than an oozing, grilled cheese sandwich and a cup of tomato soup. This is comfort food at its best.

2 slices bread

1 TB. unsalted butter, at room temperature

4 oz. shredded or grated cheese, like Gruyère or cheddar

Yield: 1 sandwich
Prep time: 5 minutes
Cook time: 10 minutes

1. Spread each slice of bread with butter. Put 1 slice down on a plate, add cheese, and top with remaining slices of bread. Set aside.

2. Warm the griddle or a pan over medium heat for at least 2 minutes. Put sandwich in the pan, and cook undisturbed for at least 2 minutes or until bread is golden.

3. Flip over, cook another 2 to 3 minutes. Press down with your spatula while cooking. Flip one more time, if desired. Remove from heat and serve.

Chicago-Style Deep-Dish Pizza from Uno Restaurant

True deep-dish pizza isn't doughy—the crust on the bottom is thin, going up the side of the pan. But what true deep-dish pizza really is, is cheesy. Deep-dish pizza has more cheese than any other type of pizza.

Yield: 1 (10-inch) pizza
Prep time: 15 minutes
Cook time: 45 minutes

¼ **cup soybean oil**

16 oz. pizza dough, at about 80°F

4 cups part-skim mozzarella, shredded

¾ **cup chunky tomato sauce**

1 tsp. freshly grated Romano cheese

1 tsp. dried oregano

1. Preheat the oven to 400°F.

2. Pour soybean oil into a 10-inch-round, deep-dish pan. Place dough ball in the center of the pan and work dough from the center outward. Press dough so it covers the bottom of the pan and work it up the sides of the pan so there is a uniform bottom and side.

3. Prick dough all over with a fork. Bake crust for 4 to 5 minutes to set. Remove crust from oven and allow to cool for 10 minutes.

4. Spread mozzarella cheese on crust, and top with tomato sauce. Sprinkle Romano cheese and oregano on top. Bake for 35 to 40 minutes, rotating pizza every 15 minutes, until crust is golden brown and cheese is bubbling.

5. Remove from oven, and cool for 3 minutes. Remove pizza from the pan using a spatula; cut and serve.

Karen Hurt's Cheesy Seafood Quiche

Rich and creamy, this quiche is perfect for a Sunday brunch, but it's also hearty enough to make an evening meal out of it.

2 large eggs

1 cup heavy whipping cream

2 cups grated Emmentaler cheese

½ cup grated Parmigiano-Reggiano cheese

1 (4 oz.) can crabmeat, drained

½ cup finely chopped white onion

2 TB. fresh chives, finely chopped

1 clove garlic, minced

Salt

White pepper

Cayenne

Unbaked 9-inch piecrust

Yield: 1 (9-inch) pie
Prep time: 20 minutes
Cook time: 50 minutes

1. Preheat the oven to 450°F.

2. In a large bowl, whisk together eggs and cream. Add Emmentaler cheese, Parmigiano-Reggiano cheese, crabmeat, onion, chives, garlic, salt, white pepper, and cayenne.

3. Pour mixture into piecrust, and bake for 45 minutes. Let quiche stand for 5 minutes before serving.

A Cut Above

Always use pure, 40 percent milk fat with no additives heavy cream. Most of the creams labeled less than 40 percent milk fat contain additives like guar gum or carrageen, which can break down when heated. (They're also the reason some creams form puddles on top of your pumpkin pies.)

Easy Broccoli and Cheese Soup

There's nothing better than a steamy, creamy bowl of this soup and a wedge of crusty bread.

Yield: 4 to 6 medium servings
Prep time: 45 minutes
Cook time: 15 minutes

Double recipe for Cheese Sauce

1 medium onion, finely diced

2 cups chicken stock or broth

4 cups chopped and steamed broccoli

1 cup whole milk

1 TB. unsalted butter

Salt

Pepper

Cayenne

1 TB. minced fresh dill (optional)

1 cup shredded cheese

Crème Fraiche

1. After making cheese sauce, heat a large stockpot over medium high heat. Add onion and sauté for 5 minutes or until translucent.

2. Add broccoli, stock, and milk. Heat and combine with cheese sauce.

3. Add dill, serve topped with fresh grated cheese and crème fraiche.

Extremely Easy Blue Cheese Dressing

Sharp and tangy, this dressing provides a creamy contrast to crisp greens. It goes especially well with romaine lettuce, tart green apples, and dried cranberries. We also love to dip carrots in it as a snack. (Inspired by Jill Prescott.)

Yield: 1½ cups
Prep time: 10 minutes

1 cup heavy cream

1 cup blue cheese like Gorgonzola or Roquefort, crumbled

1 TB. red wine vinegar

1 to 2 cloves garlic, minced

1 tsp. Cajun seasoning

1 TB. chives, minced

1. In a food processor add all ingredients except chives. Pulse on high until combined and thickened. If cream starts to solidify too much, just whisk in a little cream. Mix in chives at the end.

Elegant Cheese Blintzes

Voluptuous, decadent, and oh-so-good, these little beauties are perfect for brunch, yet also make an elegant dessert.

12 crepes

1½ cups mascarpone cheese

1 TB. caster or super fine sugar

1 TB. Grand Marnier

1 TB. grated orange zest (rind), plus 1 TB. grated orange zest set aside

2 TB. unsalted butter

2 oranges, segmented with rind, pith, seeds, and membranes removed

Heavy cream

Yield: 6
Prep time: 15 minutes (not including the making of crepes)
Cook time: 20 minutes

1. Whisk mascarpone, sugar, Grand Marnier, and orange rind together.

2. Put about 2 to 3 tablespoons of cheese mixture in each crepe. Fold into squares.

3. Heat a skillet over medium high heat, melt butter, and place crepes in pan. Turn on both sides until just brown or about 1 to 2 minutes per side.

4. Remove from heat and top with whipped cream, oranges, and garnish with extra grated orange zest.

Krissie Kierzek's Incredible Irish Cream Cheesecake

Jeanette's dear friend Krissie is an amazing baker, and one of the desserts she specializes in making is cheesecakes. Her cheesecakes are out of this world.

Yield: 1 (9-inch) cheesecake

Prep time: 45 minutes

---

2 cups graham cracker crumbs

½ cup (1 stick) unsalted butter, melted

½ cup 2 percent milk

½ cup Irish cream liquor

1 (¼-oz) pkg. unflavored gelatin

2 cups heavy cream

16 oz. Neufchâtel cheese or cream cheese

14 oz. sweetened, condensed milk

12 oz. miniature chocolate chips

---

1. For the crust: In a medium bowl, combine graham cracker crumbs, 1 cup chocolate chips, and melted butter. Mix well and press into a 9-inch springform pan. Crumbs should cover the bottom of the pan and one inch up the side of the pan.

2. For the filling: Pour Irish cream and milk into a medium saucepan. Sprinkle gelatin evenly on top. Let stand for 2 minutes.

3. Place over low heat, stirring mixture constantly until gelatin is dissolved. Remove from heat. Let stand.

4. In a separate bowl, whip the cream cheese. Add the sweetened condensed milk and ½ the gelatin/milk mixture. Whip. Add the rest of the gelatin/milk mixture and whip.

5. Fold in remaining chocolate chips and heavy cream. Pour mixture into crust. Chill at least 2 hours or freeze. If frozen, thaw before serving.

A Cut Above

A cream cheese is a cream cheese is a cream cheese, right? Not really. Some are creamier, some are crumblier. Suzy's Cheesecakes, of Milwaukee, uses two different kinds of cream cheese to achieve a perfectly silky texture. Experiment and taste different cream cheeses to find your favorite.

International Cheese Recipes

Except for some Asian cuisines, cheese is a ubiquitous ingredient in so many ethnic dishes. Typically, if you are trying a Swiss dish, you will want to use Swiss cheeses (or Italian cheeses for an Italian dish, etc.). Although this is the rule, it's not hard and fast, and you can always experiment with other cheeses, coming up with entirely new and delicious dishes.

Swiss Fondue and Raclette

Practically every Swiss canton has its own, specific Swiss fondue. This is a good, basic Swiss fondue recipe. The Swiss often thicken their fondues with cornmeal, but we've found that flour or cornstarch works just as well.

1½ lb. Emmentaler, grated

1½ lb. Gruyère, grated

½ lb. Appenzeller, grated

2 cups white wine

1 TB. kirsch (cherry liqueur)

3 TB. all-purpose, white flour or cornstarch

1 clove garlic, peeled but whole

White pepper

Nutmeg

1 crusty baguette, cubed or cut into pieces

Serves 4	
Prep time: 30 minutes	
Cook time: 10 minutes	

1. Rub inside of medium-size pot (fondue pot, preferably). Set aside.

2. Whisk cornstarch or flour into wine. Heat wine in pot for about 3 to 5 minutes: you want it hot, but you don't want it to boil.

3. Add grated cheese, handful by handful, stirring each handful in until melted. Season to taste.

4. Add kirsch. Put pot over a warmer or low flame. Dip bread into pot.

Raclette

The Swiss love this dish so much that they have a special contraption to heat the cheese and then scrape it onto plates. Many gourmet stores sell raclette machines, and some of them also offer rentals. But an alternative to using those machines is to use this recipe and broil the potatoes with the cheese on top of them.

Yield: 4
Prep time: 10 minutes
Cook time: 5 minutes

1 lb. little new potatoes, boiled

½ lb. Raclette or Emmentaler cheese, grated

1 TB. grated fresh parsley (optional)

Pickles

Picked onions

Sliced ham or sausage

1. Heat up broiler. In a ceramic casserole dish, place potatoes, then top with cheese.

2. Put under broiler until cheese melts—usually less than 5 minutes.

3. Sprinkle with parsley. Serve with pickles, pickled onions, and sliced ham or sausage.

International Cheese Sandwiches

Welsh Rarebit

A popular dish all over the British countryside, this sandwich is easy to make and quite tasty.

8 oz. hard English cheese such as cheddar, Leicester, or Cheshire, grated

½ cup beer, pale ale recommended

1 TB. all-purpose, white flour

1 tsp. Dijon mustard

6 thick slices white bread

Paprika

Yield: 3 to 6
Prep time: 15 minutes
Cook time: 2 minutes

1. Preheat broiler.

2. Whisk beer and flour together. Heat in medium saucepan over medium-high heat. Add grated cheese and mustard. Stir until melted and creamy.

3. Toast the bread. Then pour or spread cheese mixture over the bread. Sprinkle with paprika.

4. Broil until cheese is brown—about 2 minutes.

Serve two slices for hearty appetites; one slice for lighter fair.

A Cut Above

A couple of years ago, the Dairy Farmers of Canada ran a series of "Stop Cooking with Cheese" television commercial campaign. The commercials basically used crude reverse psychology to convince parents that the best way to get their adult children to move out of the house would be to not cook with cheese, and each commercial featured a grouchy old lady who yelled "Stop cooking with cheese!" The commercials were removed because they were controversial, and people thought they were anti-family.

Croque Monsieur

A standard at French bistros everywhere, this classic sandwich is a savory treat, especially when served with fries (or *pommes frites*).

Yield: 2 servings
Prep time: 10 minutes
Cook time: 5 minutes

8 oz. Gruyère, grated

2 thin slices country ham

4 slices country French bread

1 TB. Dijon mustard

1 TB. unsalted butter, at room temperature

1. Preheat the broiler. Toast the bread.

2. Spread butter thinly on both sides of both slices. On the inside, spread mustard thinly.

3. Lay slices of ham down on inside slice. Add cheese. Top with other slice of bread.

4. Place under broiler for 1 to 2 minutes, then broil on the other side for an additional 1 to 2 minutes.

A Cut Above

Croque comes from the verb *croquer*, which means "to munch," so Croque Monsieur translates to "Mr. Munchy." For a variation, to make a Croque Madame, cook an egg, sunny-side up, and top the sandwich with the egg.

Cheese Quesadillas

The cumin and Mexican oregano give these quesadillas a bit of oomph. We often serve them with guacamole, Mexican sour cream, and salsa.

2 large (12- to 14-in.) flour tortillas

8 oz. Queso Oaxaca or Queso Asadero, shredded or cubed, or 8 oz. cheddar and Monterey Jack cheese, shredded

1 tsp. dried Mexican oregano, ground

1½ tsp. cumin

Yield: 2
Prep time: 5 minutes
Cook time: 10 minutes

1. On a plate, lay one tortilla down. Sprinkle cheese over tortilla, then sprinkle seasonings and top with second tortilla.

2. Heat a large skillet over medium-high heat for about 1 to 2 minutes. Place quesadilla into skillet. Cook for about 2 minutes per side.

3. Remove from heat, slice into quarters or eighths. Garnish with chopped cilantro, sour cream, and salsa.

If you are pressed for time, microwave on high for 1 to 2 minutes instead of cooking on the stove.

Italian Specialties

Capri Salad

Sweet and tangy, this salad tastes like summer. The creaminess of the mozzarella is a perfect foil to juicy red tomatoes.

Yield: 2
Prep time: 15 minutes

2 large fresh mozzarella balls

2 large fresh tomatoes

½ red or white onion, thinly sliced

¼ cup fresh basil, minced

2 TB. extra-virgin olive oil

1 TB. balsamic vinegar

Salt

Freshly ground black pepper

1. Slice mozzarella and tomatoes. Alternate tomatoes, mozzarella, and onions on two plates. Sprinkle with fresh basil. Drizzle with olive oil and vinegar. Salt, pepper to taste.

Karen Hurt's Cheese Stuffed Shells with Vodka Sauce

Jeanette's sister Karen loves to cook and is excellent in the kitchen. Her sister Julie, on the other hand, suggested Cheez Whiz and Velveeta. Karen's recipes won out.

1 lb. large pasta shells

For filling:

16 oz. ricotta cheese

5 oz. cottage cheese

¼ lb. plus ¾ lb., small, fresh mozzarella balls, chopped

¼ cup plus ⅛ cup Parmigiano-Reggiano, grated

¼ cup fresh basil, minced

1 egg

1 tsp. Italian seasoning

For sauce:

1 (16-oz.) can crushed tomatoes

1 (6-oz.) can tomato paste

1 large white or yellow onion, diced

8 oz. fresh mushrooms, sliced

2 large cloves garlic, minced

½ cup vodka

1 cup heavy whipping cream

¼ cup fresh basil, minced

2 tsp. Italian seasoning

1 TB. sugar

Salt

Freshly ground pepper

Yield: 4	
Prep time: 60 minutes	
Cook time: 45 minutes	

1. Mix all ingredients and set aside. Boil 1 lb. large shells, cook until al dente. Let shells cool, then stuff with cheese.

2. In a large pot, sauté onions, garlic, and mushrooms over medium-high heat. Cook for 5 minutes or until onions are translucent.

3. Add rest of ingredients except for cream. Cook until simmering. Add the cream, and cook for a few more minutes.

4. Preheat oven to 425°F. In a large casserole dish, place stuffed shells, top with tomato sauce, then top with remaining fresh mozzarella and fresh Parmigiano-Reggiano. Bake for 45 minutes.

Tiramisu from Fattoria La Parrina in Tuscany

Real Italian tiramisu is creamy and light, but not overly sweet. It is the perfect "pick me up" after a heavy meal; indeed, its literal translation means just that.

Yield: 8
Prep time: 30 minutes
Chill time: 30 minutes (chilling in the refrigerator)

1 lb. mascarpone cheese

5 eggs

5 TB. sugar

2 cups espresso, cooled

3 TB. Amaretto

30 ladyfingers

½ cup cocoa powder

1. Separate the eggs. Whip the egg whites until there are soft peaks. Then add 2 tablespoons of sugar.

2. Whisk the egg yolks with the remaining 3 tablespoons sugar. Add 2 tablespoons of coffee and 1 tablespoon Amaretto into the egg yolks.

3. Combine the egg yolk mixture into the mascarpone. Then gently combine the mascarpone mixture with the egg whites. Don't overmix.

4. Combine the coffee and the Amaretto. Dip the ladyfingers into the coffee mixture—turn them 3 times in the coffee mixture.

5. Place them in the bottom of a 9×11 pan. Spread half the mascarpone mixture over the ladyfingers, then add another layer of the dipped ladyfingers, then add the last layer of mascarpone.

6. Top with cocoa powder. Chill in the refrigerator for at least 30 minutes before serving.

Greek Specialties

Roasted Kaseri (from Mt. Vikos Cheese)

Savory yet tart, this dish makes a perfect appetizer.

6 oz. Kaseri cheese   **Juice of ½ lemon**

Yield: 4
Prep time: 5 minutes
Cook time: 15 minutes

1. Preheat oven to 375°F. Place one slice of Kaseri cheese in a small baking dish or ovenproof serving dish.

2. Bake for 12 to 15 minutes until cheese is bubbly. Immediately after you remove from oven, squeeze lemon juice over the cheese.

Greek Country Salad (from Mt. Vikos Cheese)

The salad practically sings a symphony of tangy and fresh flavors. Crisp vegetables pair up well with the creamy, salty feta.

6 oz. feta cheese

3 ripe roma tomatoes, cut into wedges

1 cucumber, peeled and sliced

1 green bell pepper, seeds and ribs removed, and sliced

1 red onion, sliced

¼ cup Kalamata olives

⅓ cup extra-virgin olive oil

2 TB. freshly squeezed lemon juice

1 tsp. dried Greek oregano

Salt

Freshly ground black pepper

Yield: 4
Prep time: 15 minutes

1. Place the tomatoes, cucumber, pepper, onions, and olives in a bowl. Cut the feta into large pieces, place on top of vegetables. Mix dressing in separate bowl, pour over salad. Serve at room temperature.

Using Leftover Cheese

When you buy good cheese, you hate to see it go to waste. Fortunately, there are a few simple tricks that will help you use your good cheese.

The first trick for leftover cheese is to make *Fromage Fort* or "Strong Cheese." This is sort of a French cheese spread. Basically, what you do is combine leftover bits of cheese, butter, white wine, garlic, and salt and pepper to taste in a blender. Then serve it as a dip. The rough proportions are about 1/2 pound of cheese to 1 cup of unsalted butter, with about 1/2 cup of wine. Add the wine slowly to see how much you really need. Garlic, salt, and pepper are to taste.

The second, easy-to-make cheese leftovers is to grate the cheese you have left over from a cheese tasting and serve it over garlic bread—easy and delicious.

The third is perfect if you have dogs.

Olivia's Tuna Cheese Bites Dog Treats

Sometimes, Jeanette takes leftover cheese and makes dog treats!

1½ cup whole-wheat flour	**½ cup cheese**
1 (8 oz.) can tuna fish, with water or oil	**Water (optional)**

1. Preheat oven to 350°F. In a large bowl, combine tuna (with water or oil), flour, and cheese. Add additional water if needed to be moistened.

2. Roll into little balls. Bake for 15 to 20 minutes or until hard.

There are numerous other uses for leftover cheese. Leftover cheese can be grated and then sprinkled over soups or salads. If you have leftover blue cheese, combine it with butter and herbs to spread over bread. You can also take leftover cheese, sour cream, and caramelized onion and make a caramelized onion cheese dip. A rind of Parmigiano-Reggiano can even be tossed into stocks to flavor soup.

The possibilities for cooking with cheese—and even cheese leftovers—are only as limited as your imagination.

The Least You Need to Know

◆ Real cheese behaves differently than processed cheese when cooked.

◆ For easier meltability, cheese should be grated, not sliced.

◆ Do use traditional cheeses for cheese dishes like Emmentaler for fondues, but also experiment with different or unconventional cheeses to create new dishes.

◆ Leftover cheese can even be used to create a variety of dishes.

Chapter 26

Making Cheese

In This Chapter

- ◆ Basics of home cheesemaking
- ◆ Simple and fresh cheese recipes
- ◆ Where to go if you get bitten by the cheesemaking bug

Back in the 1970s a lot of people tried making yogurt and cheese, and then it sort of fell out of fashion. But with the resurgence of organic and regional products, combined with a growing interest in cheese, people are getting interested in making cheese at home.

Some cheeses are very easy to make at home, and you can probably make them with equipment already found in the cupboards and cabinets of your kitchen. Other cheeses require special cultures and additional equipment that can only be ordered at specialty stores.

But if you can make bread at home, then you probably can make cheese. And if you make or dabble in the making of wines or beers, then you definitely should be able to make cheese. And who knows where this new hobby could lead you?

The Basics of Home Cheesemaking

Why make cheese when you can go to the store and buy some perfectly good ones? People make cheese at home for the same reasons they make beer, wine, or bread at home—it often tastes better, and there's a certain satisfaction that comes from crafting an aged food item with your own two hands. Plus, there's nothing cooler than giving the gift of homemade cheese, beer, or bread.

Cheesemaking at home can be simple or complex. It's sort of like the difference between making a basic loaf of bread or making croissants. The beginning recipes don't require a lot of technique, equipment, or know-how, whereas the advanced recipes require all three; plus, like making beer or wine, they require aging and a place to do it.

Some companies, including the New England Cheesemaking Supply Company, Dairy Connection, and Leeners, offer various cheesemaking kits, instruction videos, and more. They also sell the supplies individually, as some of the basic or advanced kits might contain more rennet and cultures than you'd ever end up using.

Clean Is Everything

But before you even start thinking about making cheese, clean your kitchen. If you think it's already clean, clean it again. The most important thing you need to know, before you start making cheese, is that good cheese requires good hygiene. Anytime you hear those horror stories about food poisoning, chances are someone didn't clean their hands, or they didn't clean their equipment.

In every professional creamery I've visited, no matter how big or small, hygiene came first. This is so important in cheesemaking because, to make cheese (except for the really, really easy recipes), you change the constitution of the milk by adding bacterial cultures, so you want only to introduce the cultures that are going to make the cheese taste good, not the foreign stuff that got in because you didn't clean your spoon first.

That means that you will want to use boiling water and/or a bleach-water mixture to not only clean the surfaces of your kitchen, but also to sanitize your equipment: spoons, knives, bowls, and pots.

To sterilize, immerse your kitchen utensils and cheesemaking tools in a pot of boiling water for five minutes. You can also use your dishwasher for this step, but read the manufacturer's instructions, and if you are not sure, definitely do this extra step.

For a bleach sanitizing solution, you will want a ratio of one gallon of water to 2 or 3 tablespoons of bleach. Use the bleach mixture to wipe down your stove and countertops, and also keep a bowl of it and a bowl of plain water on hand, to dip your spoon in during the cheesemaking process.

Ricki Carroll, self-described cheese goddess and owner of the New England Cheesemaking Supply Company, says it best. "People have been doing this for years under all types of conditions. However, the more you sterilize your equipment, the more likely you will have a great cheesemaking experience."

The Equipment

As far as equipment goes, you will need stainless-steel, glass, or enamel utensils, bowls, and pots. At the very minimum, you will need a large steel pot—like a stockpot; a stainless-steel spoon, and a knife with a long enough blade to slice to the bottom of the pot. You will also likely need a bowl, either glass or stainless steel. And you will also need cheesecloth. Most home cheesemakers prefer butter muslin cheesecloths, made out of cotton, that are unbleached. Butter muslin is a type of cheesecloth that has the right weave to properly drain whey, and most cheesemaking supply stores sell it.

Lastly, you will need a good thermometer, because in order to make certain cheeses, you will need to know the temperature. Correct temperatures, especially for advanced cheesemaking, are crucial—if you don't heat the cheese up to the right temperature, the cultures won't grow, and if it's too high, the temperature will kill the cultures.

For advanced cheesemaking, you will also need cheese molds, a cheese press, and cheese wax. These are more specialized items that you can purchase online or at a cheesemaking supply store.

The Ingredients

The basic process of making cheese at home is the same as it is in a factory—you heat the milk, add the starter, add the rennet, let the curd set, cut the curd, re-cook the curd if necessary, drain the curds, break up the curds, salt the curds, mold the curds, press the cheese, and then age the cheese.

You will need milk, yogurt, buttermilk, and/or cream. As far as milk goes, most cheese-makers prefer raw, unhomogenized milk, which is what cheesemakers, either artisan or factory, use; then they pasteurize it if they need to.

Homogenization breaks down the protein structure of the milk and makes it harder to work with if you're making cheese. But raw milk, especially in some states, can be hard to find, and in some cases is actually illegal. If you'd prefer to work with raw milk, there are websites and information on the Internet as to where you can find good, raw milk for cheesemaking.

In any case, whether you use raw or pasteurized, you'll want to use *good* milk, and you'll definitely not want to use ultrapasteurized milk. Ultrapasteurization (UP) allows grocery stores to keep the milk longer on the shelf, but it doesn't taste as good, and the process destroys the enzymes and protein structure of the milk, which isn't what you want when you make cheese.

The milk should also be either 2 percent or whole milk. Skim or no-fat milk is used only in very specific cheese recipes like Parmigiano-Reggiano. Most cheeses require the presence of fat to get the right texture and taste.

If a recipe requires yogurt, read the label to make sure it has live cultures in it. If a recipe calls for cream, make sure it is pure cream. Most heavy creams on the market have carrageenan and guar gum, which are thickening additives or stabilizers. The additives are in creams that are less than 40 percent milk fat.

You will also need cultures and either an acid or a coagulant like rennet. There are two types of cultures used mostly in cheesemaking: mesophilic cultures, which need temperatures between 70° and 100°F, and thermophilic cultures, which work at temperatures above 100°F. Different cultures or bacteria make different cheeses, giving it different flavors, textures, and sometimes colors.

If you get into advanced cheesemaking, you will also need molds—molds of the bacterial kind, which will give your cheese that nice bloomy rind or that nice blue color. You can purchase cultures, molds, and coagulants at a cheesemaking supply shop or on the Internet. Though rennet once only came from the stomach of a calf or a kid, today it is mostly made by microbes, and it comes in tablet form. For simple cheeses, though, you do not even need rennet or a plant coagulant—you can just use lemon juice, vinegar, or citric acid.

A Cut Above

If you get really into cheese-making, you will likely get more and more into cheesemaking cultures, experimenting with different cultures to achieve different flavor profiles. You will also experiment with amounts of cultures and exactly when you introduce them into the cheesemaking process. That's the "innovative" part of making cheese.

The last food ingredient you will need is salt. Most cheesemakers use flake salt, and it's generally advisable not to use salt with iodine in it, as that will change the flavors of the cheese.

Stinky Cheese _____

If it is particularly hot or humid out, that could affect the development of your cheese if you are required to leave it out at room temperature during the process.

Simple Recipes for Making Cheese

If you have never made cheese before, you should start with the easy, fresh cheeses first. The freshest cheeses can be made without using any special cultures or coagulants, using ingredients you can get from your regular grocery store. The next step up would be fresh cheeses with cultures, and after that would be harder cheeses, aged for at least a month.

What's nice about making fresh cheeses is that they are ready to consume almost immediately after you make them. They provide instant gratification, whereas you won't be able to eat the other cheeses for a few days to a few weeks, months, or even a year or longer.

The most basic and easiest cheese to make is yogurt cheese. It doesn't require any cooking—it doesn't require anything except yogurt, cheesecloth, and a colander.

Yogurt Cheese

Yield: 1 to 2 cups	

4 cups unflavored yogurt with live cultures

2 to 4 tablespoons fresh herbs – basil, chives, etc.

1 to 2 tablespoons crushed garlic

Freshly cracked black pepper to taste

Salt (optional)

1. Line clean and sanitized colander with cheesecloth. Spoon yogurt into the cheesecloth. Tie cheesecloth up with a twist-tie or a rubber band. Leave ball of cheese in the colander, and put the colander over a clean bowl.

2. Let sit in the refrigerator for at least 6 to 8 hours or overnight. If desired, put a weight on top of the ball to press out more whey. Depending on how long you drain it, it should have the consistency of a creamy spread or cream cheese; the longer you drain it, the more it'll be like cream cheese.

3. Mix in herbs, crushed garlic, cracked black pepper, and/or salt. Serve over toast, crackers, or freshly baked bread; also good with fruit.

 A Cut Above

Rinse the cheesecloth out once with boiling water before making your cheese. This sanitizes it.

The next easiest recipe to make would be lemon juice cheese. Just milk and lemon juice, plus any herbs or flavorings that you'd like to enhance it.

Lemon Juice Cheese

2 cups whole milk, preferably unhomogenized

¼ cup freshly squeezed lemon juice

2 to 4 tablespoons fresh, diced herbs—basil, chives, etc.

Salt

Freshly cracked black pepper, to taste

1 to 2 teaspoons garlic

Sugar and/or lemon zest, about 1 to 2 tablespoons each (optional, if not using garlic)

> *Yield: about ½ lb. of cheese*

1. Heat milk to 165°F. Stir to make sure that milk doesn't burn. Then, turn the heat off and add lemon juice. Let the milk-lemon mixture sit for 20 minutes; the curds will begin to separate in the milk. The curds might appear as filmy threads.

2. Line a colander with cheesecloth, and put the colander over a bowl. Ladle cheese curd mixture into the cheesecloth and tie the cloth into a ball. Keep ball of cheese in the colander and over the bowl; let drain for at least 30 to 60 minutes.

3. Add salt, herbs, and any other ingredients you might want to flavor the cheese. For a sweet cheese, mix in fruit, sugar, and/or lemon zest. For a savory cheese, mix in fresh herbs, garlic, or cracked peppercorn. Or just eat plain, perhaps with a little salt added. The plain or sweet cheese can also be used to make a cheesecake.

Another very easy cheese to make is fresh ricotta. Not the authentic, Italian ricotta that's made with leftover whey from mozzarella production, but rather, milk-based ricotta, which is quite delicious in its own right. If you really get into cheesemaking and you find that you have the knack for making homemade, fresh mozzarella, then perhaps you should try a whey-based ricotta recipe.

But for easy and fresh ricotta, nothing beats this simple recipe, which only requires milk, buttermilk, and perhaps a dash or two of salt.

Fresh Ricotta

Yield: 1 to 1¹/₂ lbs. cheese

1 gallon whole milk,   1 quart buttermilk
unhomogenized if possible

1. In a large stainless-steel pot that's been sanitized, heat milk, gradually turning up heat. Stir constantly, and turn heat up to high. Curds will begin forming, and once temperature reaches 175° to 180°F, the curds and whey will separate. When this happens, remove the pan from heat.

2. Using a ladle with holes or a slotted spoon; skim the curds from the whey, and transfer them to a colander lined with the cheesecloth over a bowl. Let sit for at least 15 minutes.

3. Tie the cloth into a bag, and hang the cloth so that it can drain additional whey. Let drain for another 30 to 60 minutes.

4. Mix in salt in a bowl if you are adding salt. Spoon the ricotta into a container.

Ricotta is good for making lasagna, homemade ravioli, and other pasta dishes. But also use it in cheesy dips, or spoon a few dollops onto your pizzas. And if you mix in herbs, or sprinkle with sun-dried tomatoes, it can be an appetizer, served in a bowl like dip or spoon 1 tablespoon of ricotta in an endive leaf and then top with chopped tomatoes or herbs.

Mascarpone is a rather easy cheese, but it does require the addition of one rather unusual ingredient—tartaric acid. Cheesemaking supply companies sell it, as do home beer and wine making supply stores.

Mascarpone

1 quart heavy cream   **¼ tsp. tartaric acid**

Yield: 1 quart

1. In a stainless-steel double boiler, pour water into the bottom part of the pot. In the top part, pour in cream. Bring cream to a temperature of 180°F.

2. Add tartaric acid. It should start to thicken almost immediately. Stir occasionally, and let it cook for another 5 minutes. Remove from heat.

3. Pour cream mixture into a colander lined with cheesecloth over a bowl. Cover and refrigerate mixture for at least 12 hours.

A Cut Above

David Fankhauser, a professor at Clement University and cheesemaking enthusiast, says that tartaric acid can be substituted with 2 tablespoons of lemon juice.

Crème fraîche isn't really cheese, but it is a dairy product, and it's so easy to make it's not even funny.

Crème Fraîche

Yield: 1 cup

1 cup heavy cream, 40 percent milk fat   2 TB. buttermilk

1. In a sanitized bowl, mix cream and buttermilk. Cover, and let stand for at least 8 hours or until it becomes thick. Stir and refrigerate.

≈

Crème fraîche is wonderful to use in soups, desserts, and sauces, but try mixing in a little bit of sugar and Tahitian vanilla—about 1 to 2 teaspoons of each—and then serve dolloped over fresh fruit salad.

If You Really Get Into Cheesemaking

If after trying these simple, fresh cheese recipes you're hunkering for more, it's time to try out some of the aged cheeses. Aged cheesemaking requires more of an investment in time, money, and equipment, and it also might not be a bad idea to take a class or two before you start. Some artisan cheesemakers offer classes on their farms, and some cooking schools also offer classes. There are also several books on the subject, but two of the best are Ricki Carroll's *Home Cheese Making* (2002) and Tim Smith's *Making Artisan Cheese* (2005).

If you find you really enjoy making cheeses with some bite to them, you might want to consider a career as a cheesemaker. Licensing for cheesemakers is different in different states, and it often requires some professional education.

Another career option that is becoming more prevalent in large metropolitan areas is that of a maître fromager or cheese sommelier. Right now, maître fromagers need to know a lot about cheese, but they don't have the formal classes or examinations that master sommeliers must undergo. But maître fromagers are starting to get organized, and there's some talk of them setting up a master fromager examination that would mirror what sommeliers have.

But you don't have to become a professional to enjoy cheese or even to make cheese on your own. You just have to have the desire to learn and try new things.

The Least You Need to Know

◆ Sanitation and hygiene are especially important when making homemade cheese.

◆ There are several cheesemaking supply stores (also online) where you can purchase the basic cheesemaking equipment and cultures for making cheese.

◆ The easiest cheese to make at home is yogurt cheese—it only requires yogurt, a cheesecloth, and a colander.

◆ Once you've mastered the basics, try your hand at more advanced cheeses or take a course in cheesemaking.

Glossary

acidification Process in which bacterial cultures change the milk sugar or lactose into lactic acid during cheesemaking.

affinage French term for the art of aging cheese.

affineur/affineuse A person who professionally ages or ripens cheese.

aged cheese Cheese that has been ripened for several months up to several years.

aging cheese To ripen cheese.

American artisan New, often original cheese, crafted by American cheesemakers with care.

anejo Aged Hispanic cheese; aged for a period of weeks, not months or years like other aged cheeses.

annatto A South American red seed from the achiote tree that is used to color cheddar and other cheeses.

AOC Appelation d'Origine Contrôllée, French designation system of certain cheeses and their names, as well as the regulation of how they're made.

artisan Opposite of industrial cheese; cheese that is handcrafted in small batches.

aroma Smell that comes from a cheese.

bloomy rind   A cheese that has a soft, white rind like Brie.

blue cheese   Cheese in which a mold is added to create flavoring and a distinctive blue or blue-green color.

Brie   A round, French cheese with a bloomy rind and creamy interior.

brine   Salt solution that is used to make some firm and hard cheeses.

browsers   Animals, such as goats, that eat leaves, bark, twigs, shrubs, and vines.

cacio   Italian word for cheese.

Camembert   A French, bloomy rind cheese first created in Normandy; it's the most copied French cheese in the world.

caprino   Italian goat's milk cheese.

cardoon thistle   Purple thistle flower used to coagulate cheese instead of rennet, often used in Portuguese cheeses.

casein   Milk protein in cheese.

caseophiles   Cheese lovers.

caseus   Latin word for cheese.

charcuterie   French term for cured and prepared meats like sausage or pate.

cheddar   The most common type of cheese in the United States; originally an English cheese. It can be white or orange in color, aged anywhere from 2 months to 10 years.

cheddaring   Process of cutting, slabbing, and piling curds to press the whey out and create cheddar.

cheese   From the Latin word *caseus*, probably derived from the word *kwat* of the Proto-Indo-European language, a language linguists believe could be the common ancestor tongue of today's Indo-European languages. Kwat means to ferment or become sour.

cheese connoisseurs   Caseophiles or turophiles.

cheese course   A separate course within a meal that is made up of just cheese, with perhaps some bread and fruit on the side, usually served sixth out of seven courses.

cheese harp   A metal, harp-shaped paddle, strung with linear blades used to cut curds in the cheesemaking process.

cheesecloth Cotton cloth used to drain cheese curds.

chevre Fresh goat's milk cheese; chevre means goat in French.

coagulation The process in which the milk proteins stick together to form curds.

crème fraîche A type of cultured cream made with tartaric acid.

croque monsieur French ham and cheese sandwich.

cultures Bacterial cultures used to make cheese; breaks the milk down into curds and whey.

curds Solid or coagulated portion of milk during cheesemaking; the part that is aged to become cheese.

cutting the curds After the rennet has been introduced, curds are cut to expel additional whey.

Emmentaler A Swiss Alpine cheese with holes in it; what all "Swiss" cheese evolved from.

emulsifiers Chemical salts added to preserve processed cheese and make it melt smoother.

ewes Female sheep.

eyes The holes in Swiss cheese; formed as a result of propionic bacteria fermentation.

farmstead cheese Cheeses made on the same farm as where the animals are raised and milked.

fermentation The process in which milk becomes cheese or yogurt or grape juice becomes wine; it's the breakdown of carbohydrates in a food, which changes the original substance.

feta Traditionally, a Greek sheep's milk cheese. It is also made with cow's milk in the United States.

filled cheese Unnaturally diluted cheese in which some of the milk was replaced with other fats such as margarine or lard.

firm A cheese that has aged for a longer period of time than semi-soft; harder to the texture than semi-soft, but softer than hard cheese.

formaticum Roman word for hard cheese, which later evolved into the French *fromage.*

fresh   A cheese that hasn't been aged or ripened.

fromage   French word for cheese.

Fromage Fort   Means "strong cheese" in French; a type of cheese spread made from leftover bits of cheese with wine, butter, and garlic added.

girolle   A special Swiss apparatus used to shave off slices of Tête de Moine cheese.

Gorgonzola   An Italian blue cheese made from cow's milk.

Gouda   A firm Dutch cheese made from cow's milk.

grazers   Animals such as cows and sheep that primarily eat grass and clover.

Gruyère   A hard Swiss cow's milk cheese made in the Alps, known for its melting qualities.

hard   A cheese that is aged for a long period of time and has lost a lot of moisture; hard to the touch.

homogenization   Process of breaking down the fats in milk so that they are evenly distributed throughout the milk; homogenized milk is not used in making cheese.

Juustoleipa   Finnish bread cheese.

lactic acid   What is formed when bacteria eats the sugars in milk during cheesemaking.

lactose   Milk sugar.

maître fromager   A cheese expert who has studied cheese and can help navigate a restaurant's cheese selection; similar to a sommelier for wine.

mammoth cheese   A giant wheel of cheese.

mesophilic cultures   Commonly used cultures in cheesemaking that need temperatures between 70°F and 100°F.

microbial rennet   Enzyme produced by microbes or bacteria used to coagulate cheese.

oenophile   Wine lover.

paneer   A popular Indian, fresh, nonrennet cheese that is similar to unsalted, pressed ricotta; sometimes spelled panir.

Parmigiano-Reggiano   The original, authentic Italian Parmesan cheese.

pasta filata   Process of dipping curd into hot water, which causes the curds to release more whey; next the cheese is stretched and kneaded. This process is used to make mozzarella, provolone, and string cheese.

paste   The interior part of a cheese.

pasteurization   Process in which milk is heated to kill germs or unwanted bacteria.

pecorino   Generic Italian word for sheep's milk cheese. In Italy, sheep's milk cheese is more common than goat's milk cheese.

peynir   Turkish word for cheese.

plug a cheese   To remove a sample from the interior of a wheel of cheese.

poutine   A Quebecois dish made with french fries, fresh cheese curds, and brown gravy.

processed cheese   Cheese that is heat-treated and mixed with emulsifiers and other additives that keep it from breaking down when heated; not natural cheese.

propionic acid bacteria   Type of bacteria in cheesemaking that produces carbon dioxide after eating the lactose in the cheese and creates the holes in Swiss cheese.

propionic acid fermentation   The second fermentation in Swiss cheese that creates the holes.

queijo   Portuguese word for cheese.

queso   Spanish word for cheese.

queso anejo   An aged version of queso fresco.

queso asadero   A Hispanic melting cheese that's similar to provolone in taste.

queso chihuahua   A Hispanic cheese similar to Gouda, also known as queso menonita first made by the Mennonite communities who lived in northern Mexico.

queso cotija   A firm, feta-like, Hispanic cheese.

queso fresco   A Hispanic "fresh cheese," similar to a farmer's cheese; aged version of this cheese is called queso anejo.

queso oaxaca   A Hispanic cheese similar to string cheese.

queso panela   A Hispanic "basket cheese" which is molded in baskets, similar to mozzarella.

queso requeson   A ricotta-like, Hispanic cheese that's used as a filling in tamales, enchiladas, and other dishes.

raw milk   Unpasteurized milk.

raw milk cheese   Cheese made from unpasteurized milk.

rennet   Enzyme used to coagulate cheese; it once exclusively came from the stomach of a calf but today most rennet is produced by microbes.

ricotta   An Italian cheese made from the leftover whey of mozzarella production.

rind   The outside surface of a cheese.

ripening   Process of aging a cheese until it's ready to consume.

Roquefort   French blue cheese made from sheep's milk; considered the king of cheese.

salting   Part of cheesemaking process in which salt is mixed into the curds or the cheese is washed with salt.

semi-soft   A cheese that has been aged longer than fresh cheeses but still is pliable and has enough moisture in it.

terroir   French term that denotes the effects that geography and distinct environments have on food products, particularly wine and cheese.

thermophilic cultures   Common cheesemaking cultures that work at temperatures above 100°F.

trier   A tool professional cheese judges use to "plug" a cheese or remove a sample from a large wheel of cheese.

turophiles   Cheese lovers.

umami   A word used to describe the "fifth" taste; a flavor that doesn't neatly fall into the categories of sweet, salty, sour, and bitter.

unhomogenized   Milk that hasn't been homogenized; homogenization is the process of breaking the fats down and evenly distributing them throughout the milk. Unhomogenized milk is the type of milk used in cheesemaking.

washed rind   Cheese in which the rind is washed with brine, salt, beer, wine, or some other mixture to create flavors; washed rind cheeses typically have strong aromas.

whey   The protein liquid left over from cheesemaking after the curds have been separated out.

Appendix **B**

Cheese Resources

General References

Edelman, Edward, and Susan Grodnick. *The Ideal Cheese Book, First Edition.* New York: Harper and Row Publishers, Inc., 1986.

Harbutt, Juliet. *Cheese.* Wisconsin: Willow Creek Press, Inc., 1999.

Jenkins, Steven. *Cheese Primer.* New York: Workman Publishing, 1996.

Kaufelt, Rob. *The Murray's Cheese Handbook.* New York: Broadway Books, 2006.

Kosikowski, Frank V., and Vikram V. Mistry. *Cheese and Fermented Milk Foods, Vols. 1 & 2, Third Edition.* Connecticut: F.V. Kosikowski, L.L.C., 1997.

McCalman, Max, and David Gibbons. *The Cheese Plate.* New York: Clarkson Potter, 2002.

McNair, James. *Cheese.* California: Chronicle Books, 1986.

Ridgway, Judy. *The Cheese Companion: The Connoisseur's Guide.* Pennsylvania: Running Press Book Publishers, 1999.

International Cheeses

Androuet, Pierre. *The Complete Encyclopedia of French Cheese*. New York: Harper's Magazine Press, 1973.

Axler, Bruce H. *The Cheese Handbook*. New York: Hastings House, 1968.

Eekhof-Stork, Nancy. *The World Atlas of Cheese*. United States: Paddington Press Ltd. Two Continents Publishing Group, 1976.

Ensrud, Barbara. *The Pocket Guide to Cheese*. New York: Perigee Books, 1981.

Harbutt, Juliet. *The World Encyclopedia of Cheese*. New York: Lorenz Books, 1999.

Marquis, Vivienne, and Patricia Haskell. *The Cheese Book*. New York: Simon & Schuster, Inc. 1985.

Pitte, Jean-Robert. *French Gastronomy: The History and Geography of a Passion*. New York: Columbia University Press, 2002.

Teubner, Christian. *The Cheese Bible*. New York: Penguin Group, 1998.

Domestic Cheeses

Apps, Jerry. *Cheese: The Making of a Wisconsin Tradition*. Wisconsin: Amherst Press, 1998.

Roberts, Jeffrey P. *The Atlas of American Cheese*. Vermont: Chelsea Green Publishing Company, 2007.

Tewksbury, Henry. *The Cheeses of Vermont*. Vermont: The Countryman Press, 2002.

Werlin, Laura. *The All American Cheese and Wine Book*. New York: Stewart, Tabori & Chang, 2003.

———. *The New American Cheese: Profiles of America's Great Cheesemakers and Recipes for Cooking with Cheese*. New York: Stewart, Tabori & Chang, 2000.

Making Cheese and Cooking with Cheese

Carroll, Ricki. *Home Cheese Making.* Massachusetts: Storey Books, 2002.

Carroll, Ricki, and Robert Carroll. *Cheesemaking Made Easy.* Vermont: Storey Communications, Inc., 1982.

Fletcher, Janet Kessel. *The Cheese Course.* California: Chronicle Books, 2000.

Gayler, Paul. *A Passion for Cheese.* New York: St. Martin's Press, 1997.

Prescott, Jill. *Jill Prescott's Ecole de Cuisine.* California: Ten Speed Press, 2001.

Proulx, E. Annie, and Lew Nichols. *The Complete Dairy Foods Cookbook.* Pennsylvania: Rodale Press, 1982.

Smith, Tim. *Making Artisan Cheese.* Massachusetts: Quarry Books, 2005.

Werlin, Laura. *Great Grilled Cheese: 50 Innovative Recipes for Stovetop, Grill and Sandwich Maker.* New York: Stewart, Tabori & Chang, 2004.

Wisconsin Dairy Goat Association. *Moving Dairy Goats Forward.* Nebraska: Morris Press Cookbooks, 2006.

Cheese Websites

Buying Cheese/Enjoying Cheese Meals and Events

The Better Cheddar
www.thebettercheddar.com

Cheesetique Specialty Cheese Shop
www.cheesetique.com

Cheuvront Wine and Cheese Café
www.cheuvront.biz

Courtyard Wine and Cheese Bar
www.rosemarybeach.com/rosemary_beach_dining.aspx

Eno (Hotel Intercontinentals)
www.enowinerooms.com

Farmstead Cheese Shop
www.farmsteadinc.com

Formaggio Kitchen
www.formaggiokitchen.com

Fromages du Quebec
www.fromageduquebec.qc.ca/trouver_montreal.html

Grand Trunk Imports
www.grandtrunkimports.com

Ideal Cheese Shop
www.idealcheese.com

Larry's Market
www.larrysmarket.com

L'Espalier
www.lespalier.com/events/cheesetuesday.shtml

Murray's Cheese
www.murrayscheese.com

Pastoral Artisan Cheese Store
www.pastoralartisan.com

Premier Cheese Market
www.premiercheesemarket.com

Rainbow Grocery
www.rainbowgrocery.org

Vintage New York
www.vintagenewyork.com

Wasiks
www.wasiks.com

Wine & Cheese Cask
www.thewineandcheesecask.com/cheese_special.htm

The Winery Bar at the American Club
www.destinationkohler.com/restaurants/winery_bar.html

Zingerman's 888-636-8162 or
www.zingermans.com

Cheese Blogs

Cheese Diaries
www.cheesediaries.com/about.shtml

Cheese Underground
cheeseunderground.blogspot.com

Curdnerds
www.curdnerds.com

Pacific Northwest Cheese Project
pnwcheese.typepad.com

General References

American Cheese Society
www.cheesesociety.org

Artisanal Cheese Center
www.artisanalcheese.com

Dairy Business Innovation Center
www.dbicusa.org

Dairy Connection
www.dairyconnection.com

Real California Cheese
www.realcaliforniacheese.com

Vermont Cheese Council
www.vtcheese.com

Wisconsin Milk Marketing Board
www.wisdairy.com

Making Cheese and Cooking with Cheese

Cheese School of San Francisco
www.cheeseschoolsf.com

Fankhauser's Cheese Page
biology.clc.uc.edu/Fankhauser/Cheese/Cheese.html

Leeners
www.leeners.com

New England Cheese Making Supply
www.cheesemaking.com

Jill Prescott Cooking School
www.jillprescott.com

Cheese DVDs

Cheese Slices
www.lifestylechannel.com.au/shows/show.asp?id=163&presenter_id=62&tab=presenter

http://cheeseslices.com

Living on the Wedge
www.livingonthewedge.com

Index

X–Y–Z